INFORMATION STRUCTURE IN SPOKEN ENGLISH

In a series of publications in the 1960s culminating in the 1967 book *Intonation and Grammar in British English* and the three articles "Notes on Transitivity and Theme in English," Halliday proposed a system of information structure. Tonic items were presented as New or as if they were not recoverable from the context and co-text. Post-tonic items were Given or recoverable. The status of pre-tonic items was ambiguous and needed to be considered in context.

Halliday's view has proven to be reliable over the past 50 years, but this book aims to revise it. The book argues that Halliday's system was premised on two views, both of which have been questioned over the years. The first is that Halliday's notion of recoverability was influenced by Shannon and Weaver's mathematical theory of information predictability where information can be encoded in terms of bits which are transmitted from source A to source B. This is not how SFL theory sees language functioning. Languaging is not simply the transmitting of information but rather a social semiotic practice which interactants deploy to affiliate with others while pursuing their individual needs. Secondly the binary division of information as either New (1 bit) or Given (0 bit) has been questioned in recent years by work which has looked at presuppositions and implications. In addition to these issues, the book argues that Halliday's definition blurs the important distinction between referentiality and identification. The book concludes by presenting an updated Hallidayan model which is sensitive to the above issues.

GERARD O'GRADY is a professor in the School of English, Communication, and Philosophy at Cardiff University.

KEY CONCEPTS IN SYSTEMIC FUNCTIONAL LINGUISTICS

Books in this series provide monographic treatments of core theoretical concepts within Systemic Functional Linguistics, together with coverage of more recent concerns in Systemic Functional Linguistic theory and important areas of application and trans-disciplinary collaboration.

Each monograph is organized around a description of the historical factors that led to the emergence of the concept within Systemic Functional Linguistics and a detailed theoretical description of the concept within the overall architecture of the theory.

Published

Neo-Firthian Approaches to Linguistic Typology
William B. McGregor

System in Systemic Functional Linguistics: A System-based Theory of Language
Christian M.I.M. Matthiessen

Systemic Functional Translation Studies: Theoretical Insights and New Directions
Bo Wang and Yuanyi Ma

Verbal Art and Systemic Functional Linguistics
Donna R. Miller

Word Phonology in a Systemic Functional Linguistic Framework: Phonological Studies in English, German, Welsh and Tera (Nigeria)
Paul Tench

GERARD O'GRADY

Information Structure in Spoken English

A Systemic Functional Linguistics View

UNIVERSITY OF TORONTO PRESS
Toronto Buffalo London

Published by University of Toronto Press in 2025

Toronto Buffalo London
utppublishing.com
Printed in the USA

ISBN 978-1-4875-6644-9 (cloth)
ISBN 978-1-4875-6645-6 (paper)
ISBN 978-1-4875-6647-0 (EPUB)
ISBN 978-1-4875-6646-3 (UPDF)

Library and Archives Canada Cataloguing in Publication

Publication cataloguing information is available from Library and Archives Canada.

The manufacturer's authorised representative in the EU for product safety is Mare Nostrum Group B.V., Mauritskade 21D, 1091 GC Amsterdam, The Netherlands. Email: gpsr@mare-nostrum.co.uk

We wish to acknowledge the land on which the University of Toronto Press operates. This land is the traditional territory of the Wendat, the Anishnaabeg, the Haudenosaunee, the Métis, and the Mississaugas of the Credit First Nation.

University of Toronto Press acknowledges the financial support of the Government of Canada, the Canada Council for the Arts, and the Ontario Arts Council, an agency of the Government of Ontario, for its publishing activities.

Funded by the Government of Canada
Financé par le gouvernement du Canada

Contents

List of Figures

List of Tables

1 An Outline of a Theory of Information Structure

Introduction

I wrote this book for a number of reasons. The first arose from my frustration that despite having coined the term "information structure," Halliday and the Hallidayan tradition are neglected in the literature. I hope to address this issue by showing researchers within and without the Systemic Functional Linguistics (SFL) tradition how an SFL approach theorizes and describes information structure. While Halliday reserves the term information structure solely for the prosodic encoding of elements as Given or New, I use the term in a manner similar to Chafe (1976), who identified it as the structuring of sentences (here clauses and tone groups) into different kinds of information blocks. In other words, in this book information structure includes not only prosody but also syntax and lexical realization. As such I will use the acronym IS throughout the book to refer to my expanded notion, which I note is fully in line with non-SFL approaches; see Lambrecht (1994) and the chapters in Féry and Ishihara (2016) whose work on IS combines phonological, syntactic, lexical, morphological, and pragmatic approaches. My hope is that my expansive SFL-flavoured approach will be readily comprehensible to scholars of IS who are not from an SFL background.

The second reason for writing this book is to attempt to bring SFL studies into dialogue with other approaches and illustrate that despite differing terminology and underpinnings, the differing approaches share more than one might at first glance assume.

The third reason is to centre the description in authentic spoken data. While there clearly have been SFL descriptions of information structure (Halliday 1967a, 1970a; Halliday & Greaves, 2008; Tench, 1990) the vast majority of SFL descriptions on the structuring of text have focused on the system of Theme[1] in written texts, though see O'Grady (2017a) and Ping (2005). This has led regrettably to an often unstated and unwarranted assumption that Theme is Given and that the Rheme is New.[2] This, as we will see, and as was recognized by Halliday, is a gross over-simplification, and moreover, at least in spoken data, is frequently incorrect (O'Grady, 2024).

My final aim is to propose and test a theory of the IS of spoken English which argues that the interaction of syntax, lexicogrammar, and prosody structures wording into messages. It does so in order to assist the hearer in making sense of the speaker's intended meaning. By grounding the wordings within the context (verbal, physical, and generic) as well as managing expectations of what is to come, IS is simultaneously backward-and forward-looking. I will argue that it simultaneously operates on four levels. These are:

1. Relational: realized syntactically within the clause as Theme ^ Rheme
2. Identificational: realized incrementally by a clause like chain
3. Recoverable: realized prosodically within the tone group as (Given) ^ (New) ^ Focus ^ (Given)[3]
4. Propositional: realized by a clause or sequences of clauses

In order to set the scene for what is to follow, I will first briefly outline Halliday's textual metafunction as set out in the most recent edition of *Introduction to Functional Grammar* (*IFG*) (Halliday & Matthiessen, 2014). Then I will briefly sketch out the proposed theory and show how it builds upon and expands on Halliday's view. I will defer most critical reflection until the following chapters. Finally, I will complete the chapter by previewing the remainder of the book.

---

1. "Theme" and "Rheme" are capitalized in SFL literature; elsewhere in this book I have referred to theme more generally as "theme" and "rheme."
2. For instance in a discussion of written text, Fries (1997) goes as far as to contrast theme with N-rheme. The N, it hardly needs to be said, stands for New. My own papers (O'Grady, 2017a, 2024), Arús-Hita (2022), Bäcklund (1992), Ping (2005), and Taboada and Lavid (2003) are rare exceptions which focus on IS in spoken discourse. But my papers are the only ones which consider prosody.
3. The brackets signal optionality. In a tone group, the sole mandatory element is the Tonic which signals the focus.

1.1 The Textual Metafunction

In a series of publications, Halliday (1967a, 1968, 1975, 1978, 1985) proposed that there are three generalized functions which language has evolved in order to serve the needs of speakers in particular communicative situations. These are (1) the ideational metafunction which represents the external world and the speaker's inner world as meaning, (2) the interpersonal metafunction which enacts the roles and relations between the speaker and the hearer as meaning, and (3) the textual metafunction which enables the other two functions. The textual metafunction itself comprises a number of subsystems of which the most important two are Theme and Information. The other subsystems include Conjunction, Lexical Cohesion, Substitution/Ellipsis, and Reference, and while time and space preclude an in-depth discussion of these systems, they will be discussed as part of the proposed new model.[4]

Halliday borrowed Pike's (1959/2015 and 1982) description of language as *particle, field,* and *wave.* Textual meanings are wave-like. He noted that a text consists of waves of information which function at different scales – from the whole text down to the clause and the tone group (Halliday & Matthiessen (2014, p. 387). These waves as peaks of prominence are realized structurally in English by position and tonic prominence. Theme, as we will see, is realized by position.

1.1.1 THEME

In Halliday's writing, Theme is considered to be one of the two peaks of prominence which occurs in the clause. Positionally in English it occurs at the beginning of the clause, where it represents "the peg upon which the sentence is hung" (Halliday, 1970b, p. 161) or to put it another way "the ground from which the clause is taking off" (Halliday, 1994, p. 38). The two most recent editions of *IFG* define it as "that which locates and orients the clause within its context" (Halliday & Matthiessen, 2004,

4. The following example sets out where these systems are usually placed in the IS model.

System	Level
Conjunction	Propositional
Lexical Cohesion	Identificational
Ellipsis/Substitution	Recoverability
Reference	Recoverability and Identificational

p. 64; Halliday & Matthiessen, 2014, p. 89). While Theme is not defined in terms of position but rather by function, nonetheless in English it is restricted to clause initial position as in 1.1–1.3.

1.1

Themes They Subjects Important ideas Concepts which are taken for granted	occur in clause initial position
Theme	Rheme

Here, the Theme is coterminous with the subject and is realized lexicogrammatically as a pronoun, a nominal group (NG), or even a clause.

1.2

<table>
<tr><td>But
And
Although
Since
Anyway</td><td>clearly
obviously
you know
predictably
my friend</td><td>Themes
they
subjects
important ideas
concepts which are taken for granted</td><td>occur in clause initial position</td></tr>
<tr><td>Textual</td><td>Interpersonal</td><td>Topical</td><td rowspan="2">Rheme</td></tr>
<tr><td colspan="3">Theme</td></tr>
</table>

In example 1.2 even though the subject is preceded within the clause by other elements, it remains part of the Theme. The elements which optionally precede the subject are (1) textual and (2) interpersonal. Textual Themes precede interpersonal Themes and have a linking function. They may join two clauses together into a coordinating relation or signal that one clause is dependent on another. They may be followed by an interpersonal theme which functions to indicate (1) the speaker's comment, assessment, or attitude toward the message, (2) a vocative addressing the hearer, or (3) if realized as a first- or second-person mental clause, to express the speaker's opinion or seek the hearer's.[5] The part of the the Theme which is realized by the subject in 1.2 is known

5. In interrogative mood the interpersonal theme signals that a response/answer is required and may signal an expectation of the polarity of the response, e.g., the contrast between *Is Jane pretty?* and *Isn't Jane pretty?*

as the topical Theme.[6] More formally the Theme culminates in the first element that functions in transitivity. This is usually but not necessarily the subject e.g., 1.3 where the subject is found in the Rheme.

1.3

In English	Theme is always found in clause initial positions
Theme (marked)	Subject
	Rheme

In the next section, we will look at the other prominence peak – that of focus – which is realized in English by tonic prominence.

1.1.2 INFORMATION

in the Hallidayan approach, non-recoverable information is signalled by prosodic means. However, before I describe the Hallidayan view, I will first explain what is meant by information in a technical sense. In the 1940s the US scientist Claude Shannon devised a mathematical theory of information. This theory stated that for communication to occur there needed to be a sender, a receiver, and a signal. In optimal conditions the sender encoded the information while the receiver decoded it (Shannon, 1948). Figure 1.1 illustrates:

Figure 1.1: Shannon's Information Theory of Communication

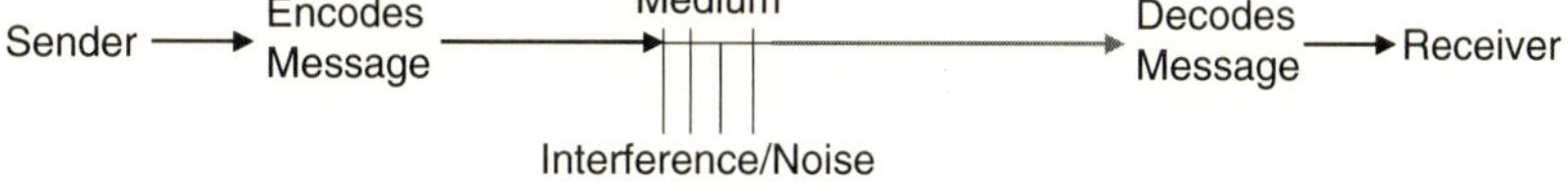

A sender decodes a message and transmits it to a hearer via a medium such as a telephone wire, a mobile phone wave, or in face-to-face conversation, a sound wave. The receiver decodes the message. However, as figure 1.1 shows, the encoded message is not identical to the decoded one and is somewhat degraded. It is interfered with by static, volume, accent, or background noise, etc. Shannon wished to measure how informative the signals encoded by the speaker were. He did so by coding it in terms of predictability; the more predictable the information, the more redundant it was, and hence the less informative it

6. Halliday (1967b) dubbed it the cognitive Theme and others such as Thompson and Thompson (2008) refer to it as the experiential Theme.

was. Information is, in other words, a measure of predictability in the signal,[7] and as we will see not be confused with meaning.

Halliday was influenced by Shannon's model and in *IFG* he defined information as:

> Information, in this technical grammatical sense, is the tension between what is already known or predictable and what is new or unpredictable. This is different from the mathematical concept of information, which is the measure of unpredictability. It is the interplay of new and not new that generates information in the linguistic sense. Hence the information unit is a structure made up of two functions, the New and the Given. Halliday & Matthiessen (2014, p. 135)

An information unit is realized in speech as a tone group which, all things being equal, is coextensive with a clause (Halliday 1967a; Halliday & Greaves, 2008; Halliday & Matthiessen, 2014).[8] Each information unit/tone group must contain a tonic prominence, and the element which carries the tonic prominence realizes the focus of the tone group. The item under focus is the entire grammatical constituent which contains the tonic prominence. The focus is the part of the New information which the speaker is drawing particular attention to (Halliday & Greaves, 2008, p. 103), or in other words the most important or newsworthy item of information conveyed by the speaker (McGregor, 1997, p. 59). Lexical content which follows the focus in the tone group/information unit is inherently Given. However, Halliday argues that the information status of items that precede the focus is ambiguous (Halliday & Greaves, 2008, p. 57).[9]

In Halliday's view, Given and New are not textual categories but rather psychological ones, and when speaking speakers project their

7. For a very informative and accessible introduction to Shannon's work among other mathematical theories of information see Gleick (2011).
8. Halliday describes a clause and a tone group as representing a quantum of information (Halliday & Matthiessen, 2014, p. 65). See also the claim in Halliday and Matthiessen (1999, p. 213) that the flow of events is chunked in quanta of change with each quantum modelled as a figure and typically realized as a clause. Halliday and Greaves (2008, p. 101) note that the segmentation of the speech signal into tone groups organizes the discourse into quanta of information.
9. McGregor (1997) offers a contrary view in that he argues that as the focus is the only part of the New which is linguistically realized, it and it alone is linguistically meaningful. See also Dik (1989, p. 277) for a similar view.

assumptions of whether particular items are recoverable or not. All focal elements, regardless of previous mention, are presented as non-recoverable. All items after the tonic similarly are presented as recoverable irrespective of previous mention. Thus, the tone group/information unit is the site of two functions: New with an optional Given component.

While the information status of pretonic items is ambiguous, there are cues which help in assigning Given and New status. Once an item has been introduced into the discourse it is considered recoverable. A pretonic accent on an item which has not been mentioned previously or is not available in the context signals that the item is presented as part of the New. Finally, unaccented pretonic items are likely to be Given (see O'Grady, 2014a). Example 1.4 details the structure of the tone group/information unit.

1.4 (Given) (New) Focus (Given)

The following examples illustrate the systemic possibilities with accented syllables underlined. In 1.5 the entire tone group is presented as New and the focus is *the shed*.

1.5 What's up?

John	painted	the shed
←———————————		Focus
Theme	Rheme	

1.6 What did John do?

He	painted	the shed
Given		Focus
——→← ———————		New
Theme	Rheme	

In 1.6 the referent of the painter is recoverable and Given. The focus is *the shed*, which represents the culmination of the New. Since "painted" has not been mentioned previously and it is accented, it is projected as New.

1.7 When did John paint the shed?

He	painted it	a few	months ago
Given		Focus	
———————	——————→	New ——→	Given
Theme	Rheme		

In 1.7 only the focus is projected as being New. However, the tonic placement on the determiner *few* signals that the noun *months* and the adverbial *ago* are themselves presented as recoverable. This example indicates that even though the NG *a few months ago* is the focus, part of the focus itself is presented as somewhat shaded. In 1.8 the focus falls on the unmarked Theme. The post-tonic elements are Given as they are recoverable from the question.

1.8 Who painted the shed?

John	painted it
Theme	Rheme
Focus	
New ←———	——— Given

In 1.9 only the focus is projected as New.

1.9 What did John do the shed?

He	painted	it
Theme	Rheme	
Given	Focus/New	Given

Examples 1.10 and 1.11 illustrate that the informational status of pretonic elements, according to Halliday, ultimately depends on prior mention or availability in the physical context. In 1.10 John is part of the New, but in 1.11 it is Given despite on both occasions receiving a prosodic prominence. I will discuss the status of "painted" after 1.14.

1.10 Wow! (Indicating unexpected exposure to a shiny shed and no previous mention of John.)

John	painted the shed	recently
Theme	Rheme	
		Focus
←———	———————	New

1.11 Wow! (Indicating the presence/previous mention of a shed plus previous mention that the speaker had employed a painter named John.)

<u>John</u>	<u>painted</u> it re<u>cent</u>ly
Theme	Rheme
	Focus
Given ——————→	New

In 1.11 the unaccented pronominal element *it* refers to the shed, which is recoverable and marks the boundary between the Given and the New elements. In 1.10 despite the shed being identifiable, it forms part of the New elements.

Examples 1.12 and 1.13 show that prominence, even a pretonic prominence on a pronominal element, can project that the element, although identifiable, is signalled as non-recoverable.

1.12 Did Jane paint the shed?

No	<u>he</u>	did
Theme		Rheme
	Focus	
New ←——————	——————→	Given

The pronoun receives the tonic accent, so it is the focus and thus presented as a non-recoverable choice from a closed set of possible painters. In 1.13 things are slightly more complicated. Here we are in a context with two possible corrective contrasts. The first is the verbal process, which is in focus in the answer. A new shed was not, as the first speaker assumed, bought. Instead, the old one was spruced up. Jane did not directly act upon the shed, though she may well have been the instigator of the material process *paint*. Instead, an identifiable male is stated as the actor of the painting. While the pronoun signals that the referent is identifiable, it is not recoverable and represents a selection from a defined set of potential painters. The set may consist of two people, with Jane being the other, or it may be that the referent identifiable by the pronoun *he* contrasts with a small group of workers in Jane's employ. The NG *the old one* is post-tonic and thus Given. Pronouns can therefore be projected as non-recoverable, while full NGs may be projected as recoverable.

1.13 Did Jane buy a new shed?

No	he	painted	the old one
Theme	Rheme		
		Focus	
Given ——→	New ←—	———	—→ Given

Example 1.14 highlights a problem with Halliday's depiction of how Given and New elements interact within the tone group/information unit. Halliday argued that the focus was the culmination of the New with the Given elements commencing on the first recoverable element. Thus, New elements contained within the Given are prohibited. In 1.14 the unaccented NG clearly refers to the previously mentioned referent *the shed*, as would an unaccented pronoun. Thus, the process *painted* must be Given information. This is problematic on two grounds. The first is that the speaker has chosen to accent it as in 1.10 and 1.11, where I noted that in the former case it was New, but in the latter it was Given. The second is that the process *painted* is no more recoverable in 1.14 than it was in 1.10. Based on such evidence, Taglicht (1984) questioned Halliday's concept of information structure, and I myself did allow New items to be detached from the focus and surrounded by Given ones (O'Grady, 2014a).

1.14 What did John do to the shed?

He	painted	the shed/it	recently
Theme	Rheme		
			Focus
Given ——→	?	———→	New

To use the wave analogy, *painted* represents a further peak of prominence within the tone group, and more importantly it is not a wave which has the same frequency as the Thematic wave. In other words when thinking of waves, we need to think of waves in terms of sound waves, which have multiple harmonics oscillating at different frequencies throughout the discourse. I will return to the wave analogy throughout the book.

1.2 A Sketch of the Proposed Model of IS

In this section I will build upon the previous sections by setting out the four components of IS proposed here. The proposed model adopts a far more catholic view of information than Halliday's. The online Oxford English Dictionary (n.d.) provides a number of glosses for *information*, some of which I reproduce below:

- The imparting of knowledge in general.
- Knowledge communicated concerning some particular fact, subject, or event; that of which one is apprised or told; intelligence, news.
- As a mathematically defined quantity divorced from any concept of news or meaning … one which represents the degree of choice exercised in the selection or formation of one particular symbol, message, etc., out of a number of possible ones, and which is defined logarithmically in terms of the statistical probabilities of occurrence of the symbol or the elements of the message.

The Hallidayan definition is clearly closest to the third gloss above, with the other two glosses referring to meaning or knowledge or what in Hallidayan linguistics might be labelled as speech function – though as I will make clear, speech function is not identical with what I mean by propositional information.

Halliday described the clause as a structure that usually contains two peaks of informational prominence – the Theme and the New. However, the proposal developed here does not quite agree. As noted above Theme is a syntactic system grounded in the clause which carries relational meaning. It can be glossed as speakers setting forth what they will talk about. New, conversely, is a prosodic system grounded in the information unit which can be glossed as that which speakers are talking about. It is the second component of the proposal, namely the system of referential meaning. While it can be mapped onto a clause, it is not a system originating in the clause and is not therefore considered here to be a prominence realized in the clause. Example 1.15, which is taken from a short interview given by Boris Johnson to Channel 4 news, illustrates.[10] In 1.15 square brackets denote Theme. Double slash brackets indicate a clause boundary. Straight brackets indicate tone groups with underlining indicating prosodic prominence. Focus is signalled by an asterisk with New enclosed in angle brackets.

10. For further details on this data see O'Grady (2022).

1.15

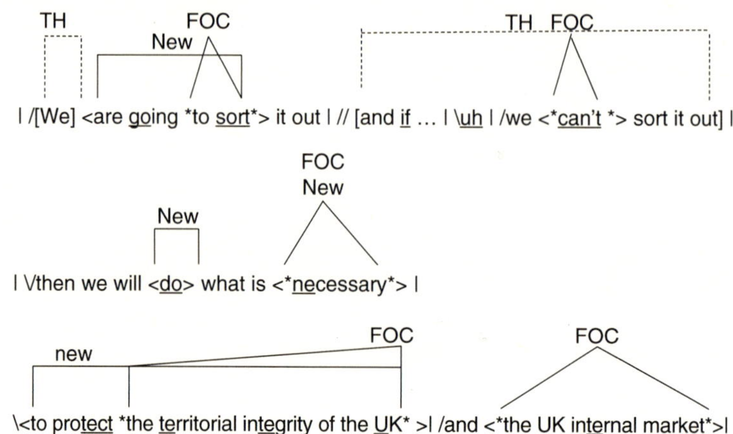

In the opening clause there is one Theme at the start and a focus toward the end conforming to Halliday's prediction. However, the following clause complex, which comprises a hypotactic clause followed by a paratactic one, has a focus contained within the Theme and three further foci within the Rheme. In other words, the fact that information units and clauses are not necessarily coextensive entails that informational (referential) waves can occur anywhere in a clause.[11]

The third component of the model is identificational information, which is realized by the presence of a topic. Like Theme it is realized by lexicogrammatical choices. Topic is identified following Strawson (1964, p. 97) as "the matter of standing current interest or concern," and it is the thing that is commented on. In most cases topics will fall within the Theme and be realized by the subject. However, we will see in chapter 2 that Theme and topic can be disaggregated in "thetic sentences." Example 1.16 illustrates identificational information and shows how it differs from referential information.

11. Givón (2017) commented on the difficulty of identifying a Theme ^ Rheme structure in discourse because as he argued spoken language is parcelled out in "spoken clauses" (which I take to be tone groups) and not realized as full clauses. I agree but have argued that Theme ^ Rheme is a clausal system which can be mapped onto the articulated tone groups. Hence, not every tone group will necessarily contain a Theme or a Rheme for that matter. Givón's view that spoken language consists of a flow of tone groups which emerge incrementally is a sound one, but I will argue that this sequence can be more or less mapped onto clausal grammar. It is this ability to map prosodic and lexicogrammatical units in speech that enables propositional information to emerge.

1.16 | \/President Biden | /\ thought you were his clone |

Topic

* FOC* New ←———— *FOC *

In the first tone group, the topic and proper noun "President Biden" is identifiable. The referent has been mentioned in the earlier co-text, but the tonic prominence on *Biden* signals the speaker's view that the referent is news as the speaker has drawn particular attention to the fact that the matter of current interest is the US president. Topics, as we will see, are commonly pronouns or definite NGs, but indefinite nongeneric NGs may be topic, and contra Lambrecht (1994) I will argue that on occasion indefinite NGs may also be. Hence, while topic, Theme, and Given are likely to be coextensive, they are logically separatable.[12]

The final component of the proposed model is propositional information. As a starting point, I assume that speakers produce language in order to share meanings that are relevant to their and their hearers' needs in particular times, places, and institutional settings. By this, I mean that their wordings are intended to create convergence between their view of the world and that of their hearers. They update the state of convergence or knowledge that they share with their hearers either by telling or asking. Similarly, they may cause the transfer of goods or services by offering or commanding (Andersen, 2017; Halliday & Matthiessen, 2014). In SFL theory, speech function is considered to fall within the interpersonal rather than the textual metafunction for the obvious reason that to tell, ask, command, or offer is to intrude on another. But equally it is obvious that for a speaker to realize a particular speech function, hearers must comprehend what is being imparted to them. They are being told something, asked about something, offered a particular thing, or commanded to do a specific act. In other words information must be exchanged and speakers must position themselves in relation to the information (see Berry, 2021a; O'Grady, 2021).

In the literature, the concept of "shared knowledge" has proven to be a slippery beast (see Lee, 2001). Scholars have argued about what it means to share "knowledge" or "assumptions." Furthermore, in order to know that what they know is known by their interlocutor, speakers and hearers must engage in an infinite regression in order to establish mutuality. Clearly, this is not feasible. Hence, some scholars such as Clark and Haviland (1977) argue for a truncation hypothesis, where

12. The clause, *At noon* (theme), *the fat man with a red briefcase* (topic) *will pick up the hidden documents,* illustrates that theme and the topic are not the same, and furthermore the topic may be produced with a tonic accent and hence be projected as New.

only a finite set of steps is required to assume shared knowledge. Others such as Sperber and Wilson (1995) propose a more radical fix and reject the entire concept of shared knowledge. In its place they argue that speakers rely on their "cognitive environments": expectations based on previous interactions and experiences coupled with a recognition that their interlocutor has needs and desires similar to their own in order to understand their interlocutor's intentions (see Premack & Woodruff, 1978, for a full discussion of the Theory of Mind). This was a view that I endorsed in an earlier publication (O'Grady, 2010). However, while I still find the view attractive, my current thinking is that it is too individualistic and ignores the fact that like language, knowledge, and cognition are distributed across society (Cowley, 2011; Hutchins, 1995; Thibault, 2011). This implies that access to knowledge may be unequal and contestable (Muntigl, 2009). Speakers position themselves and others as having more or less access to knowledge through their linguistic choices. Lexicogrammatically, such choices are negotiated incrementally through speakers' modality choices in exchanges (Berry, 2021b; Halliday & Matthiessen, 2014; Martin, 2000) and prosodically by tone movements (Brazil, 1995; Halliday, 1967b; O'Grady, 2010, 2021; O'Grady & Bartlett, 2019; Tench, 1996).

My claim here is that propositional meaning is parcelled out both as a sequence of tone groups/information units and as a lexicogrammatical syntagm which creates a series of grammatical expectations which are only satisfied when the speaker has fulfilled their communicative needs and produced an appropriate utterance. I will detail the mechanism in chapter 5, but to illustrate it is clear that 1.17 but not 1.18 may satisfy a communicative need:

1.17 John's a lucky boy
1.18 John's

In 1.18 the copula creates the expectation that speaker will identify or attribute a quality to John. The hearer is primed to anticipate the speaker's message. But consider 1.19, where the speaker produces a follow up utterance.

1.19 | John's a lucky boy | he's got a hot date | with Mary |

Here the speaker has produced two clauses and three tone groups. The second and third tone group expand on why *John is lucky.* As we will see in chapter 5, each tone group must contain a tone movement.

For the moment, following Cruttenden (1997) I shall assume a basic division between tones that fall and those that rise. Falling tones convey speaker certainty and signal that the speaker is positioning themselves as having access to the relevant information, while rising tones are hearer-oriented and signal either uncertainty or that the speaker is signalling that the hearer has prior access to the relevant information. Thus, if all tone groups contain a falling tone, 1.19 contains two tellings or two propositions, with the first functioning as the initial state to the second. The initial state of the second proposition is glossed as *The hearer has accessed the knowledge that John, someone known to the hearer, has the attribute of being lucky.* However, if the first tone group is articulated with a rising tone, the speaker has only produced a single proposition, with the first tone group functioning as information preliminary to the second. The speaker produces the message and reaches his target state by producing the third tone group. The news is *the hot date with Mary.* If only the middle tone group is produced with a fall, we also have a single proposition, but the achieved target state is slightly different. The content of the third tone group – *the identity of the date, Mary* – is presented as information that the hearer had prior access to. The telling is *the getting of the hot date,* which we can infer has been achieved after much persistence.

Thus, propositional information results from the mapping of a sequence of tone groups onto the grammatical expectations created by lexicogrammatical choices with a sequence of clauses coupled with the speaker's choice of tone movement. For a proposition to be realized it must satisfy grammatical expectations and contain a falling tone movement.

1.20 below maps out all four levels of information proposed in this book.

I John'	s a lucky \boy	I he'	s got a hot \date I	with \Mary I
Theme	Rheme	Theme	Rheme	
Top		Topic		
Proper		Pronoun		
	Foc		Foc	Foc
←	New	Given →	← New	← New
— — —	Target → ← State	Initial — — State	— — — —	— → Target State
Information to be added		Information to be added		

As can be seen, the Theme and the topic element coincide in this example with both being realized by the elements *John* and *he*. The proper noun signals that both parties of the conversation are able to identify the referent *John*. The pronoun *he* identifies the subject of the second clause as *John*. As there are three tone groups, there are three foci the speaker signals that *a lucky boy*, *a hot date*, and *with Mary* are the parts of the message that the speaker wishes to draw the hearer's attention to. Propositionally, both increments signal the speaker's view that after comprehension of the increment the hearer's access to the knowledge available to both speakers has increased. The target state achieved by the first increment is the initial state of the subsequent increment. In other words all utterances are sensitive to what has gone before (Bakhtin, 1986; Voloshinov, 1973) while at the same time shaping the future and thus, of course, our very understanding of the past.[13]

1.3 Chapter Summaries

Chapter 2 provides a critical in-depth examination of Hallidayan Theme. It first reviews work which influenced Theme and shows not only how the work of Prague School scholars influenced and motivated Halliday but also why Halliday separated Theme and information. I will review apparent inconsistencies in definitions of Theme which emerge from attempting to conflate Mathesius's three aspects of theme into Theme and Information. Theme is, as Gómez González (2001) argued, identified both by *place* and *matter* metaphors. In order to rectify the divergence, I examine the cognate notion of topic in order to motivate an analysis which codes for both Theme and topic. Topic, unlike Theme, is argued to be "the matter of current concern," whereas Theme is shown to be an orienting device which relates the clause to its context. It is shown that a clause must have a Theme but that topic is potentially optional, though in the unmarked case Theme and topic will be conflated.

Chapter 3 focuses on the system of information. It details the importance of tonality and tonicity in the speaker's projection of which lexical items are Given and which are New. Close examination of tonality choices illustrates that while tone groups/information units are often coterminous with clauses, it is more accurate to say that they also frequently correspond to clausal cores and subclausal units. Hence, there will be more tone groups/information units than clauses in a text. This

13. To illustrate now that the hearer knows that *John = a lucky boy*, he/she will naturally reinterpret and revise his/her previous familiarity with John and his/her actions in light of John being a lucky boy.

fact entails that New elements may occur at any point within a clause. While there is strong evidence equating tone groups with information units and the tonic syllables with focus, the informational status of pre-tonic lexical items is far less clear. One of the reasons for this is that the concept of recoverability is itself, on close examination, not entirely clear.

Chapter 4 provides a more expansive exploration of recoverability by examining various approaches, including Firbas's Functional Sentence Perspective, Krika's distinction between common ground management and common ground content, Prince's theory of information structure, Gundel and Hedberg's Givenness hierarchy, and Lambrecht's functional theory of information structure. The discussion centres on whether information structure is binary or ternary with inferable items neither Given or New. I also review differences between hearer/speaker Given and New and discourse Given and New, After reviewing the evidence, the issue remains unresolved, though the preponderance of evidence suggests that information structure is binary with the primary cut being between Given and New elements; however, there may well be more delicate distinctions between elements which are present and those which are inferable. The chapter concludes by arguing for a firm distinction between recoverable and identifiable elements, though it notes that both can be grouped together under a superordinate category of retrievable and that the relation between the lexicogrammatical and prosodic realization of identifiable and recoverable lexical items is a mutually reinforcing redundancy. Thus, it is shown that topical Themes are predicted to be Given, which, as we have already seen, are predicted to be thematic, though when it suits the speaker's purpose they can be separated. It will be noted that topic, Theme, and Given appear to be identical with Mathesius's three aspects of theme which I discuss in chapter 2.

Chapter 5 considers IS from a different perspective: namely predictability between classes of lexical items where an earlier item prospects a later one. In the chapter I outline a series of chaining rules which are supplemented by a number of formal devices and argue that they are sufficient to account for the dynamic and incremental flow of wordings and the chaining of tone groups in English as speakers achieve target states. The second part of the chapter reviews the concept of the mutuality of information and argues that speakers do not share information but rather signal their and their interlocutors' unequal access to information/knowledge on a moment-by-moment basis. The last chapter, chapter 6, investigates the proposed model of IS by coding real speech and analysing how the four levels of the IS model combine to enable the speakers to weave together lexicogrammatical and prosodic choices into a coherent and cohesive text.

2 Theme and Topic: What They Are, What They Do

Introduction

In order to situate Theme in the wider literature, I first outline the precursors and influences on Halliday's concept of Theme in this chapter. I do this to develop a critical discussion of how Theme functions to manage informational flow in spoken discourse and to demonstrate the strengths (and weaknesses) of the Hallidayan approach. As Theme has been extensively discussed and described in the SFL literature (e.g., Forey & Sampson, 2017; Fries, 1981; Halliday, 1967b; Halliday & Matthiessen, 2014; Hasan & Fries, 1995; Martin, 1992), I will only provide a brief description sufficient to enable comparison between SFL Theme/Rheme and terms such as topic and focus.[1] This will, however, necessitate some discussion of atypical Theme choices such as those in bi-clausal constructions such as clefts and pseudo-clefts, which have received less attention in the SFL literature.

2.1 The Emergence of Theme

The division of an utterance in terms akin to Theme ^ Rheme stretches back at least as far as the ancient Greeks. Aristotle stated that nothing could be true unless a property could be predicated of a subject (Barnes, 1977). This resulted in a double judgment with a referent first named and then something predicated about the name, as in 2.1:

1. By focus I am referring in this chapter to non-phonological glosses of focus such as the response to a Q test (Givón, 1975). Focus in Hallidayan phonological terms will be discussed in chapter 3.

2.1

John Mary The dog The astronaut	kicked the ball sang a song barked at the cat floated in space
Subject	Predicate
Theme	Rheme

In other words, we tend to name or introduce an entity into the discourse prior to commenting (saying something about it). Weil (1887/2009), a philologist specializing in the study of classical languages and Sanskrit, argued that all sentences contain a point of departure, i.e., an initial notion and a goal of discourse. He further argued that the point of departure was common ground for the speaker and the hearer. Conversely, the goal of the discourse represented the very thing the speaker wished to impart to the hearer. Accordingly, he claimed that an utterance represented the movement of the mind itself. The subject, usually found in initial position, represents the point of departure and hence is Given information. While this view is extremely problematic, as we will see, it does introduce a number of key concepts into the literature, notably that the initial elements of a sentence are of importance in relation to what follows, and that what follows comments on the point of departure. A sentence contains elements that refer to recoverable things and elements that refer to freshly mentioned things, and there is a preference for the recoverable things to precede the non-recoverable ones. Weil presents recoverable elements as cognitive categories which are realized in some unspecified manner by the lexicogrammar.

Vilem Mathesius, the founder of Prague School linguistics, was influenced by Weil's writing. In a similar manner, he identified the theme of a sentence as that which is known or at least obvious in the given situation and from which the speaker proceeds. (Mathesius, 1939, as cited in Firbas, 1964, p. 268). This view has subsequently been called "combining theme" in that it combines the criteria of linear position and informational recoverability in identifying theme (Davidse, 1987; Fries, 1981). Mathesius used three labelling criteria when discussing theme. The labels are:

1. východiště = point of departure
2. téma = topic (relevance/aboutness)
3. základ = basis or foundation

   Firbas (1987, p. 140)

He subsequently conflated základ with téma and distinguished both from východiště (Daneš, 1972, p. 217, fn2). Gómez González (2001, p. 65) notes that despite the combining overtones of his concept of theme, Mathesius on occasion recognized that the point of departure identified by syntactic positioning, the téma identified by the semantic notion of topicality or relevance (Grice, 1975; Sperber & Wilson, 1995), and the základ identified by informational criteria are not necessarily identical. In other words, the initial elements of sentence do not have to be either topical or Given, and indeed the most topical or relevant elements can be non-recoverable. Within more recent Prague School linguistics work there have been two main responses to the problem of identifying theme: the first is to use a combination of the three factors to identify the relative degree of communicative dynamism (CD) of an element within a sentence. Elements with lower CD are thematic (e.g., Firbas, 1992).

The second approach is to focus on one of the factors. For instance, Travnicek (1961, as cited in Gómez González (2001, p. 79) objects to Mathesius's thesis on the grounds that Given information and what the message is about are not the same thing. Given information is backward looking in that an element can only be recoverable in relation to the previous discourse. Conversely, what the message is about is prospective. And as such he identifies theme solely as východiště or point of departure, which he equates in an unspecified manner with the clause initial element. He recognizes that the point of departure and Givenness tend to coincide. In defence of Travnicek's argument, it is worth considering Sasse's (1987) observation that some languages such as Czech are informationally configured with the unmarked pattern showing a rise in CD throughout the clause, while others such as English are syntactically configured and require the presence of subjects, e.g., *it* in *it is raining*.[2] Thus, it may well be the case that východiště and základ in Czech are closely related and frequently coterminous though not necessarily identical. More controversially, Travnicek, like Weil before him, links theme with the order of the speaker's thoughts but does not explore the implications of this for languages, such as Gaelic, which

2. Note that while in SFL terms *it* is the subject as shown by the application of the mood tag probe (Halliday & Matthiessen, 2014): *It is raining isn't it. It* does not refer and cannot answer a question such as *What's it doing?* An alternate view is that "dummy elements" such as *it* are semiotic in that they have ambient reference and prospect the remainder of the clause as having "the greatest possible generality of meaning ... embrac(ing) weather, time, circumstances etc" (Bolinger, 1977, p. 84). Hence, they would correspond to the items with the lowest CD.

do not have the subject in initial position; for further discussion see Bartlett and O'Grady (2019).

Beneŝ (1959, p. 216, as cited in Gómez González, 2001, p. 80) differentiates theme from basis. He describes basis as "the opening element of the sentence [which] links the utterance with the context and the situation, selecting from several possible connections one that becomes the starting point, from which the entire further utterance unfolds and in regard to which it is orientated."[3] Theme is identified as the element which carries the lowest CD. Basis redefined as the point of departure depends on the previous co-text and is dependent on the unfolding textual structure of the discourse. While the basis is frequently thematic in the sense that the point of departure is an element with low CD, the point of departure may be rhematic in the sense that it is an element with higher CD. Beneŝ does not speak of the semantic factor, Mathesius's téma, but his work points the way forward for those classed as having a separating approach such as Halliday in that we can see two clearly differentiated functions: (1) basis defined as the first element and (2) theme defined as that which has low CD.

Gómez González (2001) points out that a major weakness of Beneŝ's work is that he did not work with extended texts and hence was unable to motivate why certain choices are preferred as points of departure. Nor can one see if there is a relationship between Givenness and point of departure, and if there is, when the congruent relationship is likely to be overridden. In other words, we are left wondering whether the speaker is free to choose any point of departure, based on their understanding of which elements are Given or New, or whether there are structural constraints that are also of relevance in determining what is found in initial position.

In a series of works, Daneš (1970, 1972, 1974, etc.) provides an answer. He illustrates that the patterning of the theme/rheme relationship across a text exhibits three main patterns. A theme choice is motivated by earlier choices in the text. The three patterns are:

2.2

- Linear theme progression

The rheme of the preceding clause becomes the theme of the following clause, e.g.,

The dog chased the neighbour's cat. It hid up a tree.
theme 1 rheme 1 theme 2
Both rheme 1 and theme 2 refer to the same entity: the neighbour's cat.

3. This, as we will see, is very similar to the definition of theme in Halliday and Matthiessen (2014).

• Constant theme progression

The same theme is shared by a series of clauses each with a different rheme.

The dog chased the neighbour's cat. It was disappointed not to be able
theme 1 theme 2
to catch the cat. But it cheered up again when it found a bone.
theme 3 theme 4

All four themes refer to the same entity: the dog.

• Broad spectrum theme

A general theme gives rises to a series of related or derived themes in the following clauses.

The world-renowned plaza hotel is situated right next to the main historic
theme 1
square and is famous for its traditional decor. The suites of the third floor
theme 2
replicate regency grandeur. The kitchen is renowned for its modern take
theme 3
on traditional classic dishes from the locality. The rooftop bar offers
theme 4
panoramic views.

The first theme introduces a new entity: the hotel. The other three themes talk about aspects or features of a hotel: the rooms, kitchen, and bar.

The three patterns presented above illustrate that for Daneš theme usually coincides with Given, i.e., recoverable information. Indeed, he argues for a unidirectional relationship between theme and Given; themes are usually formed from given items, but given items may occur in the theme or in the rheme (1974, p. 112).

The above discussion of Daneš's work is a gross oversimplification, but it is the part of his work which has been influential in forming SFL thinking (e.g., Fries, 1981). The system of thematic progression described above is itself formed out of three more delicate notions. The first of which is *CD*, which is represented on a scale. Unfortunately, it is not at all clear how Daneš intended to operationalize this notion beyond the obvious truism that given items have lower CD than new items. Presumably derived themes are of higher CD than constant themes, which themselves may have higher CD than linear themes owing to greater referential distance. The second notion is *information bipartition*, which argues that utterances consist of a starting point and a related core or goal of discourse. This notion combines the referential notions of Given and New, but on the other hand it argues that the core is related to the starting point. The final notion is *communicative articulation,* which equates with Mathesius's concept of téma and relates the rheme to the theme by stating the purpose of the communication. It is what the utterance is about. At the same time, by relating the relevance of the rheme to the theme, it establishes the theme as that which is being talked about. The rheme tells us why it is being talked about. It is by no means clear how these three notions work together as identifying criteria to establish theme and rheme. The following example taken from the Wikipedia entry on River Thames frost fairs illustrates:

2.3

> The River Thames frost fairs were held on the tideway of the River Thames in London, England in some winters, starting at least as early as the late 7th century until the early 19th century. **Most** were held between the early 17th and early 19th centuries during the period known as the Little Ice Age, when the river froze over most frequently. During that time the British winter was more severe than it is now, and the river was wider and slower, further impeded by the 19 piers of the medieval Old London Bridge which were removed in 1831. ("River Thames frost fairs," 2024)

In relation to theme progression, it is clear that the boldface determiner *most* plus the ellipted NG *frost fairs* is an example of constant theme. As a given item, it has low CD and thus is naturally thematic. But note that the post-verbal prepositional phrase *between the early 17th and early 19th centuries* is similarly Given owing to mention in the preceding clause, and it also has low CD. But this does not seem to make it thematic for Daneš. The concept of informational bipartition seems to mandate that the core of the utterance refers to when the majority of frost fairs were held. However, the purpose of the utterance may well have been to introduce the period known as *the Little Ice Age,* which is the answer to the Q test *What was the period between the early seventeenth and early nineteenth centuries when most frost fairs were held known as?* (Answer: The Little Ice Age). Therefore, according to the notion of communicative articulation, *the Little Ice Age* is rhematic but the status of the earlier post-verbal parts of the clause is not entirely clear. As Gómez González (2001, p. 84) states, it is not clear whether theme for Daneš is structural and clausal based or whether it is discoursal and related to textual patterns. Nor is it clear whether Daneš's conception of theme is actually separating, despite his support for the separating position. But nonetheless his work of theme progression is hugely influential and has been a major influence on SFL Themes.

In this paragraph I will summarize the above in order to show how it influenced Halliday's conception of Theme. Mathesius's theme comprised three components: point of departure, relevance, and foundation or Given/New. Some Prague School scholars, e.g., Travnicek, Beneŝ, and perhaps Daneš, proposed a separating theme and drew a distinction between theme ^ rheme as a relational clausal structure and as a referential inter-clausal relation. The clause initial element was identified as the site of the point of departure, but prior to Daneš's study of extended texts, no motivation was provided for why speaker/writers chose particular elements as points of departure.

Halliday, as noted by Davidse (1987), was a separator of Theme with Given and New treated as the system of information structure. In English the Given ^ New structure is identified by intonational choices. I will review Hallidayan information structure in chapter 3. Following Travnicek, Halliday identified Theme in English as the clause initial element. In the following section, we examine Hallidayan Theme in relation to the criteria of point of departure (východiště) and relevance (téma). The evolution of the concept from the 1960s onwards will be examined in order to address criticisms of the approach, and to contrast the Hallidayan Theme with the Prague School separating theme.

2.2 Halliday's Theme

In 1967 and 1968 Halliday published a series of three interlinked landmark articles entitled *Notes on Transitivity and Theme in English* (1967b, 1967c, 1968). In the second of these he spelled out his conception of Theme, and in the following paragraphs I will briefly summarize his ideas. Halliday (1967b, p. 200) stated that he avoided the terms topic and comment because of their combining overtones: topic in his view conflated Given and Theme. He clarified the distinction by stating that "given means what you were talking about (or what I was talking about before) 'theme' means what I am talking about" (p. 211). Halliday emphasized the separateness between Theme/Rheme and Given/New in the following:

> The Information systems, in other words, specify a structural unit and structure it in such a way as to relate it to the preceding discourse; whereas thematization takes a unit of sentence structure, the clause, and structures it in a way that is independent of what has gone before. This structuring is into two parts, a theme and a rheme, and is realized simply by the

> sequence of elements: the theme is assigned initial position in the clause, and all that follows is the rheme. (Halliday, 1967b, p. 212)

Theme was defined solely in terms of the relation between the Theme and Rheme and identified in English as consisting of the initial elements of the clause. In Halliday (1970b, p. 161) he emphasized what he meant by glossing Theme as "the peg on which the message is hung." In this sense we see that as well as being the point of departure, Theme functions to present an entity and then something is said in relation to that entity. To quote Halliday (1994, p. 37), Theme is "the element which serves as the point of departure of the message; it is that which the clause is concerned." Gómez González (2001, p. 94) noted that the above definition comprises both a place and a matter metaphor. These are not necessarily comparable as we will see. But it is clear that Halliday's theme as set out above is a direct descendant of Mathesius's notions of *východiště/téma*. Gómez González criticizes Halliday's gloss as being unhelpful, not only on the grounds of the potential incompatibility of the two elements of the gloss, but also on the grounds that it does not explain why certain elements are chosen as the point of departure (see criticism of Beneŝ above). I will return to this point once I have set out the systems of Theme in Halliday (1967b).

The first point to consider is what Halliday meant by clause initial elements. Martin et al. (1997, p. 24) state that "the first element" of the clause is the first one that expresses representational meaning.[4] More technically, they add that it is the first element that functions in the transitivity structure of the clause. Their definition entails a number of things. First the Theme does not necessarily consist only of the actual first element, which may be a conjunction or a modal adverb, but rather culminates in the first experiential element known as the topical Theme.[5] Second, as the subject may not be the first element which functions in transitivity, it does not necessarily function as Theme. Thus, Halliday notes that there are Themes which represent unmarked and marked choices. Unmarked Themes are defined as "the element which

4. "The Theme extends from the beginning of the clause (up to and including) the first element in transitivity. This element is called the 'topical' Theme; so we can say that the Theme of the clause consists of the topical Theme together with anything else that comes before it" (Halliday, 1994, p. 43).
5. This element was labelled cognitive theme in Halliday (1967b) and presumably to avoid confusion with "topic" it has been labelled the experiential theme by others such as Thompson (2013). But as topical theme is the term used in the latest edition of *IFG*, I too will employ it here.

Table 2.1: Topical Theme and Mood

Mood	Theme	
	Unmarked	Marked
Declarative	Subject, e.g., pronoun, nominal group, non-finite clause.	Complement, Adjunct, e.g., preposition phrase, adverbial group.
Interrogative Y/N	Finite plus subject,[1] e.g., finite operator ^ subject.	As above.
Interrogative Wh	Wh element, e.g., nominal group, preposition phrase or adverbial group functioning as interrogative element.	As above.
Imperative	(Let's) plus predicator, e.g., verbal group.	As above.

[1]Note in (1967b) the theme was finite only. A different approach is taken in Martin et al. (1997, p. 25), who class the finite as the interpersonal theme on the grounds that it is the element which signals that a response is required. They would similarly class the Wh interrogatives as a fusion of interpersonal and topical theme.

the speech function would determine for the point of departure of the clause" (1967b, p. 213). To illustrate, declarative mood comprises subject ^ finite order and hence the subject represents the unmarked Theme choice in that mood. Halliday and Matthiessen (2014, p. 97) provide a semantic gloss that the unmarked Theme represents the expected choice and is chosen as Theme unless there is a good communicative reason for not doing so. In a similar manner I glossed marked Theme as showing that the perspective being developed within the clause is approached from an unusual angle (O'Grady, 2017a, p. 276). Table 2.1 outlines the typical options.

Some examples may help with the Theme underlined.

2.4

Unmarked	Marked
John drank beer	On Friday night John drank beer
Jane sang well	Sing well Jane did
Are you going out?	Later are you going out?
Did you eat the cake?	The cake did you eat it?
Why did you write to Mary?	After marrying Jane why did you write to Mary?
Who played tennis yesterday?	Yesterday who played tennis?
Let's play tennis	Next week let's play tennis

Gómez González (2001) has noted that the place and matter components of Theme may not coincide. For instance, in the examples *Yesterday who played tennis* and *After marrying Jane why did you write to Mary,* the elements identified as Theme by Halliday clearly correspond with the point of departure, but it's much less certain that they are the matter of concern. It seems plausible that the matter of concern or relevance is that something will be said about the identity of the tennis players and the reason why the man wrote to another woman; the initial elements are settings in which "the that which" the clause is concerned with develops.

As well as the simple Themes outlined above, Hallidayan Theme recognizes that textual and interpersonal elements may precede the topical Theme. Such elements cannot exhaust the thematic potential of a clause as the following topical Theme "will also have thematic status almost if not quite as prominently as when nothing else precedes" (Halliday & Matthiessen, 2014, p. 110). In other words, the argument seems to be that as textual elements such as *and, but, if, when, however,* etc. are inherently thematic, and interpersonal elements such as vocatives and modals are characteristically thematic – their presence at the start of a clause cannot use up the clause's thematic potential. Instead, they function to establish logical and semantic relations with the preceding co-text such as expressing the speakers' angle and opinion vis-a-vis the development of the concern of the clause.

In Halliday (1967b) four further thematization options are presented which relate to how Themes are highlighted or related in clauses/ clause complexes to Rhemes. They are:

- Equative Theme (pseudo-clefts)
- Predicated Theme (clefts)
- Substitute Theme
- Reference Theme

In the passages that follow, I will describe each in its own terms and where relevant draw connections to more recent work outside of the SFL literature in order to highlight similarities and differences between SFL and other approaches.

2.2.1 Thematic Equative (Pseudo-cleft)[6]

Halliday (1967b) used a famous advertising slogan, *What we want is Watneys,* to illustrate his concept of equative Theme. He noted that as

6. I am in full agreement with Dik (1978, p. 27), who noted the unfortunate connotations of the term cleft with movement and derivation. My use of the term cleft is

the agnate clause, *We want Watneys* does not convey a message of exclusivity. The brewer's choice of slogan was inspired. Like all identifying clauses, Thematic equatives are reversible, e.g., *Watneys is what we want*. Halliday notes that Thematic equatives (pseudo-clefts) set up a relationship where the Theme equals the Rheme.[7] The structure specifies what the Theme is and equates it with the Rheme. It is this equation which signals the exclusiveness of the pseudo-cleft construction (Halliday & Matthiessen, 2014, p. 95). The *Watneys* example illustrates that the nominalization *what we want* can occur in either the Theme or the Rheme. The nominalization fulfils the function of the identified. It is the other element, the identifier, which is to be identified by its relationship with the identified nominalization.[8]

Pseudo-clefts are a type of identifying clause. Thus, as token and value are functions in identifying clauses, they must carry a token (variable) and value relationship. Token/value can be mapped on the identifier/identified in two ways:

2.5 (a) decoding: token = identified and value = identifier
(b) encoding: token = identifier and value = identified

Halliday (1967b, p. 237) has convincingly shown that in pseudo-clefts the relation is an encoding one; he notes that it is not possible to predicate the value in an equative relation. To illustrate using our example, *What we want is Watneys*, the utterance is a response to the question:

2.6 Q: *Is what we want Watneys?*
A: *Yes Watneys is what we want/ Yes what we want is Watneys.*
It is not an answer to the question:
Q: *What do we want?*

---

simply because of the widespread acceptance of the term. Like Dik, I do not see that clefts are derived from basic clauses and pseudo-clefts are derived from clefts.

7. This implies that strictly speaking the copula is not part of the Rheme but is rather transitional. However, I will follow SFL convention and notate it as part of the Rheme, though see discussion of Firbas (1992) in chapter 4.
8. In earlier work Halliday had used the labels *known* to refer to the *identified* and *unknown* to the *identifier*. Owing to the confusion between these terms and the terms Given and New he changed them (1967, p. 244, fn5). While on the whole this is a welcome clarification if *known* and *unknown* as terms are understood only in relational terms, with Given and New understood in referential terms then the argument may be clearer if the original terms are used.

Table 2.2: Pseudo-clefts: Theme/Rheme Structure Mapped onto Given/New in a Single Tone Group Following Collins (1991/2015)

There is a value	*what is it?*	
What we want	**is Watneys**	
Identified (known) Value	Identifier (unknown) Token	*As Halliday*
Theme (Given or New)	Rheme (New)	
There is a token	*what is its value?*	
Watneys	**is what we want**	
Identifier (unknown) Token	Identified (known) Value	*Not as Halliday*
Theme (Given or New)	Rheme (New)	

Thus, the structure of the pseudo-cleft assigns an encoding relationship. Collins's (1991/2015, p. 68) report that in his corpus no examples of decoding pseudo-clefts were located provides empirical support for the argument that pseudo-clefts carry an encoding relation.

Halliday argues (1967b, p. 226) that where the pseudo-cleft is spoken as a single tone group (information unit) – see chapter 3 – there is an unmarked relationship between the intonation focus (tonic syllable) and the identifier.[9] This, as we will see in chapter 3, entails that in the sequence identified ^ identifier the identifier consists of New information. The information status of the identified is ambiguous, but may well, depending on the context, be New. Collins (1991/2015, p. 118) provides some empirical support for Halliday's claims in that he finds that over 86 per cent of non-reversed pseudo-clefts are realized as a single tone group and mark the tonic syllable in the rheme. However, in the case of reversed pseudo-clefts, articulated in a single tone group, Collins reports that the tonic syllable is found in the rheme in 95.5 per cent of occasions. Thus, as table 2.2 indicates, Halliday's expectation is in need of correction. In the utterance *Watneys is what we want*, it seems that the tonic syllable does not naturally fall on the token *Watneys*, but rather falls within the value.

It should be noted that in the case of clefts articulated as single tone groups in Collins's corpus, reversed clefts outnumber non-reversed clefts by a factor of 12.5 to 1. Where the pseudo-cleft is articulated as more than one tone group, there is more than one intonational focus

9. For a contrasting view see Lambrecht (1994, p. 123), who argues that *Wh-pseudo-clefts* are synonymous with subject accented sentences, e.g., *what WE want is Watneys.*

and in most cases New information is signalled to occur in both the Theme and Rheme. This is the case regardless of whether the cleft is reversed or not. However non-reversed clefts are more frequent and outnumber reversed clefts by a factor of 4 to 1. In chapters 5 and 6 I will discuss the issue of competing tonic foci.

Collins's (1991/2015) corpus study classifies three types of structures as comprising pseudo-clefts, e.g., *Wh-clefts, All-clefts,* and *That-clefts.* Example 2.7 illustrates that *That-clefts* usually have the nominalization as Rheme. Martínez Lirola (2006, 2007, 2008) reports a corpus study of two novels by Alan Paton where she found that reversible *That-clefts* functioned to make the narrative vivid by referring to anaphoric information. Previous mention usually presents the referent of the pronoun as Given. Note though that speakers are free to make the token and not the value tonic if it suits their individual communicative desire. This brief digression is designed not only to point out the strength of a separating approach, but also to show that the information structure of spoken language is the result of nuanced interplay between prosodic and lexicogrammatical choices.

2.7 What we want is Watneys
All we want is Watneys
That's what we want.

Following Collins (1991/2015, p. 32) we can gloss the difference between the *Wh-cleft* and the *All-cleft* as

2.8 What (the thing) we want is Watneys
All (the only thing) we want is Watneys

Thus, Halliday's gloss of the *Wh*-cleft is need of some modification. While it may convey exhaustiveness, it does not have to. Collins (1991/2015, p. 33) states that *Wh*-clefts as identifying constructions convey an implied notion of exhaustiveness. So the utterance *What we want is Watneys* implies that we do not require anything further. However, Declerck (1988, p. 55) notes that an utterance such as *What we want is Watneys and some crisps* may convey either a specificational reading, i.e., we want more things, cf., Lambrecht's (1994) listing reading, or a predicative reading where the beer and crisps merge into a single substance which we can gloss as "pub fare." But on the other side of the argument Erteschik-Shir (2007, p. 81) provides the following example, which she describes as marking a contrastive focus.

2.9 What I saw was A BIG WASP (original capitalization)

Thus, it seems that for her that the exhaustive reading is to be preferred with the identifier (token) referring to a choice from a limited set of insects. Collins (1991/2015, p. 155) disagrees and criticizes what he labels the misconception that the identifier always signals contrastive meaning. Though of course in context it may well do so. Collins notes that as the inference of exhaustiveness is not encoded in the lexicogrammar, it is defeasible. Compare the following two examples and note that the later utterance is not acceptable in English as the *All-cleft* encodes exhaustiveness.

2.10 What we want is Watneys among other things
All we want is Watneys among other things[10]

Quirk et al. (1985, p. 426) argue that pseudo-clefts attract adjectives such as *crucial, important,* etc. as in *what is important is this feeling* or *this feeling is what is important.* This suggests that the identified or value is graded against an exemplary instance of a semantic category (Martin & White, 2005, p. 137). Hence the identifier (token) is identified by its relation with an exemplary referent and in the non-reversed clefts the Theme is a blend of the interpersonal and ideational. The identifier is the target of the positive appraisal inscribed in the identified. Such a view is contrary to Halliday, who argued that as Theme in pseudo-clefts isolates one of the two members which function in an equative relationship, it is primarily ideational (see Collins, 1991/2015, p. 84).

The identified or value is commonly held to represent a presupposition with only the identifier or token not identified. Thus, in our example it is presupposed that *we want something,* and the cleft identifies the something as *Watneys.* In the Hallidayan view, presuppositions are not synonymous with Given information. A presupposition is a proposition, knowledge of which is assumed. Given information, as we will see in chapter 3, refers to the recoverability of lexical elements which form into propositions. Though as presupposition in non-reversed pseudo-clefts corresponds with Theme, and as Theme is frequently composed of Given material, there is a close correspondence between the two terms (Prince, 1978),[11] but they should not be confused.

---

10. The utterance *All we want is Watneys and some crisps* is acceptable as it can only have a predicative reading.
11. Gundel (1985) states that in pseudo–clefts, that the topic is always initial and indicates a correlation between topic and referentially recoverability. We will examine the difference between topic and Theme in Section 2.4.

The above discussion supports the separateness of the Hallidayan approach, and there can be little doubt that his proposal originally formulated in (1967b) stands the test of time. However, there are three possible areas where revision may be necessary. The first relates to the notion of exhaustiveness, and Collins suggestion of a defeasible implicature seems sensible. The second relates to the unmarked intonation pattern of reversed pseudo-clefts produced in a single tone group, and the third is to recognize the interpersonal thematic potential of pseudo-clefts.

2.2.2 Predicated Theme (Clefts)

Halliday and Matthiessen (2014, p. 122) state that what they label "predicated Theme" is a further resource which "figures prominently" in assigning Theme / Rheme structure and thus in organizing the clause as a message. Halliday (1967b, p. 237) illustrates with the examples:

2.11a It was John who broke the window
2.11b There was John who broke the window.

He explains the difference between the examples and the agnate form *John broke the window* by saying that structurally the predication maps the function of the identifying onto that of the Theme. The Theme carries the focus of information and is conflated with the New (Halliday, 1967b, p. 237; Halliday & Matthiessen, 2014, p. 123). There is an alternative Theme analysis (Halliday & Matthiessen, 2014, p. 124) which recognizes that the cleft itself is composed out of a matrix clause and a relative clause, and the subjects of both clauses represent the unmarked Themes as shown in 2.12.

The difference between 2.11a and 2.11b is one of exclusiveness. In (a) the Theme *it was John* is uniquely specified: he and he alone broke the window. In (b) however, the Theme is not uniquely specified and can be glossed as "John, possibly among others" (Halliday, 1967b, p. 238). For reasons that are not clear to me, there is no further mention of *There-clefts* in Halliday's writings. Indeed, the literature on *There-clefts* is vanishingly small. I will return to the issue of *There-clefts* below, but first I will discuss *It-clefts*.

Example 2.12 presents the utterance with the assumption that it was articulated as a single tone group. The underlining of *John* indicates that it is the tonic syllable in the spoken utterance.

2.12

It	was John	who	broke the window
Theme 1	Rheme 1	Theme 1	Rheme 1
Theme		Rheme	
Identifying (value)		Identifier (variable)	
New		Given	

Davidse (2000, p. 111), Lambrecht (2001, p. 43), Huddleston & Pullum (2002, p. 1416), and Bourgoin et al. (2021, p. 486) agree with Halliday that *It-clefts* are formed of a matrix clause and a relative clause. The cleft relative clause (CRC) does not form a constituent with its antecedent. The antecedent is the full complement NG and not the subject of the matrix clause. In other words, the subject of the CRC in this example is *John*. The complement of the matrix clause specifies a value (John) for a variable, the gap expressed by the proposition in the CRC "X broke the window," by identifying X as John.

Bourgoin et al. (2021, p. 487) note that despite apparent similarities between what they label Halliday's "functional approach" and Lambrecht's "formal pragmatic approach," the theories rest on different theoretical underpinnings. For Lambrecht information structure is the pragmatic structuring of propositions, whereby the assertion differs from the presupposition in terms of focus. The assertion as focus is typically accented, though prosody is not part of this definition of focus. So regardless of how it is articulated for Lambrecht, *John* is the focus, and *it was John* is the assertion. For Halliday (1967a, 1967b) and Halliday and Greaves (2008), focus is coded by the articulation of a tonic accent. In the Hallidayan model, speakers are not constrained by syntax in their choice of how to manage information structure. Thus, a speaker could, if appropriate, signal the intonation focus on the variable and not the value, or they could articulate the utterance in two tone groups with two foci.

Bourgoin et al. (2021) is the first large-scale corpus study of *It-clefts*[12] which combines syntactic and prosodic information. They extracted 143 *It-clefts* from the LLC1 corpus and found that in only twelve cases

12. The article examined full and reduced *It-clefts*, e.g., Who broke the window? *It was John (who broke the window).* Only the matrix clause is overtly uttered. In the discussion that follows I will focus only on full clefts.

Table 2.3: The Distribution of Intonation Foci in *It-clefts* from Bourgoin et al. (2021)

Single tone unit = *It-cleft*	#	More than one tone unit = *It-cleft*	#
Focal + Non-focal, e.g., I it was John who broke the window I	12	Focal + Focal, e.g., I it was John I who broke the window I	91
Non-Focal + Focal, e.g., I it was John who broke the window I	34	Non-focal + Focal copula + Focal, e.g., I it was John I who broke the window I	6

were the clefts produced as a single tone group with focus on the value. Table 2.3 summarizes the findings.

Such evidence strongly supports Halliday's functional approach and in particular the wisdom of separating Theme from information; the interplay of Theme and information allows speakers the freedom to subtly manage their information structure needs. The following four examples with the identical Theme ^ Rheme structure demonstrate.

2.13

I It was John	who broke the window I
Theme	Rheme
value	variable
Focus	Given
← New	

The identifying clause or value is mapped onto the Theme, and the identifier (variable) is mapped onto the Rheme. In 2.13 the Theme and the New are conflated. The variable is presented as Given information. The sole element which is non-recoverable is the identity of the window breaker.

2.14

I it was John I	who broke the window I
Theme	Rheme
value	variable
Focus	Focus
New	Given ← New

Here there are two foci as the cleft is produced as two tone groups. I will reserve discussion of a potential information hierarchy when there is more than one focus until chapter 3. For now I will assume that as all foci are in separate tone groups, they have equal status. In the first tone group, which corresponds with the Theme/value, the identity of John is introduced and presented as non-recoverable information. Then in the following tone group, the complement of the CRC (variable) is introduced and presented as non-recoverable information. The information status of the preceding part of the CRC is ambiguous and depends on whether the verb has in the context of utterance been previously mentioned. The effect of this is to signal that not only the identity of the value is New but also the result of the action encoded in the variable and possibly the action itself is also New. Thus, the clause may present a non-recoverable value uniquely specified by a freshly introduced variable.

2.15

ǀ it was John	who broke the window ǀ	
Theme	Rheme	
value	variable	
		Focus
Given	←	New

In 2.15, the cleft is presented as a single piece of information as in 2.13 but differs in that the speaker presents the identity of the value as recoverable while the variable is presented as not recoverable. Thus, relationally a Given value is specified for a freshly introduced variable.

2.16

ǀ it	was	John	ǀ who broke	the window ǀ
Theme			Rheme	
value			variable	
Given	Focus	Given	Given	Focus
	New		←	New

As in 2.14 above, the cleft in 2.16 is presented as two pieces of information. The complement of the matrix clause is presented as Given. Instead, the copula receives the tonic accent. Thus, while the value is recoverable, its temporality is signalled as non-recoverable. A reasonable pragmatic explanation is that by making the copula tonic the speaker wishes to emphasize that it is in fact the value X that equates with the variable Y. In this reading the speaker may be anticipating that the speaker will object to the identity of the value and doubt that *John* could equate with the value specified for the variable, which is itself not recoverable. These four examples clearly illustrate the strength of the separating approach.

As noted above, there has been little work either in or outside the Hallidayan tradition on *There-clefts*. Davidse and Kimps (2016), Davidse and Njende (2019), and Davidse et al. (2023) have, however, produced Hallidayan-inspired, corpus-grounded analyses of *There-clefts*. They have also suggested reasons why *There-clefts* have been ignored: chiefly the use of written and not spoken data and the lack of recognition of reduced *There-clefts* as clefts rather than as existential clauses. Their analyses have shown that what may seem to be existential constructions are in fact clefts.

2.17 His nomination of formative influences gives a clue. **There is Brian Ashton and Jack Rowell.** (WB Times, from Davidse & Njende, 2019, p. 160)

Here it is tempting to analyse the clause in transitive terms as an independent clause of the type *there ^ process ^ existent*. However, as Davidse and Njende (2019, p. 184) point out, there is a textually evoked, implied variable and the clause can be reconstrued as

There is Brian Ashton and Jack Rowell	who are nominated as formative instances
Value	Variable

This example clearly shows the importance of analysing utterances in context, a particular strength of the Hallidayan approach. Two types of *There-clefts* are identified. The first (2.17) has a listing function where the value is listed as instances of the variable; Ashton and Rowell among unnamed others are the presupposed formative instances. The second type (2.18) is a quantifying *There-cleft*. In these examples the value quantifies how many instances are identified by the variable. The following examples are corpus examples of quantifying *There-clefts* reported in Davidse and Kimps (2016).

2.18 Perhaps there was one who didn't lecture
There are only about three people who are sort of teenagers

In the small numbers of cases where sound files were available, a tonic syllable occurred on the value. However, as in the case of *It-clefts*, *There-clefts* may be articulated as more than a single tone group, e.g.,

2.19 | Perhaps there was one | who didn't lecture |[13]
| There are only about three people | who are sort of teenagers |

Thus, it seems likely that in the case of *There-clefts* as in *It-clefts* that the interplay between the lexicogrammatical choices and the intonation choices combine to enable a speaker to produce rhetorical effects appropriate to their individual communicative needs. Once again the power of the separateness approach in describing how people make meaning is apparent.

2.2.3 Substitute Theme[14]

Halliday (1967b, p. 239) provides the following three examples, which he classes as dialectal variants with Theme underlined:

2.20 He is always late, John[15]
He is always late, is John
He is always late John is

The substituted element is a delayed Theme; hence the clause has two points of Thematic prominence. The speaker is free to make the delayed Theme tonic thus conflating the Thematic meaning of *the angle of the clause* with the informational meaning *of freshly introduced*. This pattern has been widely discussed outside SFL,[16] where it is labelled right dislocation (again an unfortunate term as it implies both an invariant word order and movement; see for example, Aijmer, 1989; Lambrecht, 2001; López, 2016). The function of right dislocation has been defined as functioning to keep the attention of the hearer by sustaining a relation-

13. In this example the original coding was a compound tone. This is an analysis I reject as will be detailed in chapter 3. See Halliday and Greaves (2008) for arguments in favour of a compound tone analysis and Tench (1996) and O'Grady (2010) for arguments against.
14. For reasons that are unclear substitute Theme and reference Theme are not discussed in *IFG*.
15. The presence of a comma suggests the expectation of a tone group boundary.
16. There has been much discussion of right dislocation by user in the variationist sociolinguistics literature; see, for example, Durham (2011), and indeed in other languages, e.g., French and Catalan, where it has been labelled the tail, e.g., Vallduví and Engdahl (1996).

ship between the Given referent and a proposition (Lambrecht, 2001, p. 1076). Lambrecht claims that the dislocated element and the substitute are already ratified, or in Hallidayan terms, recoverable. In SFL, however, substitute Theme can, depending on the speaker assessment of the hearer's shared knowledge, be presented as Given or New. A New substitute Theme functions as an online correction to what had previously and erroneously been considered a shared state of affairs. López (2016) proposes that there are two types of right dislocation, which he dubs hanging (h) and displaced / contrastive (d).

2.21 John met her, my mother (h)
2.22 He met my mother John (d)

The contrastive topic is identical in form to Halliday's substitute Theme. The contrastive type dislocations are, López claims, integral to the clause[17] and always Given in the sense that they refer back to an antecedent. Following Rochemont (2016), Givenness is defined as tying some linguistics property of an expression, its syntactic form or position or its prosody, to the information or cognitive status of its denotation, which is already present in the discourse model in some sense. Thus, it may be previously mentioned, unmentioned but inferable, or contrastive. The displaced item can, in SFL terms, be presented as recoverable or not recoverable. López's view, albeit from a very different tradition, is clearly compatible with Halliday's sketch of substitute Theme. In the next section, we will examine the relationship between topic / tail and Theme.

An intriguing finding of a function of right dislocation is found in Aijmer (1989). Her corpus-grounded study provides evidence that right dislocations (or in her words, "tails") as Given elements functioned in-

17. This argument is based on case agreement from a range of languages. To illustrate using an example originally in Anagnostopoulou (1997, as quoted in López, 2016, p. 406).

I	mitera	tu,	kathenas	tin	agapai	(h)
The.nom	mother	his	everyone	her.acc	loves	
Tin	mitera	tu,	kathenas	tin	agapai	(d)
The.acc	mother	his	everyone	her.acc	loves	

The second example is classed as a (d) dislocation because the variable is bound by the quantifier. The clause is in accusative case, which matches the case of the resumptive pronoun (her).

terpersonally to create an affective bond and not to transmit information. Aijmer found forty-nine instances of right dislocations, and so her findings must be taken as no more than suggestive. Interestingly, in around 35 per cent of the examples, the right dislocation was uttered in the same tone group as the rest of the clause. In the remaining examples, it was found in an independent tone group which contained rising tone. I will discuss in chapter 5 that rising tone signals an assumption of common ground in that the proposition expressed in the tone group is known to both speaker and hearer. Cruttenden (1997) labels it a hearer-focused tone. Thus, Aijmer's findings are suggestive that the displaced Theme is either recoverable or functions to express a state of affairs known to the speaker and hearer and that the speaker is reaching out to their interlocutor. This study resonates with the SFL view that clauses carry interpersonal as well as experiential meaning, and hence that Theme/information structure should not be seen simply as a resource for weaving together experiential meaning. It also signals the interpersonal weave in a text.

2.2.4 Reference Theme

Halliday (1967b, p. 241) briefly describes this Thematic resource and provides the following examples. The first is unmarked the second marked.

2.23 <u>Britain</u> it is all roads
2.24 <u>The sound that came out on the air</u> I didn't know I had it in me

While noting that the resource is restricted by register and channel, Halliday argues that the use of the non-Thematic anaphoric pronoun functions to isolate the Theme from the remainder of the clause. In his words the Theme is not needed as a participant in the clause structure. He therefore predicts that the Theme would be articulated in a different tone group than the rheme. Using López's description, these Themes are examples of (h) left dislocations. The Themes are promoted, and by being in a separate tone group, they must conflate with a tonic syllable which signals a point of information focus within the Theme. Thus, we can see that Halliday's view is largely in accord with other views. However, these examples illustrate a paradox. Namely, that while we can see that the interplay of intonational and lexicogrammatical choices allow speakers to project subtly different assumptions of information and thematic structure, information and thematic choices that co-occur lose some of their independence. The meaning of reference Themes, for example, is dependent on tonality choices. In chapter 3 we will consider how, while it is possible to tease apart the thematic from the informational, in practice combinations of thematic and informational choices recombine to project contextually appropriate speaker assumptions of the information they share with their hearers as they weave their wordings into coherent and appropriate propositions.

In this section, we have seen that Theme functions as a linking and an organizing resource. In the next I will first look at how Theme choices weave clauses into a coherent message.

2.3 *Theme as Weaver of Meaning*

In Halliday (1967b) Theme is identified as an intra-clausal feature which relates the initial part of the clause, which in declarative mood in the unmarked case is everything up to and including the subject, to the remainder of the clause. Nothing is explicitly stated about how a specific Theme choice is itself constrained by the prior co-text. Yet, it is obvious that each clause is itself a response to what has come before. The immediately preceding co-text[18] creates a set of expectations which constrain the choice of Theme. While Halliday's (1967b, p. 212) claim that "the Information systems, in other words, specify a structural unit and structure it in such a way as to relate it to the preceding discourse; whereas thematization takes a unit of sentence structure, the clause, and structures it in a way that is independent of what has gone before" may seem to suggest that each Theme choice is independent of the preceding discourse, that is not the case. While the speaker has the freedom to change the discourse topic, disagree, or say something unexpected, their contribution must be relevant to and motivated by what has gone before. Fries (1995), in a widely cited paper which was heavily influenced by earlier work on thematic progression (e.g., Daneš, 1974), proposed that in order for a Theme to represent a point of departure, it had to depart from somewhere established by the prior co-text. Hence, rather than thinking of Theme as a clausal element as Halliday (1967b) had, Fries argued that it needed to be considered as a discoursal feature. His hypothesis was that there will be a correlation between thematic progression and the structure of the text and that this will correlate with different genres, e.g., some genres will favour con-

18. The language we produce is in reality subject to different time scales: (1) the immediate context and co-text, (2) the generic conventions established by a particular subgroup over a number of years, and (3) the forms of the language used in a speech community which have emerged through generations of interactions.

stant Theme progression and others linear Theme progression. Fries, while following Halliday in separating Theme from Given, recognized that Theme and Given frequently co-occur. This means that like Halliday, he recognizes the fact that speakers are free to introduce novel points of departure if appropriate.

In the first two editions of *IFG* (Halliday, 1985, 1994, p. 34), Theme was defined as "the element which serves as the point of departure of the message: it is that with which the clause is concerned." In the more recent two editions, the definition has been changed to "The Theme is the element which serves as the point of departure of the message; it is that which locates and orients the clause within its context" (2004, p. 65; 2014, p. 89). This is a welcome recognition that Theme choices are sensitive to context. In a similar manner, Halliday and Martin (1993, p. 244) described Theme as enabling the text's angle on the field, and Matthiessen (1995) described Theme in terms of being an enabling resource for the logogenetic growth of ideational meaning within texts and phylogenetically for the evolution of ideational meaning open to interpersonal negotiation. However, despite the promotion of the enabling function of Theme as a discourse resource, it is fair to say that Gómez González's (2001) critique of the tension between the metaphorical descriptions of Theme as place (point of departure) and matter (topic) is still valid.

In the recent edition of Halliday and Matthiessen (2014), when discussing the variations of the clause *The Duke gave my aunt this teapot*, Halliday discusses three different types of "subject" which he labels: (1) psychological subject or Theme, (2) grammatical subject or subject, and (3) logical subject or Actor. He notes that in the case of 2.25 the three kinds of "subject" coincide.

2.25

The Duke	gave my aunt this teapot
Theme Subject Actor	

But in 2.26–2.29 they do not coincide.

2.26

This teapot	my aunt	was given	by the duke
Theme	Subject		Actor

2.27

My aunt	was given	this teapot	by the duke
Theme Subject			Actor

2.28

This teapot	the duke	gave	my aunt
Theme	Subject Actor		

2.29

By the duke	my aunt	was given	this teapot
Theme Actor	Subject		

On page 83 of *IFG4*, we find the quote:

> The Theme functions in the structure of the **clause as a message**. A clause has meaning as a message, a quantum of information; the Theme is the point of departure for the message. It is the element the speaker selects for "grounding" what he is going on to say. (Halliday & Matthiessen, 2014)

The Theme is both the point of departure and the element that speaker selects as that which he is going to talk about. The second part of the definition equates the Theme with the matter metaphor. More specifically, on page 80 we find the following description of 2.26 above:

> In *this teapot my aunt was given by the duke*, the psychological Subject is *this teapot*. That is to say, it is "this teapot" that is the concern of the message – that the speaker has taken as the point of embarkation of the clause. (Halliday & Matthiessen, 2014)

Again the Theme is equated with the concern or topic. It is also of interest that in this quote the Theme is described as psychological in a manner akin to the 1967 description of cognitive Theme. It has some mental reality, which has been described notionally as the *peg* or *hook* on which the message is hung (Halliday, 1970b, p. 161). In the following section we will review the concept of topic as presented by non-SFL scholars in order to illustrate similarities and differences between topic and topical Theme and argue that the peg metaphor is more appropriate for the function of topic, not Theme.

2.4 Topic

In a footnote, Halliday and Matthiessen (2014, p. 89, fn1) explain that their use of Theme/Rheme differs from others' use of the terms topic/comment in that Theme/Rheme represents a separating approach while topic/comment represents a combining approach. Yet the use of such terms as Giv(en) Top(ic) and New Top(ic) in the work for functional scholars such as Dik (1978) shows that this cannot be the complete story.

Lambrecht (1994) is a hugely influential work and its ideas have been picked up and accepted by numerous functional approaches such as Functional Discourse Grammar (see Hengeveld & Mackenzie, 2008) and Role and Reference Grammar (see Van Valin & LaPolla, 1997). Like Halliday, Lambrecht sees topic as a grammatical category which operates at clause rank and is related to but is not identical to subject. That said, there are significant differences between the Lambrechtan and Hallidayan approaches. Lambrecht, unlike Halliday, uses the pragmatic test of "aboutness" to identify topic. Strawson (1964, p. 97) defined a topic as a matter of standing current interest or concern. A statement can only be informative if it imparts information that is relevant to the topic. Lambrecht (1994, pp. 121–2) argues that there are distinct sentence patterns with two types of information structure. The first type of sentence contains a topic and a comment. Lambrecht argues that this is the unmarked or expected presuppositional sentence structure with the subject as the unmarked topic, such as in 2.30. He refers to one of the other types as "identification sentences" (see 2.32), and argues that they, along with thetic sentences, are topic-less. I will discuss thetic constructions in section 2.5; see also discussion of the quality scale in chapter 3.

Thus, in the following example taken from Lambrecht (1994), Theme/Rheme and topic/comment are identical.

2.30

The children	went to school
Theme topic	Rheme comment

However, the structures only overlap if the sentence is a response to the question *What did the children do next?* (Lambrecht, 1994, p. 121). As Lambrecht states, example 2.30 "pragmatically presupposes that the children in question are a 'matter of standing interest and concern' … and asserts about these children that they went to school. With traditional logic we might say that the predicate 'went to school' expresses a property attributed to the subject 'the children'" (1994, p. 121).

Yet in a different context the topic comment structure diverges from the Theme/Rheme structure.

2.31

Context: Who went to school?

The children	went to school
Theme comment	Rheme topic

The matter of standing current interest or concern is *went to school,* which is the topic. An alternative wording with a marked complement Theme, *To school the children went,* illustrates that *to school* is the expression of standing interest. My analysis differs from that presented by Lambrecht (1994, p. 122), who argues that there is no topic in the sentence. His logic is that such sentences function "to identify a referent as the missing argument in an open proposition." He claims, and I agree, that the subject NG is a focus expression and that its status as a non-topic is signalled by a prosodic prominence. However, I reject Lambrecht's analysis on the grounds that a matter of standing interest may be an event or action; topichood is not necessarily restricted to a nominal referent.

2.32

Context: What happened?

The children	went to school
Theme	Rheme

The matter of standing current interest or concern is the open proposition, which does not refer to a referent, event, or action. We cannot therefore assign a topic comment structure to this sentence. The sentence reports an event or happening. As it does not contain a matter of standing concern it is topic-less, though as we will see it introduces potential topics to the unfolding discourse.

2.33
Context: John was busy that morning.

After the children went to school	he	had to clean the house
Theme (marked)	Rheme	
Topic scene setting	topic	

In 2.33, the matter of current standing or interest is John, and the pronominal *he* is the topic. In Hallidayan terms the setting is a marked Theme, and the subject is found in the Rheme. In section 2.5 we will see that some scholars working with the SFL tradition would include the subject *he* as part of the Theme. Lambrecht's (1994, p. 127) example shows that a topic can appear in more than a single location in the clause.

2.34

Pat	said	they	called	her	twice
topic				topic	
Theme		Rheme			
Theme 1	Rheme 1	Theme 2	Rheme		

In 2.34 there are two possible Theme ^ Rheme structures. If we treat the projecting and projected clause as a nexus, the projecting clause is the marked Theme. *Pat's saying* is the point of departure for *their calling* and functions as a setting for the action expressed in the clause. Conversely, if we treat the clauses as separate, the subjects *Pat* and *they* are the unmarked Themes. For Lambrecht the tonic prominence on the adverbial element *twice* entails[19] that Pat and the referential object pronoun are topical in that it is the woman named Pat who is the topic which the different propositions comment on. However, had the speaker produced the following example:

19. We can infer that a tonic prominence on the verb *calling* or the pronoun *they* would have resulted in *Pat* and *her* functioning as topics.

2.35

Pat	said	they	called her twice
topic		topic	
Theme		Rheme	
Theme 1	Rheme	Theme 2	Rheme

The intonational focus on *her* would necessitate that it was not a topic expression. Instead, the nominative pronoun *they* is the referent, which functions as the point of current interest in the projected clause. This brief description of topic as described by Lambrecht has shown that a referent must at the time of speaking be a matter of ongoing concern and topics tend to correlate with Given items. Lambrecht (1994, p. 165) schematized the relationship as follows:

2.36 The Topic Acceptability Scale

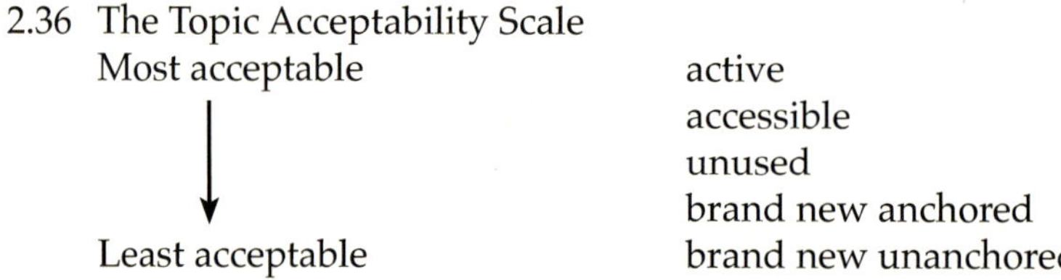

He notes that the most acceptable topic referent is one that is active in the discourse and the one that is least acceptable is one that is brand new and unanchored. I will discuss and critique these terms in chapter 5. But for present purposes, it is sufficient to note that the top three terms in the scale refer to recoverable referents, while the bottom two terms refer to non-recoverable referents. Lambrecht provides the following examples:

2.37 A boy is tall
2.38 A boy in my class is tall

He argues that the indefinite referent *a boy in my class* is more acceptable as a topic than the indefinite referent *a boy* because the anchoring phrase *in my class* is a referential link to the speaker. It represents a subset of students of whom the speaker is one.[20] He argues that 2.39 is

20. An indefinite NG without anchoring is acceptable as a topic if it is construable as having a generic and hence identifiable referent, e.g., *A German Shepherd is strong willed.*

a more acceptable sentence than 2.37 above because of the presence of a dynamic rather a stative predicate: in SFL terms a material rather than a relational process. Despite 2.39 being more acceptable, Lambrecht refuses to class the indefinite subject NG *a boy* as a topic and analyses it with 2.32 above as a topic-less sentence.

2.39 A boy was run over by a car

Instead, he argues that the subject NG in 2.39 is to be construed as a participant in an event. There is no aboutness relation in the sense that the listener does not need to identify the referent in order to assess the relevance of information expressed. This is clearly correct but missing the important insight that sentences are not usually produced in isolation, and that the propositions expressed in them act as the starting point for further propositions. Thus, if we examine the following paradigm, it is odd that only the sentence with the indefinite NG is considered not to have a topic comment structure and to construe an event.

2.40 He was run over by a car (active)
The man was run over by a car (accessible)
My friend John was run over by a car (unused)
A man in my class was run over by a car (brand new + anchor)
A man was run over by a car

In fact I contend that all of the sentences in 2.40 construe an event: the same one in fact. There is someone and that someone was run over by a car. What differs though is the hearer's presumed knowledge of the identity of the unfortunate man. But in each case, there is a male person who is presented as the matter of current interest. The indefinite determiner NG signals that the identity of the topic is not yet known or activated but prospects that the identity will be revealed in the subsequent discourse. Therefore, I propose that the role of topicality is not restricted to previously identifiable referents, though it usually is. This suggests that the speaker / writer must have motivated reasons for such an unexpected choice.

There is widespread agreement that an analysis of the function of topic must take account of how communication functions (Féry & Ishihara, 2016; Krifka, 2008). In other words, why do speakers need to signal that certain referents and expressions encode topicality? Scholars such as Büring (2016), Chafe (1994, 2018), Erteschik-Shir (2007), Féry and Ishihara (2016), Vallduví (1992), etc., propose what I will gloss as a file card metaphor.[21] Every topic is akin to a mental file card or frame with each one representing a discourse referent. The frames are organized so that the most recently activated file cards / topics are most easily retrievable. In the previous paragraph, we have seen how this is encoded in English in Lambrecht's topic accessibility scale. When a speaker activates a new topical referent to the discourse, the hearer opens a new file card which then becomes the most accessible one. Topics refer to the identifiable information in a proposition which merges with the non-presupposed information to fulfil a communicative need.

I propose that this metaphorical description of topic has the potential to enrich SFL theory. As the example below indicates, the three types of subject identified in Halliday (1967b) are not necessarily conflated. Here the grammatical and psychological subjects are conflated but separated from the logical subject or actor. It is also worth pointing out that "non-identifiable" refers to the identifiability of a referent and not to whether it is "present in the discourse." Hence it may or may not, depending on the speaker's tonicity choice be presented as the information focus of the clause.

2.41

A man	was run over by	a car
Topic (Non-ident)		(actor)
Theme	Rheme	If tonic = focal new.

Lambrecht (1994), as noted above, has argued that not all clauses have a topic. He proposed a class of clause labelled identificational – see 2.32 above, where I rejected his argument – and 2.42 below which Lambrecht reports to have seen in a handwritten message on a partially ripped poster on a university campus protesting the Reagan government's murderous assault on Central America. In SFL terms the subject Nazis is the unmarked Theme.

2.42 Nazis tear down anti-war posters

Lambrecht (1994, p. 133–4) argues that the first reading of the sentence is likely to construe *Nazis* as a generic topic, and the proposition as a comment on the actions of the *Nazis*. According to this reading,

21. Similarities with Halliday's peg metaphor are apparent as I'm sure readers will have noticed.

which he stigmatizes as "inattentive," the writer intended to do no more than express what is an accepted truth. But he argues that in the context where the sentence was written on a torn anti-war poster that the writer did not wish to make a generic comment on Nazis. Instead, the sentence should be construed as *People who tear down anti-war posters are Nazis* or perhaps *Only Nazis tear down anti-war posters.* However, I find this argument rather unconvincing for a number of reasons. The first is that it is premised upon the view that topics must refer to identifiable referents. Instead, there is nothing to suggest that the writer did not want to make a comment on those he/she perceived as Nazis. Furthermore, after seeing the torn anti-war poster, the writer may well have assumed that the identity of those who ripped the poster was inferable. Therefore, even using Lambrecht's own reasoning which requires an accessible referent to encode the topic *Nazis*, the writer may have intended to refer to a generic group of warmongers operating on the campus. In any case the reading of *Nazis* requires the readers to open or assess a mental file card to which further propositional information is entered.

There is though a class of sentences in English where the lack of a topic is overtly coded according to Lambrecht. However, his argument only holds water if one accepts that topic can be signalled by lack of tonic prominence. This is obviously not a view I subscribe to. Briefly, the argument is based on an observation in Schmerling (1976), who heard the radio announcements of the deaths of two former US presidents as follows (these examples are discussed in much more detail in chapter 5):

2.43 Truman <u>died</u>
2.44 <u>John</u>son died[22]

Lambrecht argues that the tonic syllable on Johnson means that it represents the focus of the sentence. To preview the next chapter, I agree with this point but find the rest of Lambrecht's argument circular and based once again on the premise that topics must have identifiable referents. For Lambrecht, Truman is an inferable referent, but Johnson was a brand new unanchored one. There seems to be no reason why Johnson is not a topic as the sole difference between *Johnson* and *Truman* is that the hearer will need to activate a mental file card for *Johnson*. In

22. Truman died on December 26, 1972, after a long illness, and his death had been widely expected and foreshadowed. Johnson conversely died unexpectedly on January 23, 1973, after a heart attack.

other words, Johnson becomes the matter of standing interest or relevance at the moment of uttering. As such, he is the referent which the proposition tells us about. Moreover, the proper nouns "Johnson" and "Truman" are identifiable as members of the class of former American presidents. The sole difference in informational status between the examples is referential and not topical; both utterances contain topics though "Truman" alone is presented as being recoverable, or to paraphrase Halliday, in the air.

In the next section, we will examine a further class of sentence types which have been claimed not to contain a topic; though of course in SFL terms there must be a Theme.

2.5 *Theticity*

In some languages such as Japanese, topics are encoded by morphological means. Kuroda (1972, p. 176) labelled the distinction between the two following sentences as thetic and categorial (containing an overt topic).

2.45 Inu ga hashite iru (thetic and translated)[23] as *There is a dog running.*
2.46 Inu wa hashite iru (categorical and translated) as *The dog is running.*

The distinction is based solely on the presence of the respective particles *ga* and *wa.* To illustrate in Japanese, we can find the following examples which can all be translated as *On my birthday I drank a beer.*

2.47 *Tanjoobi ni* biru o nonda
Birthday to beer acc drank

In 2.47 the subject and actor are elided with the hearer inferring that the referent is the speaker.

2.48 *Tanjoobi ni* watashi ga biru o nonda
Birthday to I nom beer acc drank

In this example the same information is encoded but the subject is overtly expressed. However, the subject particle "ga" signals that the

23. While I am obviously not a native Japanese speaker, this is a rather free, albeit apt, translation. For me *There is a dog running* would translate as *Hashitte iru inu ga imasu.* Kuroda's argument as to the presence or absence of a topic though is sound.

sentence is to be construed as an event. The speaker does not signal that the sentence is about any particular referent. Shimojo (2024, p. 11) states that when topics are "zero-coded" it is because the topic is so salient that it does not require overt mention.[24] Zero-coding of topic contrasts with 2.49, where the pronominal element is clearly marked as topic. The sentence concerns the referent, and the birthday is the setting.

2.49 *Tanjoobi ni watashi wa* biru o nonda

Such examples illustrate that as topic is overtly codable by the system of Japanese grammar, it is possible in a Lambrecktan framework either to identify sentences as having topic comment structures or as being thetic and hence topic-less. The following two examples show that the speaker has the option of making birthday the topic: it is that and not the speaker which is the matter of current interest.

2.50 *Tanjoobi wa* biru o nonda
2.51 *Tanjoobi wa* watashi ga biru o nonda

Teruya (2004, p. 231) notes that in Japanese Theme is identified as culminating in a Theme marker usually *wa*.[25] In the examples (2.46) to (2.51) I have underlined the Theme. Of interest is that the Theme position is at or near the start of the clause. The element marked as the grammatical subject by *ga* is not thematic and that as a result there would appear to be numerous clauses in Japanese, such as *biru o nonda*, where the function of Theme is not overtly coded. In English by contrast, except in minor clauses the Theme function is coded in all independent clauses.

Sasse (1987) proposed a distinction between statements which are categorical and those which are thetic. His reasoning built upon work of Brentano and Marty (1918) at the turn of the twentieth century, who challenged the notion that all statements had to be composed of double judgment: a topic is introduced and then the rest of the statement is predicated about the topic. They argued that there are sentences (such as this one) which simply expressed an event, state, or situation.[26] 2.52 to 2.59 list some examples of "thetic statements" with the underlining

24. An analogous example from English is where the second mention of a subject is zero-coded in a sequence of two paratactic clauses, e.g., Gerard went to the supermarket and bought some coffee.
25. For a full list see Teruya (2004, p. 231).
26. I will also discuss this issue in terms of a quality scale in the review of Firbas's FSP in chapter 4.

indicating the Theme. Sasse, like Lambrecht after him, argues that theticity may be expressed by intonation as in 2.56 to 2.59 below, where in all cases it is claimed that the subject/Theme would receive tonic prominence. Sasse's argument is that the tonic placement on the subject signals the fusion of the referent denoting an individual and an element denoting an event (1987, p. 522). The selection of the individual and the predication occur almost simultaneously (1987, p. 521). I argued above that such reasoning confuses the recoverability of a referent with its identifiability. *The dog* and *my neck* can therefore be considered to be the matter of standing concern or interest, and the rest of the clause comments on the topic. The informational status is coded by tonic placement in a manner akin to that of the US presidents discussed earlier.

However, the two metrological examples 2.57 and 2.58 are clearly paraphrasable in a manner akin to group 2.52 to 2.55. Furthermore, while one can ask a question concerning the identity of the *barker* and the location of *the hurt,* is it not possible to ask a question about the subject of *the falling* or *shining*? In Sasse's term there is fusion between the individual element and the event, and therefore there is evidence that some examples of subjects followed by intransitive verbs, but by no means all, are thetic.

2.52 It is raining. Rain!
2.53 There goes Johnny Johnny!
2.54 Here comes Johnny. Johnny!
2.55 In a land faraway there lived a great warrior. A great warrior
2.56 The dog's barking. What's barking? The dog (is).
2.57 The sun's shining. (It is bright)
2.58 Night is falling. (It's getting dark)
2.59 My neck hurts. What hurts? My neck (does).

In 2.52 to 2.55 the clauses present the existence, emergence, or disappearance of an element. The speaker presents an element and introduces it into the discourse. Once introduced into the discourse, the element provokes the hearer to open or create a mental file card for the referent which becomes a potential topic for the following clauses. Within the clause itself, the element underlined as Theme has the function of signalling the point of departure; the "dummy" subjects *it* and *there* locate the clause within its context as scene setting for what is to come. In (2.54) the existential element is preceded by a marked Theme which grounds the clause temporally and physically in its context while presenting a potential topic as a matter of standing interest or concern which is available to any party to the discourse to comment on.

The argument here then is that such presentative thetic sentences do not have a topic comment structure, though they do present a referent which then becomes available as a subsequent topic. Like all English clauses, however, they have a Theme ^ Rheme function with the Theme locating the clause in its context and orienting it towards what is to come. The presented topic is found in the Rheme. Davidse et al. (2023) argues that an unstressable *there* along with ambient *it* are definite exophoric pronouns and not dummy elements. They refer to the ambient surroundings in which the speech event occurs. As such they are meaningful semiotic elements and not merely dummy elements mandated by the conventions of the English grammatical system. They ground the clause in the speaker's internal perspective of their surroundings and any changes within it (Bolinger, 1973; Halliday & Hasan, 1976). In 2.52 the ambient *it* grounds the point of departure in the time and location of the act of speaking and the ambient meteorological conditions. In 2.53 the *there* pronoun refers the hearer to the speaker's view of their physical surroundings and orients the hearer to *Johnny*'s emergence. To quote Langacker (1991), *there* is a "setting subject"; it designates a setting but not a participant. The participant in the clause is the presented subject. In these examples it is *Johnny, rain,* or *a great warrior* that are presented as matters of current interest.[27]

Thus, we propose the following analyses:

2.60

There	goes	Johnny
Theme	Rheme	
		F/Topic

27. Erteschik-Shir (2007, pp. 16–17) describes *there* and *it* in such examples as "stage topics." Her argument is that to investigate whether X or Y are true, a hearer must physically look and check to see if there is *rain* or *Johnny* is appearing. In her thinking, *rain* or *Johnny* are not topics. Furthermore, as all possible utterances are produced by speakers in definite temporal and physical locations, she rejects the class of thetic sentences, as according to her argument, all sentences can potentially have an implicit stage topic. She would argue that the presence of the marked Theme, for her an overt topic, is on its own insufficient to serve as the setting used to evaluate the truth of the sentence and requires the presence of the ambient *there*. Yet, in 2.55 very little meaning, other than an overt signalling of existence, would have been lost had the existential not been produced. *In a land faraway lived a great warrior* grounds the clause in the temporal and physical distance of the location. However, the marked Theme is not the matter of current concern. It is the setting for the presentation of the matter of current interest, namely the existence of *a great warrior.*

Table 2.4: Theme and Topic Compared and Contrasted

Theme	Topic
Restricted to clause initial position	Usually located in clause initial position
Orients the clause to context (relational meaning)	Functions as that which is commented on
May contain textual and interpersonal elements preceding topical Theme	Does not include textual or interpersonal elements
Usually conflates with Given information	Usually conflates with Given information
In the unmarked case equates with the subject and the most common realization is a pronoun	In the unmarked case equates with the subject and the most common realization is a pronoun
Is identified as culminating in the first experiential element found in the clause	Is identified as the matter of current interest encoded in the clause
Is obligatory in English major clauses	Is usually present in English major clauses

Johnny is presented as a future topic one which is made available for comment by the discourse participants in the following discourse.

2.61

In a land faraway	there lived	a great warrior
Marked Theme	Rheme	
Setting		F/Topic

In 2.61 there is a marked Theme which serves as the setting for the future topic. The disassociation between Theme and topic, unusual though it is, is caused by the different functions Theme and topic have in weaving clauses into a text. Theme as point of departure relates the beginning of the clause to the rest of the clause, while topic construes an element and presents it as the current concern of the clause. Unlike Theme it does not necessarily relate one part of a clause to another but rather identifies what its relevance is to the clause in the unfolding discourse. The unmarked topic is a subject, and as we saw the prototypical topic is a pronoun which identifies an element present in the text. As we will see in chapter 3, this element is, in the vast majority of cases, informationally Given, but it need not be. The element identified as topic is available to be commented on and thus potentially may, like Theme, signal relational meaning. Table 2.4 summarizes:

Marked Theme examples, according to Halliday, are marked precisely because the point of departure does not contain the subject. Others have argued that Theme in English should include subject. Some such as Berry (1995, 1996, 2020), Downing (1991), Fawcett (2000), Huang (2017), and Ravelli (1995), whose interests were grounded in text analysis, argued that the subject, regardless of what preceded it, was the culmination of the Theme. Thompson and Thompson (2008) argued that both approaches are valid but dependent on the analyst's goal. When examining the unfolding method of development in a text, it is important to keep track of the participants, especially the subject (see Martin, 1992). Conversely, when looking at intra-clausal Theme, motivations for the choice of Theme are irrelevant. All that matters is how the Theme orients the Rheme to a local context. To sum up, the tension between the approaches is caused by Berry's focus on text development and her need to explain how a particular Theme related to what came earlier and Halliday's more narrow syntactic view which only focused on how a Rheme is oriented to its local context.

The view presented here is supportive of Halliday but recognizes the function of topic, which identifies the elements which function as the matter of current interest and as such are motivated by the preceding co-text and context in which the language is produced. I do not argue for the extension of the Theme to include the subject because of the existence of "thetic sentences"; see examples 2.60 and 2.61. Rather I argue that the system of Theme operates alongside the function of topic in weaving clauses into a coherent text. They are two closely related but separate choices. Prior to discussing a third related choice, that of Given and New, I will summarize what has been said in this chapter.

2.6 Conclusion

In this chapter I have illustrated the wisdom of Halliday's decision to propose a "separating Theme," and I have shown that the combination and recombination of thematic and informational choices has the potential to create novel meanings in individual contexts. While Theme and information frequently conflate, they are separate systems. I have gone further, or perhaps returned back to Mathesius's original tripartite division via Gómez González's concern that point of departure and matter had been conflated in SFL Theme, and proposed a further system of identificational meaning realized by the presence of a topic. I have shown that the topic which is identified as the matter of current interest may be found outside the Theme. While every major clause in English must have a Theme, there are clauses however, which do not contain topics. I have accepted the metaphorical description of topic as the peg on which a message is hung or as a file card which locates the referent which is to be commented on. However, I have disagreed with Lambrecht's view that only referents which are available can function as topic. Instead, I have argued that unidentifiable referents, regardless of whether they are accessible, may function as topics for what is to follow. Topic is a system of the clause but is motivated by communicative needs and sensitive to the wider discourse.

We have now seen two of the four information waves occurring in the unfolding of a discourse which I propose are necessary for a full explication of IS; theme signalled by its syntactic position and topic signalled by its relevance to the message. In the following chapter, we will examine the referential wave signalled by prosodic prominence.

3 The Prosodic Realization of Given and New Information

Introduction

As shown in the previous chapter, the system of Theme has been extensively studied within the SFL tradition. While in earlier work, such as Halliday (1967b), Theme as a system was restricted to clause rank, work such as Martin (1992) and Martin and Rose (2007) have extended the function of Theme upward to paragraphs (hyperTheme) and indeed whole texts (macroTheme). This was a welcome move; it recognized that the patterning of discourse is far more complex than the simple accretion of clauses. Rather the text producer has a message to impart, and in order to help convey the message selects Theme choices which create a receptive path for the listener/reader. These choices are used to orient listeners/readers through the text and guide them towards the intended meaning (Coffin & Derewianka, 2008). In other words, Themes, depending on their location in a text, may make bigger or smaller waves and their ripples may extend far beyond a clause. In chapter 5 when discussing the propositional component of IS, I will look at how IS functions above the clause and explore how these larger ripples function.

As a function, Theme has been frequently opposed to New with Theme representing the first peak of clausal prominence and New the final one. This was a view which I rejected in the previous chapter. In this chapter I will further demonstrate that Theme and New are not oppositional functions within IS, especially when we consider how the referential component of IS is encoded within non-clausal units.

This chapter will show that, by contrast to Theme, there has been limited work done on identifying New and defining its functions. This is partly the result of the fact that while there has been extensive work on Theme in written texts, far less work has been done on New or indeed

Theme in spoken texts. It has simply been assumed that unmarked thematic elements are not New[1] and that the New is found within the Rheme, though see O'Grady (2017a, 2024), who argues that the full semogenetic potential of Theme in spoken English can only be understood by examining its prosodic realization. This is a very different approach from scholars such as Martin Davies (1989, 1992, 1994), who have assumed that information structure in written English operates in a very similar manner to how it does in spoken English. For instance, Davies assumes that New functions to oppose Theme and seems to think that clauses and tone groups are one and the same. More crucially he does not see that relational and referential information are two separate though overlapping components of the IS model. Much of the evidence provided by Davies comes from the reading aloud of written verse with Theme preceding the New. However, it is questionable, to say the least, to argue that read aloud written verse is typical of spoken English (Brazil, 1984; Esser, 1988).

In the following sections, I will describe Halliday's system of information, pointing out issues that have been raised with the details of Halliday's system; I will also argue that for the most part Halliday's claims are sound. Information is part of the textual metafunction, and it is realized by prosody in a lexicogrammatical unit called the information unit which Halliday states is parallel to the clause. Information units and clauses are not identical but will tend to be coterminous in extent. The information unit is realized by the phonological unit the tone group, which itself functions grammatically to realize a quantum of information in speech.[2] Halliday labels the chunking of speech into information units the system of tonality, which I will outline in the following section.

3.1 Tonality

Halliday (1967a) and Halliday and Greaves (2008) proposed a phonological rank scale for English of tone group, foot, syllable, and phoneme, with the higher ranks being composed of the lower ones. The

1. Halliday and Matthiessen (2014) makes it clear that topic/comment is not same as Theme/Rheme and argue that topic and not Theme tends to conflate with Given. The previous chapter shows that I regard Theme, topic, and Given as three distinct though overlapping components of IS.
2. Halliday and Matthiessen (2014) somewhat confusingly also describe a clause as realizing a quantum of information.

tone group itself can, like a clause, form into a tone group complex.[3] The tone group as the realization of an information unit may contain a mixture of New and optional Given information. It represents a quantum of information. A tone group is a stretch of speech which contains a complete pitch contour, which in English is realized by one of the five primary tones. It may be bounded by a pause, but the presence of a pause does not necessarily imply a tone group boundary. Within the SFL tradition, Tench (1996) has proposed a number of phonetic criteria which can assist in delimiting the location of a tone group boundary. First, the presence of a major pitch movement entails the presence of a tone group, and hence a boundary must lie between the presence of the two major tone movements. In addition, tone groups contain one or more prominent syllables, with the last one, the tonic syllable, being the site of the major tone movement; thus, the boundary will lie between the tonic syllable and the following prominent syllable. There is a change of tempo between tone groups with syllables produced at the end of a tone group being articulated with a slower rate of acceleration: thus, a change in tempo is a cue to the presence of a tone group boundary. Syllables produced after the tonic syllable are articulated with decrescendo; a change in volume after the tonic signals a boundary. Finally, as mentioned above, the presence of a pause frequently co-occurs with a tone group boundary. Barth-Weingarten (2016), a thorough and minute analysis of the phonetics of tone group boundaries, notes that at times it is impossible to know with full confidence where a tone group boundary lies. Such a view has led some, such as Brown et al. (2015), to abandon the concept of a tone group in favour of units which can be more easily delimited by the presence of pause.

I, however, see no reason to abandon the concept of the tone group/ information unit for four reasons. The first is that the tone group is not the only phonological rank with indeterminate boundaries. For instance, are /tʃ/ as in church and /tɹ/ as in train single phonemic units or is /tʃ/ a phoneme and /tɹ/ a sequence of two phonemes, /t/ followed by /ɹ/? While convention suggests the latter, there is actually no clear phonetic criteria for rejecting the former view. At syllable

3. It is true to say that the criteria for identifying tone group complexes is much more opaque than that for identifying clause complexes. This is chiefly because phonological structure, unlike lexicogrammatical structure, is flat and hence there can be no question of hypotactic or rankshifted tone groups. For a useful discussion of the flatness of phonological structure, see Ladd (2008).

rank, it is unclear where the syllable boundary lies in words such as *extra, colour,* and *basket.* Is it /ˈɛks-tɹə/ or /ˈek-stɹə/, /ˈkʌ-lə/ or /ˈkʌl-ə/, /ˈbæ-skət/ or /ˈbæs-kət/?[4] Different speakers will have different answers. But what matters is that all speakers will be able to recognize that the above words all contain two syllables.[5] Second, informationally significant items are neither post-tonic nor found prior to the first prominence in the tone group. Thus, the actual location of the boundary is not functionally significant (Greaves, 2007). Third, as the tone group is the realization of the information unit, the fact that its boundaries are indeterminate does not entail that the boundaries of a corresponding information unit are indeterminate.

Fourth and most significantly, Halliday (1967a) argued for the psychological reality of the information unit. His argument was based on a series of studies of speech errors which claimed that errors such as Spoonerisms were sensitive to tone group boundaries; they occurred within tone groups but not across them. Therefore, we find examples such as: | you have **t**asted a **w**orm | instead of the intended | you have **w**asted a **t**erm | but not | you have **t**asted | a **w**orm | where the verb and complement are found in different tone groups. Such findings led Boomer & Laver (1968, p. 8) and Laver (1970, p. 68) to claim that tone groups are handled as single behavioural acts by the central nervous system. However, this is not a universally accepted view. For instance, Levelt (1993) argues that speakers, in order to achieve their individual communicative needs, microplan and macroplan the content of their utterances. Microplanning is defined as the assigning of information structure to a discourse (Levelt, 1993, p. 109). However, in his model Levelt does not assign any importance to a unit such as the tone group: microplanning occurs as activation spreads across local lexical and sublexical features with no need for any higher prosodic units. More recently however, Levelt's findings have been challenged by Croot et al. (2010), who argue that as speech errors are less frequent in items containing prominences that this is evidence for the specification of higher-level prosodic units such as tone groups prior to the phonetic and phonological encoding of word forms. Choe and Redford

4. My answers, for what they are worth, are /ˈɛks-tɹə/, /ˈkʌ-lə/, and with limited confidence ,/ˈbæ-skət/.
5. Halliday and Matthiessen (2014) report examples of speakers disagreeing about the numbers of syllables in words such as comfortable (three or four), seldom (one or two), cigarette (two or three), but that is likely to be the result of dialectal differences and not related to indeterminacy in the system of the speech community of the speakers.

(2012) generated a dataset of read aloud tongue twisters and found that the speech errors overwhelmingly occurred within and not across tone groups. They interpreted their data as suggesting that the patterning of errors identified supports the view that tone groups have psychological reality as planning domains.

The literature on the comprehension of speech suggests that the chunking of speech into tone groups aids comprehension; see Cutler et al. (1997) and Frazier et al. (2004) for more details. Carers talking to young children produce language chunked into short tone groups in order to aid the child's comprehension and bootstrap learning (Kempe et al., 2010; Martin et al., 2016; Payne et al., 2019, etc.). In a similar manner, others (Chun, 2002; Morgan et al., 1987; Rothermich et al., 2019, etc.) report that foreigner-directed speech and TESOL language-teachers deploy similar strategies when conversing with beginning learners regardless of the age of the language learner. This illustrates that these speakers are trying to aid their hearers by parcelling out their message in small chunks of information.

Thibault (2004a, p. 281) cautions that much description and theorizing of language has occurred in the absence of a proper understanding of its biological underpinnings. He suggests that we must treat current descriptions as provisional. Thus, at the very least, if we are to argue for the psychological reality of information units, we need to show that they are consistent with what is known about human cognition. Humans are biologically programmed to be social creatures, a facet which orients us towards dialogic communication. Hence, if information units are to have psychological reality, they must be cognitively feasible, and they must be shown to function in a manner which assists individuals in achieving their communicative needs in dialogue. I will return to the second point in chapter 5.

Thibault, grounding his work in Flohr (1991), proposes a three-level approach to mental representation. Input from the sensory organs is routed through the thalamus, resulting in the formation of associations of neurons with specific signals leading to a strengthening or weakening of links between neurons. This is in line with Hebb's law, which, crudely put, states that "neurons that fire together wire together"[6] Hebb (1949). Stimulus and feedback lead to changes in the synaptic weights, which over time form into relatively stable neural networks

6. More technically the law states that when an axon of cell A is near enough to excite cell B and repeatedly or persistently takes part in firing it, some growth process or metabolic change takes place in one or both cells such that A's efficiency, as one of the cells firing B, is increased.

which we experience as mental representations.[7] Evans (2015, p. 68) has noted that tone groups occur within the Hebbian perceptual moment where neuronal firing binds objects together. Tone groups/information units are learned patterns of behaviour such as the unmarked correlation between clause and information unit; see below for further discussion. Hebbian learning is clearly one way of explaining how clauses and information units are associated.

Thibault (2004a, p. 294) links the content stratum to which information units belong (see O'Grady, 2020) with the central nervous system and the expression stratum with the peripheral nervous system. The articulation of information structure by prosodic means such as increased vocal fold vibration to signal prominence is the result of excitatory signals in the peripheral nervous system resulting from relatively stable configurations of neurons firing simultaneously in the central nervous system. As the theoretical relation between the content and the expression is one of realization, we can predict a degree of redundancy in the projection of information (Halliday, 2002). Thus Theme/Rheme and Given/New will at times overlap as outputs of a biological system with the following metaredundancy relations: stimulus patterns / assembly formation // representation of spatio-temporal patterns. In other words, the representation of the spatio-temporal pattern on the expression stratum redounds with assembly formation on the content stratum which redounds with stimulus patterns routed through the thalamus.

A further constraint on human cognition is the limited nature of working memory. Miller (1956) introduced the magic number of seven, but recent research has indicated that in relation to words the memory span is around fifteen if the words form a meaningful sentence (Baddeley, 2010). This extended span reflects the contribution of long-term memory and of meaningful semiotic patterns. Yet remembering the wording of constructed sentences in an experiment is not the same as producing speech. Miller & Buschman (2015) do not put a number on what can be contained in working memory as they claim that the num-

7. This has two implications which I will explore later. The first is that information value is somehow related to predictability. Articulation of certain elements results in the expectation that other elements will follow, and over time it is these elements which form the tightest neural connections. The second is that as the signal is routed through the thalamus, it must include sensory information related to the experiencer's feelings towards the stimulus as well as the experiential content of the stimulus (Damasio, 2010). As Thibault (2020a) says, "languaging conveys complexes of thoughts, feelings, beliefs, desires" and not just thoughts. So, too, must information structure.

ber fluctuates depending on other competing cognitive tasks. And as speech is almost always performed as part of an assembly of cognitive tasks, we can assume that competing tasks will lead to constraints in working memory span.

However, considering the length of tone groups, there seems to be no plausible reason why speakers could not hold a tone group or even a tone group complex in working memory. Reviewing the evidence, it seems that the argument in favour of the psychological reality of information units, while strong, is not yet proven and probably cannot be until more is known about how the brain processes and produces speech.

Linguistic theorists other than Halliday have also proposed that prosodic units encode a single chunk of information. For instance, Cruttenden (1997) says that tone groups function as "presentation units" in which speakers manage the flow of information. Chafe, in a series of publications (1974, 1994, 2018), has proposed that spoken language flows as a series of idea units which are physically realized as tone groups. Chafe uses the term intonation units and states that they are identifiable by the presence of a complete intonation contour. Hence, they seem identical to what we are referring to as tone groups. Each idea unit contains one and only one idea. Chafe's view, as we will see, is comparable to Halliday's, though we have also seen that his identification of information is not identical to Halliday's.

In order for a tone group to realize a quantum of information, it must encode sufficient semantic information which is realized by a clause or a major grammatical constituent. Halliday and Matthiessen (2014, p. 120), as stated above, argue for an unmarked relation between clause and tone group. Though, as they admit, things are not always equal, and adjuncts, marked themes, and longer subjects are likely to be articulated as their own tone group, for instance. So, we could predict tonality divisions as shown in the following examples with 3.2, 3.3, and 3.4 being technically examples of marked tonality.

3.1 | John gave the book to Mary |
3.2 | On Friday | John gave the book to Mary |
3.3 | Finally | John gave the book to Mary |
3.4 | John the chap who she met last week | gave the book to Mary |

Support for Halliday's view can be found in Watson & Gibson (2004), who from the formalist tradition provide an approachable account of what Selkirk (1984) labelled the "sense unit condition of intonational phrasing," which states that an intonational unit (tone group) must form a sense unit by equating to grammatically valid constructions, e.g.,

3.5 | John gave the ball to Mary |
3.6 | John | gave the ball to Mary |
3.7 | John gave the ball | to Mary |
3.8 | John gave | the ball to Mary |*
3.9 | John gave | the ball | to Mary |*

Examples 3.8 and 3.9, which contain tone groups "John gave," are not valid as the tone group does not contain a complete grammatical constituent.[8]

Corpus evidence on the coextensiveness of clause and tone group is, however, rather sparse. Halliday & Greaves (2008, p. 101) report that 60 per cent of tone groups are mapped onto complete clauses, though they do not provide any evidence for their claim. Some supporting evidence though can be found in Croft (1995), which is a small corpus investigation of oral narratives, *The Pear Stories,* in English. He found a relation between tone groups and what he labelled grammatical units. Croft's corpus showed that the relation between tone groups and grammatical units in his corpus was strong, occurring 91 per cent of the time. However, he identified a number of tendencies, presented below in order of importance, where the one-to-one relationship between clause and tone group did not hold: (1) parallelism, (2) syntactic complexity in general, and (3) distance.[9] The examples are illustrated below.

3.10 | John plays the piano | and electric guitar |
3.11 | The new musical wonderkid | plays the piano |
3.12 | He gave the book | to Mary | or | He was dressed | in a black cloak |

8. In the formalist tradition, unlike SFG, the complete verbal phrase contains the direct object *the ball.* Note that as this is a rule related to language competence, the rule does not preclude speakers producing tone groups such as /john gave/. Gussenhoven (2004) employs an optimality analysis where he recasts the sense unit rule as a series of constraints.

9. By "distance" Croft refers to the concept of syntactic closeness. For example, a direct object is closer to the verb than an oblique one, or a complement is closer than an adverbial clause. This, of course, explains why adjuncts may occur within their own tone groups.

In a follow-up paper exploring the relation between tone groups and grammatical units in the Australian Aboriginal language Wardaman (Croft, 2007), he found a similar relationship which he argued was evidence for his hypothesis that the constructions which are stored in the mind are the grammatical units that are normally articulated as a single tone group. Croft's work, while interesting and suggestive, remains in need of empirical validation in larger corpora, especially one of spoken English.

To this point I have illustrated the Hallidayan (and others') position that a tone group is an information unit which encodes a single quantum of information, but I have not stated in this chapter what is meant by the term information. It is time to put that omission to rest. Halliday and Matthiessen (2014, p. 116) define information as follows:

> It is the tension between what is already known or predictable and what is new or unpredictable. This is different from the mathematical concept of information, which is the measure of unpredictability. It is the interplay of new and not new that generates information in the linguistic sense. Hence the information is a structure made up of two functions, the New and the Given.

While the following section will detail the internal structure of the tone group in order to illustrate how Halliday conceived the interplay between New and Given in speech, we can say that every tone group/ information unit contains some information which is unpredictable. Halliday's use of the term unpredictable is, as he says, not a prospective measure but rather a retrospective one. To illustrate the presence of a determiner anticipates the presence of a noun, and in that sense occurrence of the noun as a structural element is entailed and hence informationally predictable. However, while the presence of the nominal is predictable, the value encoded by the nominal may or may not convey a recoverable referent. It may be that the value encoded by the nominal has been mentioned in the previous co-text or is available in the context. Each information unit must contain at a minimum one lexical item which encodes a non-recoverable value. As noted above, phonology, unlike lexicogrammar, has a flat non-recursive structure, which means that each information unit is of equal rank and that the discourse unfolds as a temporal sequence of information units.[10]

---

10. There will be a discussion of compound tone groups which consist of an information unit followed by a minor information unit after extract 3.3.

In the next paragraphs, we will examine the flow of information units in a number of short texts in order see if the speakers' tonality choices were mostly unmarked and if the cases of markedness are explained by Croft (1995, 2017). Information units are marked by slashes with ranking clauses in boldface. In the interests of readability, I have not marked the internal structure of the tone groups/information units. The first text is a prepared monologue spoken by Gordon Brown as his opening remarks in the first televised election debate in 2010. The second is a primed conversation by three female undergraduate students who had been tasked with watching a silent video on recent flooding in the UK and discussing it and their experiences of the flood. The third is a spontaneous conversation taken from the London Lund 1 corpus.

Extract 3.1

1. | These are no ordinary times |
   [unmarked]
2. | **and this is no ordinary election** |
   [unmarked]
3. | **We've just been going through the biggest** |
   [marked-other]
   global financial crisis | in our lives |
   [marked-other] *[marked-distance]*
4. | **and we're moving** | **from recession to recovery** |
   [unmarked] *[marked-distance]*
5. | **and I believe** | **we're moving on a road to prosperity for all** |
   [marked-complexity] *[unmarked]*
6. | **Now, every promise you hear** | **from each of us this evening**
   [marked-complexity] *[marked-complexity]*
   | **depends on one thing** | a strong economy |
   [marked-complexity] *[marked-parallelism]*
7. | **And this is the defining year** |
   [unmarked]
8. | **Get the decisions right now** |
   [unmarked]
9. | **and we can have secure jobs** |
   [unmarked]
10. | **we can have standards of living rising** |
    [unmarked]
11. | **and we can have everybody better off** |
    [unmarked]

12. | **Get the decisions wrong now** |
[unmarked]
13. | **and we could have a double-dip** | **recession** |
[marked-other] *[marked-other]*
14. | **And because we believe in fairness** |
[unmarked]
15. | **as we cut the deficit** | over these next few years |
[unmarked] *[marked-distance]*
16. | **we will protect your police** | your National Health Service |
[unmarked] *[marked-parallelism]*
17. | **and we will protect your schools** |
[unmarked]
18. | **I know** | **what this job involves** |
[marked-complexity] *[unmarked]*
19. | **I look forward to putting my plan** | to you
[marked-complexity] *[marked-distance]*
| this evening |
[marked-distance]

Table 3.1: Tonicity Choices in Extract 3.1, Unmarked and Marked

Information Units/Clauses	Unmarked	Marked			
		Complexity	Parallelism	Distance	Other
32/19	15	6	2	5	4

Only the tonality division in clauses 3 and 13 did not accord with expectations, as there is a tone group boundary in the middle of the NGs *the biggest global financial crisis* and *a double-dip recession*. These very marked choices result in a double focus on the fact of the recession/crisis and on its severity. Table 3.1 summarizes the findings.

It is clear that there is a tendency of the obligatory elements of clauses to be coextensive with information units though, as clauses 3 and 13 show speakers have the ability to override the expected relationship if it suits their communicative interests.

The second example is taken from an informal conversation by three female undergraduate students chatting after watching a silent video depicting recent winter floods in the UK. All of the participants had themselves been affected by the flooding.

Extract 3.2

A: 1 | Yeah **I guess what you were saying about like**
[marked-complexity]
| **Portland and stuff** |
[marked-complexity]
2 | coz **I didn't know where it was** but |
[unmarked][11]

C: | Yeah | (OVERLAP)
| **it is in Dorset** | near Weymouth |
[unmarked] [marked-distance]
3 **That's quite bad**
[unmarked]
4 | but it was … but then … **it kind of looked really really bad on the video** |
[unmarked]

C: 5 | Yeah | **but it was only hitting one side of it** though so |
[marked-minor] [unmarked]
6 | **it kind of made it look worse than it actually was** |
[unmarked]

A: | Yeah | (minor clause/acknowledgment)
[marked-minor]

C: 7 | because … because **the rest of it is sheltered** |
[unmarked]
8 | **it was just only like one** | **portion** |
[marked-other] [marked-other]
9 | **which obviously is really bad for people that live there** |
[unmarked]
10 | but | **it probably wasn't as** | **bad** |
[marked-other] [marked-other] [marked-other]
as other places |
[marked-distance]
11 | which they | probably didn't **they didn't really show in the clip** |
[marked-other] [unmarked]

11. Technically the *but* does not belong with this clause. The same issue arises in number 5 with the conjunctive elements *though so* belonging to a following clause. In example 11 the information unit also contains extraneous material as a result of the speaker realizing that her original modality section was in need of revision.

12 | whereas there they were like | **this is this inn** |
[marked-complexity] [unmarked]
that's been like attacked |
[marked-complexity]
13 | **and it's still standing** |
[unmarked]
14 | this modern road | **it was more like** |
[marked-parallelism] [marked-complexity]
that was more specific than | **the other clips** |
[marked-complexity] [marked-complexity]
15 | where **it was just** | **people talking about what they have seen** |
[marked-complexity] [marked-complexity]
16 | and **they're sat in their cars** |
[unmarked]
17 | yeah **it did show you** kind of like | **how** |
[marked-complexity] [marked-complexity]
the sea front | **was more protected than inland** |
[marked-complexity] [marked-complexity]
with rivers | with like rivers were just pouring
[marked-parallelism] [marked-distance]
over (unclear overlap)
A C: | Yeah | (Minor clause acknowledgment)
[marked-minor]
B: 18 | and like **the river banks were just gone** |
[unmarked]
19 | **and like coming up the paths** | **where as you could see with the sea** |
[marked-complexity] [marked-complexity]
20 | **they have like flood** | **massive barriers** |
[marked-other] [marked-other]
yeah | **that protect that** |
[marked-minor] [marked-complexity]
21 | **so I guess it's quite a contrast** |
[unmarked]
A: 22 | Hm | (Minor clause/acknowledgment) (overlap)
[marked-minor]
B: | in that respect |
[marked-distance]

Table 3.2: Tonicity Choices in Extract 3.2, Unmarked and Marked

Information Units/Clauses	Unmarked	Marked				Minor
		Complexity	Parallelism	Distance	Other	
49/23	14	16	2	3	9	5

In this extract again we see that the speakers' tonality divisions basically conform to expectations. In fourteen out of the twenty-three clauses, the information unit is coextensive with the obligatory clausal elements. The marked information units again mostly accord with Croft's predictions and hence are coextensive with grammatical units below clause rank. As in the first extract, speakers are free to produce information units which are not coextensive with grammatical units in order to emphasize particular pieces of information, such as the number of portions as in 8, the size in 11, or as way of co-involving the hearers by inviting them to predict the following lexical item as in 10. This example illustrates how speakers can deploy the parcelling of information in order to strengthen/create interpersonal links. In this extract there are five cases where the information unit is coextensive with a minor clause. Halliday and Matthiessen (2014) define minor clauses as clauses without predicators. In the above the speakers produce the informal polarity marker *yeah*. This functions in this extract in two ways. The first in C's overlap to clause 2 is to acknowledge receipt of the information: the information unit conveys interpersonal information. The second as in clause 21 functions textually as an organizing piece of information (Sinclair & Mauranen, 2006) in that it signals that the speaker's message is incomplete.

The third extract is taken from a conversation in the London Lund 1 corpus.

Extract 3.3

A: 1 | from Marlborough | **she has hit Reading** | at half
[marked-complexity] [unmarked]

B: | splendid | (overlap)
[marked-minor]

A: past eight in the morning |
[marked-complexity]

B: 2 | splendid | agreed | **but you're not** | (incomplete)
[Marked-minor] [Marked-minor]

A: 3 | that is **that is the other side of** Reading |
[unmarked]

B: | **going into Reading** |
[unmarked]

A: 4 | **It will be the other side of Reading** going into Reading |
[unmarked][12*]

12. Technically the insertion of the extra material in this tone group means that there is no one-to-one correspondence between clause and tone group. However, because

5 | **that's where she hit the traffic** |
[unmarked]
| traffic | going in |
[Marked-parallel] [Marked-other]
to Reading | from either side |
[Marked-other] [marked-complexity]

B: 6 | no | **you've missed the point** |
[marked-minor] [unmarked]

7 | **the traffic you are worried about** | **is the traffic** |
[marked-complexity] [marked-complexity]
going towards London |
[marked-complexity]

A: 8 | no Petey | at half past eight in the morning |
[marked-minor] [marked-complexity] + ellipsis

B: 9 | **there is not a mysterious line** | which divides traffic going
[unmarked] [marked-complexity]
to London | immediately at Reading |
[marked-distance]

A: 10 | no | **but there is traffic** |
[marked-minor] [unmarked]

11 | **there is a traffic rush hour at Reading** |
[unmarked]
when traffic piles into Reading |
[unmarked]

12 | **and it is about eight thirty** | that my mother has gotten stuck |
[unmarked] [unmarked]
in traffic trying to get into Reading |
[marked-distance]

B: 13 | **most of it** | **is going to London** |
[marked-complexity] [marked-complexity]

A: 14 | what from the other side of Reading | (ellipsis)
[marked-complexity]

B: | yes |
[marked-minor] (ellipsis)

Table 3.3: Tonicity Choices in Extract 3.3, Unmarked and Marked

Information Units/Clauses	Unmarked	Marked				Minor
		Complexity	Parallelism	Distance	Other	
35/15	12	11	1	2	2	7

---

the clausal core is found within a single tone group/information unit I have classed it as unmarked.

Once again there is clear evidence for the coextensiveness of the obligatory core clausal components with information units. Again, the marked information units are, with two exceptions, coterminous with grammatical units such as prepositional phrases, NGs, etc. In clause 5 speaker A says:

3.13 | that's where she hit the traffic | traffic | going in | to Reading | from either side |

The speaker produces an unmarked information unit but then sees the need to elaborate and produces an elaborating hypotactic clause which is articulated as four information units. It is clear that the speaker feels that for her communicative need to be met, the hearer must focus on the forward direction of the traffic into the town and the origin of the traffic from either side of the town. Thus, the speaker parcels out the information units in a manner which allows for a focus on the direction and destination. In this extract there are seven minor clauses which are coterminous with information units, three of which signal negative polarity. Unlike the examples discussed in extract 3.2, the negative polarity information units in this extract convey experiential as well as interpersonal information. The remainder of the clause has been ellipted and the speaker presents the tense and referential information as being available to the speaker and hearer alike. In line 2 speaker B produces the two minor clauses | splendid | agreed | and articulates them as two information units. It is clear that the speaker has ellipted material though it is not entirely clear what has been presented as available to the hearer.

Unlike this book, Halliday and Greaves allow for the presence of compound or fused tone groups which have twin foci. The second tonic is minor and always accompanied by a low rising tone. Halliday and Greaves (2008, p. 44) argue that the two tone groups are fused together by the absence of a choice for any pretonic prominences in the second tone group. Informationally they argue that the second focus is minor and adds a gloss to the first focus. Following Tench (1990) I consider all tone groups to have a single focus and treat compound tone groups as sequences of two tone groups. Tench (1990) noted that even in Halliday's own examples it is possible to find those with an intervening prominence in the pretonic, and second that the presence of a compound tone disturbs the symmetry of one information unit being realized by one tone group. I further argue that in the pursuance of communicative goals, tone groups often coalesce into larger sequences on a moment by moment basis and that within this larger sequence the choice of tone is one factor, but only one factor, in establishing the local hierarchy of foci needed for the speaker to impart their message (O'Grady, 2010, 2020; O'Grady & Bartlett, 2019).

In the next section we will examine how the articulation of lexical items in information units presents them as recoverable or non-recoverable. But first it is time to recap and point out what remains to be investigated. Evidence has been shown suggesting the psychological reality of tone groups/information units and that there is an unmarked relation between grammatical units such as the clause and information unit. But we have also seen that grammar does not determine the extent of tone group/information unit; speakers are free to package their information up into the chunks which they assume best convey their message to their audience. However, it is equally clear that the lexicogrammar and the prosody are in a mutually reinforcing redundancy relationship. We have also seen that phonology has a flat structure, so each information unit is of equal rank. Once we have examined the internal structure of information units, we will examine how information units form into larger complexes and say more about the redundancy relation between the lexicogrammar and the prosody.

3.2 *Tonicity*

Halliday (1967a) and Halliday and Greaves (2008) represent the clearest statements of the Hallidayan view of how speakers use prosody to package their words into items that are Given and items that are New. As illustrated in chapter 1, the tone group is the highest unit in the phonological rank scale and is itself composed of one or more feet. As we noted, feet in English function as a unit of rhythm. English rhythm is trochaic, and the foot is composed of an obligatory ictus followed by a remis. The ictus commences either with a strong or silent beat while the remis is composed of weak syllables; see Kohler (2009) for an overview. I illustrate using a sequence of tone groups from extract 3.2 above with foot boundaries notated by / and silent beats by ^. The feet are numbered, and the tonic syllables are italicized.

3.14 | **where** they were like | ^ this is this / **inn** | that's /been like
1 2 3 4
at/**tacked** |
5

The three information units are coextensive with five feet, but it is noticeable that the boundaries are not identical. To illustrate, the first foot commences with the ictus *where* and is followed by the remis *they/were/like.* As *where* is also the tonic syllable, this foot is known as the tonic foot. The second foot commences with a silent ictus and contains the syllables *this/is/this* in the remis. The third foot is a tonic foot and contains the syllable *inn* as ictus and the syllable *that's* as remis. The fourth foot commences with the ictus *been* and is completed by the syllables *like/a* in the remis. The final foot is a tonic foot and contains the syllable *tacked*. If we look at figure 1, we note that the tone group / information unit 3 had been transcribed as containing material which is in the remis of foot 3 as well as feet 4 and 5.

Figure 3.1: Tone Groups and Feet

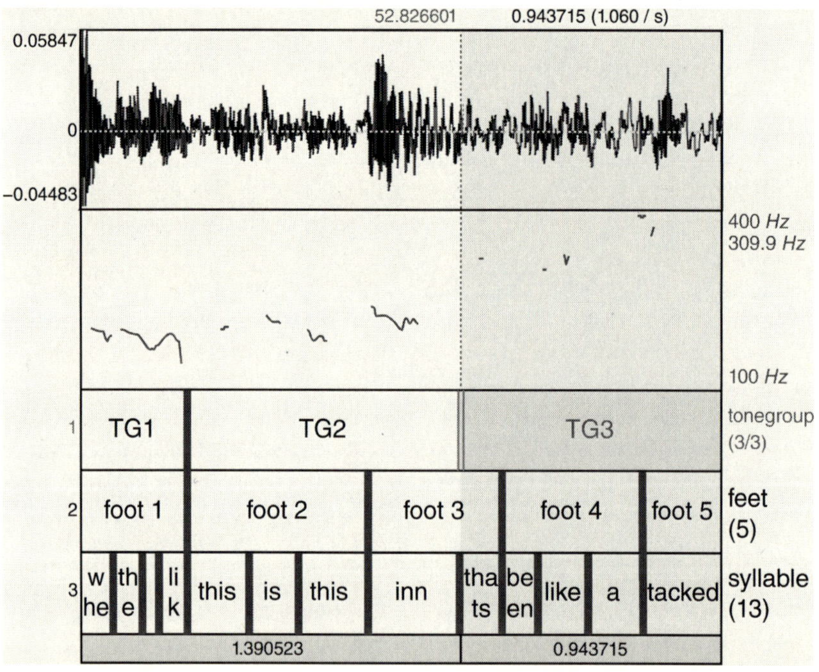

We see that the boundaries of the tone groups formed from feet and tone groups which are coextensive with information units are not always coextensive. Thus, as information units are grammatical units which are realized by tone groups, and as they are in the unmarked case coextensive with tone groups, we cannot expect prosodic units and lexicogrammatical units to dovetail 100 per cent of the time. Furthermore, this is not of significance in that no informationally salient material can appear post-tonic or before the first salient syllable (filled ictus) in the following tone group (Greaves, 2007; O'Grady, 2014a). We can also see that lexical items may appear in more than one foot.[13] Despite this, the entire lexical item *attacked* is the focus of the third tone group. This is the second reason we will not take feet and rhythm into further account. Work outside the SFL tradition by Ladd (2008) has noted the co-occurrence of salient syllables and rhythmical beats, and thus, when I discuss the function of salient syllables in the following paragraphs, I am indirectly, albeit without considering the role of feet, discussing rhythm. Martinec (2000), Van Leeuwen (2011) , and from outside SFL, Szczepek Reed (2007, 2010a) provide excellent accounts of the organizing function of rhythm.

In the next few paragraphs, we will describe the form of a tone group before examining its function. Each tone group must contain a tonic or nuclear syllable and can contain optional syllables before and after the tonic syllable. Syllables after the tonic must be non-salient while those before the tonic may be salient or non-salient. In English salient syllables are generally produced on a higher pitch, have longer duration, and are louder. The tonic syllable is, in addition, the locus of the major pitch movement within the tone group which starts on the tonic and continues until the end of the tone group (Tench, 1990, 1996). The structural potential is schematized as follows with ( ) bracketing indicating optionality and ^ indicating sequence:

(pretonic syllables) ^ tonic ^ (non-salient post-tonic syllables).

Post-tonic syllables are known as the tail. Non-salient pretonic syllables before the first salience are known as the pre-head, while the stretch of syllables between the first salient syllable and the tonic is known as the head.

If we look at the sequence of tone groups below, we see the possibilities with salient syllables underlined and tonics underlined and in bold.

3.15 | <u>**where**</u> they were like | = tonic ^ tail

13. This is of course in line with the standard SFL view that there is no lexical word rank in the phonological rank scale, though it does beg the question as to whether there is or needs to be a concept of phonological word in English. The existence of a phonological word is prime facie incompatible with a rank scale containing trochaic feet (see Tench, 2014, 2017).

3.16 | this is this **inn** | = pre-head ^ tonic
3.17 | that's been like at/**tacked** | = pre-head ^ head ^ tonic]

Tone groups can take other possible forms, which are illustrated below by tone groups taken from the conversation about flooding between the three female undergraduates.[14]

3.18 | **por**tion | = Tonic
3.19 | which obviously is really bad for **peo**ple that live there | = pre-head ^ head ^ tonic ^ tail
3.20 | as **oth**er places | = pre-head ^ tonic ^ tail
3.21 | trying to help get the **pow**er back on | = head ^ tonic ^ tail |

The tonic syllable signals focus within the information unit. By focus Halliday means the part of the information unit that the speaker "draws particular attention to." It is "the culmination of the New"; everything after it in the same information unit is Given (Halliday & Greaves, 2008, p. 103). Phonetically the tonic focus is realized within a tonic syllable, but in fact informationally it is the grammatical item which contains the tonic focus that the speaker draws attention to. I reproduce the examples above with information focus notated in bold and post-tonic Given elements shaded in grey.

3.22 | **where** they were like | = *Where* is the focus and *they were like* is Given
3.23 | this is **this inn** | = *This inn* is the focus
3.24 | that's been like **attacked** | = *Attacked* is the focus
3.25 | **portion** | = *Portion* is the focus
3.26 % | which obviously is really bad **for people** that live there | = *For people* is the focus, and *that live there* is Given
3.27 % | **as other** places | = *as other* is the focus and *places* is Given[15]

14. For wider context the tone groups are in bold here and shown in their immediate context:
because ... because the rest of it is sheltered	it was just only like one	**portion**	**which obviously is really bad for people that live there**
but	it probably wasn't as	bad	**as other places**
there was like people out	**trying to help get the power back on**	and get rid of the water

15. Readers will have noticed that *as other places* is an NG, according to what has been written above the entire group should be in focus. But this is not the case. The following discussion on marked tonicity will clarify.

3.28 % | trying to help get **the power** back on | = *The power* is the focus and *back on* is Given

I will return to the status of the pretonic items in a moment, but first I need to introduce a distinction between marked and unmarked tonicity. The examples above preceded by % are marked. In cases of unmarked tonicity, the tonic focus falls within the last element in the information unit which has lexical content. Marked tonicity is where the tonic focus is realized elsewhere in the information unit. While Halliday's identification of marked and unmarked is clear, applying the definition to text is more complicated. For instance, in 3.28 the predicator consists of two elements: the light verb *get* followed by the particle *on* with an intervening adverb. It is arguable that the elements *back on* have lexical content as part of the predicator, but equally arguable that their lexical value is entailed by the verb *get*. In 3.26 the final element with lexical content is *live*, and hence the earlier tonic placement is marked. In 3.27 the nominal element *places* is the final element with lexical content, and the earlier tonic placing is marked. This example illustrates that while the tonic focus remains within the same grammatical element – in this case an NG – the focus is only on part of the group. Tonicity, while described as a system operating at information unit rank, clearly also operates at group rank and here draws attention to the adjective *other* with the nominal presented as Given.

Yet, in 3.26 had the tonic focus been placed on the verb *live*, the message would have carried an additional contrast with the emphasis on the post modifying specification of the status of the people. Similarly in 3.28 a focus other than on the nominal would have led to drawing attention either onto the predicators *try* or *help* and focused on the failure to restore electricity. Had the accent been post-tonic, it would have signalled what Ladd (1980, 2008) labelled a default accent. This is one where the tonic is placed onto a semantically empty element in order to avoid an unwarranted contrast. An example from Lambrecht (1994, p. 254) illustrates:

3.29 A: *Let's go the kitchen and get something to eat*
B: | there's nothing **to** eat |

Lambrecht argues that the placement of the tonic on "the semantically empty function word *to*" arose by default. Any other tonic placement would have resulted in an unwarranted contrast. If the speaker had chosen to make *no(thing)* tonic, their utterance would have signalled either an explicit contrast between *no* and *some* and represented an explicit face-threatening denial of the previous utterance or a complaint.

A tonic placement on *eat* would have left open the theoretical possibility that there might be something to drink in the kitchen. The tonic choice in 3.29 alone signals a non-face-threatening correction. Regardless, it is difficult to consider *to* as recoverable. This is a point I will return to in the following chapter when I examine the relational nature of the tonic syllable which operates within a tone group to signal the most informationally salient element in a stretch of speech.

Within the broader literature, there has been a recognition that, irrespective of lexical order, nouns are more likely to receive the tonic focus than verbs. Some scholars such as Bolinger (1972) argue that this reflects the fact that nouns usually carry greater semantic weight or interest than do verbs. Or to put it another way, speakers are usually more focused on actors and things rather than actions and events. Others such as Schmerling (1976) argue that it is a grammatical principle that verbs receive a lower stress than subjects or direct objects in what she calls "news sentences."[16] Ladd (2008) is an accessible account of the competing views. But for present purposes what is of most relevance is that contra Halliday these scholars would consider the tonicity choices in 3.30 and 3.31 to be the most likely. Within the intonation literature, eventive sentences are widely considered to be uttered with a tonic on the subject and not the verb (Cruttenden, 1997, p. 78; Gussenhoven, 1984, p. 25ff; Ladd, 2008, p. 244ff), again contrary to Halliday's concept of unmarked tonicity. The following examples illustrate:

3.30 | the **ba**by's crying |
| the **ket**tle has boiled |

3.31 | the baby's **talk**ing |
| the kettle has broken |

Schmerling (1976), as noted above, would see the information units in group 3.30 as examples of news utterances and in 3.31 as topic com-

16. In her system she has two types of sentences: (1) "news sentences" which are by far the most frequent and "topic comment" sentences. In the latter case the subject is a topic. It is by no means easy to relate her notion of topic to Halliday's work, but the topic is, broadly speaking, something that refers to a matter of current concern. To illustrate, Schmerling drew a distinction between two sentences she heard on the radio of the deaths of two former US presidents. The utterances were | Truman died | with the tonic on the verb and | Johnson died | with the tonic on the subject noun. She states that both patterns are predictable with the Truman example being a topic comment sentence: Truman had fallen into a coma and his passing was expected. Johnson's demise on the other hand was unexpected. Such an account is both different and similar to Halliday's, who would consider the Johnson example to be a case of marked tonicity while agreeing with Schmerling that Truman: in his terms the Theme is unlikely to be tonic. I will return to this issue in the next chapter.

ment sentences. Halliday would see the 3.30 examples as being marked with the focus on the subject with the process projected as being recoverable. Bolinger (1986, pp. 112–26) presents four reasons why speakers de-accent content words of which the first two can be used to explain the tonicity choices in the 3.30 group. The first is that the meaning is implied in the context. The second is that the meanings are so culturally ubiquitous that they can be taken for granted. Kettles function to boil water and babies are renowned for crying. The third reason is that the meaning is sacrificed to a nearby focal-meaning as in

3.32 | your **mo**ther called | 3.33 | your mother **call**ed |

In 3.32 the identity of the caller is what matters and not the fact that she called. Conversely 3.33 conveys that there is something unexpected in the calling. Bolinger's fourth reason is that speakers, for their own pragmatic purposes, choose to play down some meanings. Halliday (1994, p. 298) is in agreement as he sees tonicity distribution as reflecting speakers' projected assumptions of what is and what is not recoverable.

Turning to 3.31, we can see that the verbs *talking* and *broken* convey information that is out of the ordinary. It is not every day that babies start to talk: it is an event that parents will wish to see and linguists perhaps to record. The kettle breaking likewise signals a disruption to expectations that the normal daily activity of making tea or coffee is available. The next pair illustrates the meaning potential of changing the focus:

3.34 | the **ba**by's crying | 3.35 | the baby's **cry**ing |

In 3.34 the focus of the information unit is on *the baby* and the baby's *crying* is backgrounded as something that is recoverable from the hearer's previous interaction with babies. By contrast, in 3.35 the focus is on the action which is signalled as not being recoverable from the hearer's previous interactions with babies; the crying is not normal baby crying. It is an action that requires attending to.

The following two examples, adapted from Newman (1946), further illustrate the meaning potential of tonicity choices.

3.36 | I have in**stru**ctions to leave | 3.37 | I have instructions to **leave** |

In 3.36 the speaker informs that they have written or oral instructions to relay, while in 3.37 someone has instructed the speaker to depart. Unlike in the earlier examples, there is no question of the 3.37 information unit being somehow more surprising than the 3.36 event. Nor indeed is it the case that the 3.36 event is marked. To sum up, we can see that there is no doubt that tonic placement signals the focus of the information within the information unit. But equally it is clear that there is little point in discussing the distribution of information as being marked or unmarked. The distinction is clearly only relevant in examples such as the following taken from Halliday and Greaves (2008, p. 58):

3.38 | too many cooks spoil the **broth** | unmarked
3.39 | too many cooks **spoil** the broth | marked
3.40 | too many **cooks** spoil the broth | marked

Here it is obvious that a tonic placement other than on *broth* signals a focus on either the process or actor.

While we have seen that tonic placement signals the focus of the information unit and that post-tonic items are inherently Given, nothing yet has been said about the status of pretonic elements: would the information status change if *cooks* in 3.38, *instructions* in 3.37, or *baby* in 3.35 had been made prominent? Halliday and Greaves (2008) state that boundary between Given and New is not signalled solely by prosody but depends instead on the prior linguistic and situational context. However, Halliday (1967a, pp. 206–7) also argues that recoverable information tends to be represented anaphorically by reference, substitution, or ellipsis. The presence of a pretonic prominence is likely to signal New information while the absence of a pretonic prominence signals Given information.

In all of the examples below, *Jane* is presented as the focus: the part of the information unit which the speaker draws particular attention to. To illustrate:

3.41 What's happening?

Mary is shopping with Jane		
	Focus
←	New

3.42

She is shopping with Jane		
	Focus
Given → ←	New

In 3.41, assuming that there has been no previous mention of Mary, the entire information unit is projected as containing New or non-recoverable information. In 3.42, the pronoun *she* represents Given information. Had the speaker replaced *she* with a non-prominent realization of *Mary*, Halliday would argue that the boundary between Given and New would be unchanged. I will return to the issue as to whether the presence of the proper noun *Mary* or the substitution of the pronoun *she* results in an identical information structure in chapter 6 and argue that the connotations are different.

3.43 Is Mary there?

| Mary is shopping with	Jane |
	Focus
Given ——→	←—— New

3.44 Is Mary there?

| She is shopping with	Jane |
	Focus
Given ——→	←—— New

In 3.43 and 3.44, because of the prior mention of *Mary*, it can be seen that the distribution of the information is identical in Halliday's view regardless of whether or not *Mary* is articulated or substituted by a pronoun.[17]

3.45 Is Mary there?

| Jane |
Focus
New

Yet in this case, 3.45 in context seems the most natural response and consists only of New material. As earlier the presence of pretonic prominences is claimed to be redundant. Mary and her activity have been established and are recoverable from the context, thus if chosen

17. The prominence on Mary in 3.43 enables the speaker to produce an independent key choice. The significance of key choices are discussed in chapter 5.

the pretonic must contain only recoverable elements. This implies that if an element is available in the context which the speaker wishes for some reason to draw attention to, they must make it focal.

The following bullet points summarize Halliday's position as outlined above.

1. Every information unit must contain a focal New element and may contain optional Given elements;
2. The tonic element represents the culmination of the New and is the focus of the information unit;
3. Post-tonic elements are Given;
4. Pretonic elements may be Given or New;
5. Pretonic prominent elements are New unless they are recoverable from the context or co-text;
6. The pretonic New starts at the first non-recoverable element and as noted above culminates in the tonic, or to put it another way the Given culminates with the final recoverable element in the pretonic.[18]

The following example based on the criticism in Taglicht (1984, p. 34) presents a problem with Halliday's system.

3.46 What happened?

| John danced with	Mary |	| and Peter danced with	Jane |
	Focus		Focus
←———————	New	Given ——→←———	New

The first information unit is presented as containing all New information. In the second information unit, the presence of *danced*, which was mentioned in the prior information unit, must therefore be Given. This entails that *Peter*, despite being as prosodically prominent as *John*, must be presented as Given even in contexts where mention of *John* does not entail mention of *Peter.* Taglicht comments that the different treatment of *John* and *Peter* is awkward for Halliday's theory. And indeed even more so if one considers that had the order of the information units been reversed, *John* would be presented as the Given referent. Had the

18. Halliday (1967a) states that certain items such as closed system items like verbal auxiliaries and prepositions are inherently Given unless made tonic. This view implies the possibility of some discontinuity in the New. However, this was not a point that was subsequently developed.

speaker wished to signal that all four referents were New according to Halliday they could have produced the examples below.

3.47

<table>
<tr><td>| John danced with</td><td>Mary |</td><td>| and Peter with</td><td>Jane |</td></tr>
<tr><td></td><td>Focus</td><td></td><td>Focus</td></tr>
<tr><td colspan="2">←————————— New</td><td colspan="2">Given ———→←——— New</td></tr>
</table>

While in this example *Peter* is presented as New, the ellipsis of the verb *danced* suggests that there could be no ambiguity about the activity jointly carried out by *Peter* and *Jane*. The verb is so present that it does not need articulation. And while we are dealing only with the projection of binary referential information and not considering the relational nature of information (to be discussed in the following chapter), it does seem odd that the overtly articulated *danced* is classed as a Given element which blocks *Peter* from being classed as New while the ellipted verb does not. Two further possibilities are:

3.48

<table>
<tr><td colspan="2">| John danced with Mary |</td><td colspan="2">| and Peter |</td><td colspan="2">| danced with Jane</td></tr>
<tr><td></td><td>Focus</td><td></td><td>Focus</td><td></td><td>Focus</td></tr>
<tr><td colspan="2">←——————— New</td><td colspan="2">Given→←New</td><td colspan="2">Given→←——New</td></tr>
</table>

3.49

<table>
<tr><td>| John |</td><td colspan="2">| danced with Mary |</td><td colspan="2">| and Peter |</td><td>| danced with Jane |</td></tr>
<tr><td>Focus</td><td></td><td>Focus</td><td></td><td>Focus</td><td></td></tr>
<tr><td>New</td><td colspan="2">←——— New</td><td colspan="2">Given→←New</td><td>Given→←—New</td></tr>
</table>

However, in 3.48 there is an unwarranted focus on *Peter* which also results in marked tonality and signals a distance between *Peter* and *Jane*. In the second case, as well as there being a distance between the dancers, there is also a parallel focus between the two males which adds information to that found in the original utterance. We can provisionally conclude here that the status of pretonic new elements is not settled and that Halliday's view is either in need of revising or of finding additional support. I will return to the issue of pretonic prominences in chapter 4, but for the remainder of this chapter I will examine the related issue of what Halliday means by recoverability.

As illustrated above, a tone unit must contain some non-recoverable information and may contain recoverable information. Halliday (1967a) suggests that once an element has been introduced into a discourse, it has the potential to remain recoverable until the closure of the discourse. In support of his claim, he reports that the lexical item *students* remained recoverable despite not being mentioned for eighty-three information units. Prince (1992, p. 309) goes further and argues that once a lexical item has been introduced into the discourse, it remains recoverable until the completion of the discourse.[19] Others, however, disagree. For instance Givón (1983, 2020) argues for a limit of twenty spoken clauses beyond which a lexical item is no longer recoverable based on a cross linguistic survey. His spoken clauses would seem to be our tone groups. Halliday's typology of recoverability differs in that as noted above recoverability is not a textual feature but rather something that the speaker projects to suit their individual communicative needs.

There are cases in Halliday's data where the same lexical item is articulated with a nearby tonic, suggesting that the speaker, for their own communicative purposes, wished to ensure that a particular lexical item is presented as the very information which the speaker wishes to draw the hearer's attention to. As there seems to be no reason why a speaker might not wish or need to draw a hearer's attention to a referent which was available in the context or co-text, it is not entirely clear that tonic syllables always signal non-recoverability. The next two examples illustrate. In example 3.50 from Halliday (1970a), the lexical item under discussion is *train*. For reader ease, I have notated *train* and coreferential pronouns in small caps.

3.50 | TRAINS could manage the gradients much more **eas**ily and the | … [20 information units] | all the TRAINS have been withdrawn | now if they decided to keep the track in good con**di**tion and | run the TRAINS at the speeds at which THEY **could** have been run | … [3 information units] what you **need** for | this **pur**pose is a | self-drive **TRAIN** | … [5 information units] | and **then** | instead of running TRAINS as THEY're run at **pre**sent | as public **ve**hicles | you hire **out** | small **TRAINS** to | individual

19. We will see in chapter 5 that Prince does not think of information in binary terms. Her proposed typology of information structure is a ternary model contrasting given, inferable, and new. In addition her cognitive model proposes a distinction between discourse status and hearer status.

drivers | [6 information units] | so that once a TRAIN gets into a **sec**tion | no other TRAIN can move **on** to that section and | ... [10 information units] there'd be **fam**ily TRAINS for | ... [3 information units] | you'd have your own **TRAIN** and you'd |

Table 3.4: Alternative and Non-marked Realizations of Example 3.50

	Realization	Possible Pronoun Comment
1. Trains	none	first mention
2. All the trains	all of them/they	no change to extent of New
3. The trains	them	no change to extent of New
4. They	N/A	
5. A self-drive train	one	de-accent and move focus to type of train
6. Trains	them	no change to extent of New
7. They	N/A	
8. Small trains	ones	de-accent and move focus to type of train
9. A train	it	no change to extent of New
10. No other train	one	de-accent and move prominence to type
11. Family trains	ones	post-tonic so no change to IS
12. Your own train	one	de-accent and move focus to type of train

The lexical item *trains* is first introduced into the monologue as a pretonic prominence and in Theme position. In the text the lexical item is referred to a further eleven times across a span of sixty-four information units. Only two references are articulated as a non-prominent pronoun. One reference is the non-prominent noun. However, three references are tonic and the remaining six are pretonic prominences. The above table illustrates that the experiential meaning would not have been altered had the speaker substituted pronouns.

As the above commentary indicates, had the pretonic prominence on *trains* in 2, 3, 6, and 9 been substituted with an unaccented pronoun, the information structure would not have been changed according to Halliday. This is because, as noted above, Halliday recognizes that anaphoric referential items, while inherently Given, may be found within the New.[20] In 8, 10, and 12, while representing the same event, substitution would have resulted in a different information structure with a

20. Intuitively this seems awkward and is another reason why the presence or absence of pretonic prominences requires further investigation.

Table 3.5: Alternative and Non-marked Realizations of Terrorist/Terrorism in Example 3.51

Realization	Possible Pronoun	Comment
1. Terrorism	this	change of focus to results of action and not action itself
2. This terrorism	zero	change of focus to specific attack
3. Terrorist attack	zero	de-accent and move prominence to present tense change of focus to time
4. Terrorist attacks	zero	no change to IS
5. Terrorism	this	change of focus to action *engaged*

narrowed focus on the type of train. Hence, while no recoverable information would have been lost, the focus would have shifted.

3.51 of the effects of **TER**rorism | and all the **lead**ers | as they will **in**dicate | a little bit **la**ter | share our complete reso**lu**tion | to defeat this **TER**rorism | … [8 information units] | just as it is reasonably **clear** | that this is a TERrorist attack | or a **se**ries of TERrorist attacks | … [9 information units] | it's important how**ev**er | that those engaged in **TER**rorism |

The above extract 3.51 covers a span of twenty-eight information units. The tonic lexical item *terrorism* in the first tone group is recoverable in that the extract is part of a monologue describing and condemning a series of bombings on the London transport system (see O'Grady, 2014a, for further details). Within the extract there are five mentions of the *terrorism/terrorist*. Of these, four are tonic and one is post-tonic.

We can see that in 4 even the deletion of the word *Terrorist* would not have changed either the experiential meaning or indeed the information structure where only the quantifier *series* was presented as focal New. Yet, the speaker's inclusion of the epithet *terrorist* here and also in 3 conveys a negative evaluation (Martin & White, 2005). The claim that the distribution of information inside the information unit was unaltered does not seem correct; the experiential has been wrongly prioritized. We will return to this point when we discuss information in chapters 5 and 6 in terms of "thought feeling complexes" (see Thibault, 2017, 2020a, 2020b). But for now, we simply wish to raise questions about the notion of recoverability and what is signalled by intonational prominences.

In two important but sadly neglected papers, Geluykens (1989, 1991), while agreeing with Givón that a distance of twenty clauses usually requires the reintroduction of a referent, also notes that recoverability is not solely dependent on referential distance. Other factors such as a change of topic, change of speaker, and dysfluency also play a part. I suggest that a further factor is take-up of the item. In pre-planned speech such as radio and television news broadcasts, speakers signal a change of topic by chunking their speech into paragraph-like units known as paratones (Brazil, 1997; Esser, 1988; O'Grady, 2014a, 2014b; Tench, 1996; Wichmann, 2000). A paratone is realized by boundary features of an initial high pitch reset and a closing low pitch. It may optionally be bounded by pauses. Tench (1996) notes that because of the spontaneity of much spoken discourse, paratones tend to be restricted to pre-planned speech such as lectures, oral narratives, news reports, audiobook reading, and speeches. In O'Grady (2014a) I analysed the paratone structure of the entire speech from which 3.51 is taken.

The initial mention of *terrorism* occurs in paratone 7 with the following mention five information units distant and in the same paratone. The next mention of *terrorist attack* is ten information units distant and found in paratone 9. The final tonic mention is in paratone 10 and eleven information units distant. Thus, there is some evidence indicating that a topic change may result in but not determine, as the two mentions in paratone 7 clearly indicate, whether the referent is presented as Given or New. We will examine the effect of a change of speaker in chapter 6.

The following example taken from the conversation about flooding between three different female undergraduates (see O'Grady, 2016, for full details) illustrates how dysfluency may impact the articulation of a second mention.

3.52 a | but her garden is at**tach**ed to it |
b | so her garden's **sloped** |
c | so as soon as it started over**flow**ing |
d | at the river |
e | it started … pouring down her **gar**den |

The referent *garden* is mentioned three times in five information units. It is clear that the speaker is not entirely sure how to relay her message that her friend's garden slopes up to a riverbank. Hence, she made *garden* the focus in information unit (e) in order to emphasis the topography of the garden. Incidentally this example illustrates that recoverability cannot always be equated by distance. In information unit (b), had the speaker substituted the pronoun *it* for *garden*, the identity of the referent that was sloped would not have been clear. This though does not explain the pretonic prominence on *garden* in (b).

The next example, taken from Crystal and Davy (1975), illustrates how the lack of take-up results in a second mention not being de-accented. Here the speaker's second mention of *worried* and *flames* are tonic. This is likely to be because the speaker feels that that the first two information units of her message had been unattended or unheard, and hence she needs to repeat them. Had she wished to escalate the degree of worry or her lack of enjoyment, we would expect that in (d) the adverbial would be tonic and in (e) the verb *enjoy* would be tonic.

3.53 a | and I was so **WORRIED** |
b | the the **FLAMES** |
c | were going right up to the lower branches of the **tree** |
d | and I was so **WORRIED** |
e | that I didn't really enjoy the **FLAMES** |
f | very **much** |

3.3 Conclusion

This chapter has described the systems of tonality and tonicity in some detail. I have shown that there is solid evidence in favour of viewing information units as having a psychological reality. I further showed that in the unmarked case, information units are coextensive with major grammatical units, and frequently with the clause itself. The picture for the system of tonicity is less clear. I have identified a number of issues to do with the status and function of pretonic prominences. The concept of recoverability has been examined and shown to be somewhat problematic for a number of reasons: chiefly to do with the repetition of tonic lexical items, the status of pretonic accents, and consideration of the possible relations between accented syllables and the interpersonal metafunction. I have also suggested that while a tonic syllable signals referential meaning in discourse, within the more confined scale of the information unit, it also signals relational meaning by being the most newsworthy part of the information unit. I will return to these issues in chapter 6 after I have considered other views of information structure in the following chapters.

4 Is Information Binary?

Introduction

In this chapter I will detail the theory of Functional Sentence Perspective (FSP) and compare it to Halliday's work. This is done in order to motivate the proposed four component theory of IS and to show that it represents a natural extension of both Halliday's work and FSP. FSP, as we will see, can be considered to be a non-binary theory of information, and the latter half of the chapter will examine whether information is binary. I will do this by drawing a sharp distinction between speaker-oriented and textually grounded notions of recoverability in order to provide a more expansive description of recoverability grounded in Krifka's (2008) distinction between "Common Ground content" and "Common Ground management." At the end of this chapter, I will provide a summary of the proposed model as set out in this and the previous two chapters. This is done to enable us to move on to chapter 5 where we will discuss information at the propositional rather than the lexicogrammatical level. After all, the purpose of human communication is not to signal the informational status of lexical elements but rather to signal informational status in order to convey communicatively appropriate meanings which are packaged as propositions.

4.1 Firbas's Functional Sentence Perspective

FSP is a relational theory of information structure; elements are more or less dynamic than other elements within the same distribution field (Adam, 2007; Firbas, 1987, 1992). We will see that while there are many similarities between FSP and the Hallidayan theory of Theme, that FSP theme is more encompassing than Hallidayan Theme. This is because Halliday splits off the theory of information structure from that of

Theme and includes both as components of the Textual metafunction. Davidse (1987) describes Halliday's approach as separating Theme and the FSP approach as combining theme.[1] In the made-up example 4.1, the tonic placement on *John* in SFL means that it represents the culmination of the New, and thus in this case the Theme is coterminous with the New, and the Rheme is coterminous with post-tonic Given. Examples 4.2 to 4.5 represent FSP analyses of the same clause. In 4.2 the element *with Jane* is the element with the highest CD, and it is the element towards which the clause is perspectivized. However, in 4.3 the tonic accent on *John* results in a re-evaluation of which element is being perspectivized and the rheme is in initial position. This analysis contrasts with 4.1 and illustrates the basic difference between separating and combining approaches.

4.1

John	danced with Jane
Theme	Rheme
Focus New	Given

4.2	John	danced	with Jane	(Written form only)
	theme	transition	rheme	
4.3	**John**	danced	with Jane	
	rheme	transition	(dia)theme	
4.4	John	danced	with Jane	before Mary (Written form only)
	theme	transition	rheme	rheme proper
4.5	John	danced	with **Jane**	before Mary
	theme	transition	rheme proper	rheme

The examples illustrate a number of important points. First FSP, or at least the version most closely associated with Firbas and his colleagues at Masaryk University, is not strictly binary. There are elements which belong neither to the theme or the rheme but are instead transitional. Third, as the FSP examples illustrate, the degree of CD within the theme and the rheme is relative. Fourth, the place of the tonic accent (or Intonation Centre in Firbas's terms) can lead to a re-evaluation of CD within a distributional field. Thus, for FSP practitioners, contra SFL

1. The use of an initial capital signifies SFL Theme with FSP theme is written without an initial capital.

approaches (such as Davies, 1994), intonation is not a factor in the assignment of CD in written texts. While this book concerns the information structure of spoken English, consideration of the factors behind the assignment of CD to written text is a useful entry into the theory, and hence I will start there.

4.1.1 THE ASSIGNMENT OF CD IN A WRITTEN TEXT

In the interests of satisfying communicative needs, writers signal which elements function to push the message forward: the message is perspectivized towards one element within a distributional field. As the name FSP implies, the distributional field is usually a sentence, but it can come in other forms. For instance, in the NG *the dogs*, the determiner has lower CD than the noun and is thus thematic within the NG. There are three factors in determining the CD of a written clause: (1) the contextual factor, (2) the semantic factor, and (3) linearity. These are not equal: the contextual factor is the most significant and linearity is the least significant. Firbas (1992), however, acknowledges the existence of a "basic FSP distribution" where the CD rises throughout the distribution field. This view aligns with Halliday's argument that Given elements usually precede New ones (see also discussion in chapter 1). However, non-basic distributions are not uncommon.

Turning first to the contextual factor, the key thing to note is that as thematic elements are those which contribute least to the development of the message, the elements which are recoverable (Firbas's term is retrievable) must be thematic. Unlike SFL approaches to recoverability, retrievability is an objective measure identified solely by referential distance (see discussion in chapter 3). While acknowledging that defining the absolute limit of a retrievability span is impossible, FSP scholars argue, based on text analyses, that it is short and unlikely to exceed seven clauses (Firbas, 1995; Svoboda, 1983). However, it must be borne in mind that the data used by the FSP scholars was mostly fictional prose, and hence other factors such as turn-taking, topic shift, uptake, etc. were not fully taken into consideration. I will return to this point when discussing the distribution of CD in spoken language. Returning to the contextual factor, while retrievable elements are thematic, it is possible to find examples where non-retrievable elements are thematic, e.g.,

4.6	From Marlborough	she	has hit	Reading
	theme	theme prop	transition	rheme

Assuming that *Marlborough* is not available in the immediately prior context, it cannot be retrievable. But as it fulfils the setting function, it is thematic though it has higher CD than the pronoun *she*. The rheme is the non-retrievable *Reading*, and thus despite both locations being non-retrievable only one of them is rhematic.

The second factor is the semantic factor, which basically states that verbs cannot finish the development of the message in the presence of a successful competitor. As noted above, a successful competitor must be non-retrievable. Firbas (1992, p. 42) states that non-retrievable objects and complements exceed the verb in CD except in exceptional cases. Technically speaking, FSP describes elements as outcompeting one another. To illustrate:

4.7 He kicked a ball
4.8 He kicked the ball
4.9 He kicked it

In 4.9 the retrievable pronouns are outcompeted as they do less to push the message forward than the verb; the utterance is perspectivized towards the *kicking*. In 4.7 the utterance is perspectivized towards *a ball*. 4.8 without further context is ambiguous, but assuming that *the ball* is non-retrievable, *the ball* is the element with the highest CD.[2]

Four exceptions are stated by Firbas (1992, pp. 45–6) to the general tendency for sentences to perspectivize towards context-independent objects. The first is where the object does not amplify the meaning conveyed by the verb and is itself realized by an indefinite pronoun. However, note in 4.11 the adverb extends the meaning, and it is therefore considered to have the highest CD: *nice* is the rheme. In the following examples, the element with the highest CD is presented in SMALL CAPITALS.

4.10 She PLAYED something
4.11 She played something NICE

The second is where the object precedes the subject and both are non-retrievable. It is likely that the marked syntactic ordering signals

2. We note here the unfortunate blending of what I separate out into referential and identificational information. Both the pronoun *he* and the NG *ball* must be identifiable though they may not be recoverable.

that *cats* carries the highest degree of CD, though if spoken a tonic accent on *milk* would lead to it being re-evaluated as the rheme.

4.12 Milk CATS like.

The third is where the object introduces a phenomenon which has been expressed by the subject. Here the context-independent subject presents the appearance of a phenomenon which covers the setting expressed by the object. I will return to this point when describing the presentation scale below.

4.13 DESOLATION AND LONELINESS enveloped his body.

The fourth exception is where the object expresses an idea which contrasts with an idea equally expressed by an initial element, and where the verb is non-retrievable. Firbas (1992, p. 45) gives the following example:

4.14 The towns they DAMAGED and the villages they BURNT.

Firbas argues that in the initial context the object *the villages* in the second clause is outcompeted by the verb *burnt* because the verb expresses a notion which contrasts with another notion previously expressed, in this case *damaged*. These examples can be contrasted with 4.15 where the NG *the villages* has higher CD than the verb and outcompetes it. In the second distributional field, the message perspectivizes towards the thing that was burnt.

4.15 They damaged THE TOWNS / and burnt THE VILLAGES

There are two other instances where the verb is outcompeted. The first (4.16) is where the distributional field comprises a non-retrievable subject and an intransitive verb, or where it comprises (4.17) a transitive verb and a retrievable object or complement.

4.16 JOHN smokes (see discussion of eventive sentences in chapter 3).
4.17 JOHN told him

The second is where the clause is completed by a non-retrievable adverbial element. Compare:

4.18 He lived IN LONDON In London he lived WITH HIS WIFE
4.19 The dog unexpectedly JUMPED The dog jumped UNEXPECTEDLY

4.20 In a rage she LEFT She left IN A RAGE

The examples illustrate that where the adverbial extends the meaning expressed by the verb, it adds new meaning. It outcompetes the verb and is the element with the highest CD.

4.21 He lived with HIS WIFE in London

Linearity is outcompeted by the extension of verbal meaning in 4.21; though again in spoken language a tonic accent on *London* would lead to a re-evaluation of the distribution of CD in this example. I will return to this point when I discuss how FSP contrasts settings and specifications. But first I will detail the final factor, linearity. As noted above, the basic CD pattern involves a rise from the start to the end of the distribution field. This implies that if two elements are non-retrievable and both out compete the verb, then the final one will outcompete the other and be the rheme.

4.22 A teacher praises A PUPIL
4.23 A pupil praises A TEACHER

In both examples the nominal elements outcompete the verb. In 4.22 the message is perspectivized to the nominal element *a pupil* while in 4.23 it is perspectivized to *a teacher*. In these examples the linearity factor determines the CD.

To conclude this examination of CD distribution in written texts, we have seen how the three factors interact in the assignment of CD. In the next section, I will describe the scales which are grounded in these factors and used by FSP theorists to assign CD to written texts.

4.1.2 The Scales

Firbas (1992, p. 68) notes that within each clause, communication is perspectivized towards a phenomenon presented by the subject or towards a quality or further specification of the quality expressed by the subject. To illustrate:

4.24	**BIRDS**	flew	overhead	
	Phenomenon	Process	Setting	
4.25	The Birds	sang	**SWEETLY**	in the trees
	Quality Bearer	Ascription Of Quality	Quality	Setting

It is clear that the phenomenon must exist prior to the role of quality bearer. Consider the rather contrived sentence: *Birds flew overhead and then sang sweetly in the trees.* This implies that the birds had to be first introduced into the text prior to the ascription of a quality. This led Firbas to propose the following scales with CD increasing from left to right.

4.26 Presentation Scale

Setting	Process	Phenomenon
Overhead	flew	Birds

4.27 Quality Scale

Setting	Quality Bearer	Ascription	Quality	Specification	Further Specification
In the trees	birds	sang	sweetly	of love	IN A TIME OF HOPE

The scales can be combined into the following with not all elements needing to be realized.

4.28 Combined Scales

Setting-Process-Phenomenon-Quality bearer-Ascription of Quality-Specification-Further Specification.

An example would be as follows:

Birds	flew	overhead	and then	sang	SWEETLY	in the trees
Phenomenon	Process	Setting	Setting	Ascription	Quality	Setting

The scales as set out by Firbas apply only to non-retrievable information: non-retrievable elements outcompete retrievable ones even if they are lower on the scale. Extract 4.1 is an analysis based only on the written text, and for those interested in comparing it with an SFL Theme/Rheme note that I have italicized the SFL Theme.

Extract 4.1

1. *These* are NO ORDINARY TIMES
   setting process phenomenon
   theme rheme
2. *and this* is NO ORDINARY ELECTION
   setting process phenomenon
   theme rheme
3. *We*'ve just been going through the biggest global financial crisis IN OUR LIVES
   setting process phenomenon specification
   theme rheme rheme proper

4. *and we*'re moving from recession TO RECOVERY
process phenomenon specification
theme rheme rheme proper

5. *and I believe we* 're moving on a road
setting process phenomenon
theme rheme
to prosperity FOR ALL
spec further spec
rheme proper

6. *Now, every promise* you hear from each of us this evening
setting bearer ascription
theme
depends on one thing A STRONG ECONOMY
quality specification
rheme rheme proper

7. *And this* is THE DEFINING YEAR
setting process phenomenon
theme rheme

8. *Get* the decisions right NOW
process phenomenon specification further specification
theme rheme rheme proper

9. *and we* can have SECURE JOBS[3]
process phenomenon
theme rheme
Or
Get the decisions right now and we can have SECURE JOBS
setting process phenomenon
theme theme proper rheme

10. *we* can have standards of living RISING
process phenomenon specification
theme rheme rheme proper

11. *and we* can have everybody BETTER OFF
process phenomenon quality
theme rheme

12. *Get* the decisions WRONG now
specification
theme rheme theme

13. *and we* could have a DOUBLE-DIP RECESSION
phenomenon
theme rheme

3. There are two possible analyses for 8 and 9 (also 12 and 13). The first is to consider each clause as its own distributional field. The second is to consider 8 to be the setting for a clause complex with the first clause functioning as a condition.

Or

Get the decisions wrong now and we could have a DOUBLE-DIP RECESSION

setting process phenomenon

14. *And because we* believe IN FAIRNESS

ascription quality

theme rheme

15. *as we* cut the deficit OVER THESE NEXT FEW YEARS

process phenomenon specification

theme proper rheme rheme proper

16. *we* will protect YOUR POLICE YOUR NATIONAL HEALTH SERVICE

process phenomenon 1 phenomenon 2

theme rheme

17. *and we* will protect YOUR SCHOOLS

phenomenon

theme rheme

18. *I* know WHAT THIS JOB INVOLVES

bearer ascription quality

theme rheme

19. *I* look forward to putting MY PLAN to you this evening

process phenomenon specification setting

theme proper rheme theme

The extract shows in most cases rising CD correlated with sequential positioning, though in the case of 19 the final element was interpreted as a *setting* and hence as having lower CD than the phenomenon. In 12 the final element *now* was interpreted as retrievable and hence thematic. As can be seen in, for example, 15, where the rheme has more than a single element, the element with the highest CD is labelled the rheme proper. Similarly, in theme the element that contributes least to the development of the communication is the theme proper.[4] For fuller information on how to encode the CD of written texts see Firbas (1992) and Drápela (2011). The extract above, though while very likely born as a written text, was produced as an oral one. In order to fully understand the distribution of CD in spoken texts we need to consider prosody. There is some disagreement among FSP scholars as to what

4. I have not attempted a complete FSP analysis of the text as my purpose is only to show how FSP relates to SFL's theory of information structure. For instance the setting this evening in 19 is actually a diatheme – a thematic element which has the potential to be rhematic – rather than a theme. The sole point of interest is that the final element in 19 is not rhematic.

prosody's role is.[5] For instance Firbas argues that where a clause and a tone group are coextensive the presence of a tonic accent signals the element with the highest degree of CD, as does Chamonikolasová (2018, p. 50). Daneš (1972, p. 229) disagreed about the importance of prosody in assigning degrees of CD; prosody is reflective of different underlying topic comment structures. He provided the following minimal pair:

4.29a He also visited Prague (Others visited Prague and so did he)
4.29b He also visited Prague (He visited Prague and some other places)

He claims that the assignment of the tonic accent redundantly reflects an underlying information structure. For instance in 4.29a, the fact that others had visited Prague is recoverable information. Firbas (1992) disagrees and argues that there are utterances where the interplay of FSP factors creates potentiality and hence allows for multiple interpretations such as 4.30.

4.30	I	have	instructions	to leave
	bearer	ascription	quality	specification rheme
	bearer	ascription	quality rheme	setting

In such cases he claims that tonic placement resolves the issue and removes the potentiality. He describes two ways in which tonic placement may alter the existing CD relations. The first is prosodic re-evaluation where the placement of a tonic accent results in the tonic accent outcompeting all other elements in the distribution field. Firbas notes that the element containing the tonic accent is deshaded, while the other elements are shaded. To illustrate, I interpreted the final element of extract 4.1 in 4.31 as a specification and hence the rheme proper.

5. Chamonikolasová (2018, p. 50) reports that tonic placement in English and Czech achieve the same communicative function, tending to signal the presence of the element with the highest degree of CD (1995, p. 49). This is despite English, but not Czech, being a plastic language where tonic accent and not word order signals focus (Vallduví & Engdahl, 1996, p. 503). Chamonikolasová's study also cautions us that because clauses are not necessarily coterminous with tone units, tonic accents cannot always signal the highest CD element in a clause.

4.31 as we cut the deficit OVER THESE NEXT FEW YEARS
ascription quality specification
rheme rheme proper

But had the speaker produced it with a tonic accent on the quality, the final specification would have been reinterpreted as a setting, e.g.,

4.32 as we cut THE DEFICIT over these next few years
ascription quality setting
rheme theme

The second way is prosodic intensification, where the placement of a tonic accent remains on the element with the highest CD but within that element moves:

4.33 and we could have **a** DOUBLE-DIP RECESSION
quality
rheme

4.34 and we could have a DOUBLE-DIP recession
quality
rheme

While the communication remains perspectivized towards the nominal, what has changed is that it no longer focuses on the nominal as a quality; rather, it focuses on specifying the kind of recession. Extract 4.2 examines the CD distribution in the spoken version of Brown's speech in order to show how it differs from the analysis above

Extract 4.2

1. | These are no \ORDINARY times |
prosodic intensification
2. | and this is NO ORDINARY \ELECTION |
no change
3. | We've just been going through the \/biggest | global \financial crisis | IN OUR \LIVES |
No change but three tone groups
4. | and we're /moving | FROM RECESSION TO \RECOVERY |
No change but two tone groups
5. | and I \believe |we're moving on a road to prosperity FOR \ALL |
No change but two tone groups
6. | Now, every promise you \hear | from each of us this \evening |
deshade deshade

\depends on one thing | A STRONG \ECONOMY |
shade no change but four tone groups

7. | And this is THE DEFINING \YEAR |
no change

8. | Get the decisions right \/NOW |
no change but tone is evidence for setting analysis

9. | and we can have SECURE \/JOBS |
no change

10. | we can have standards of living \RISING |
no change

11. | and we can have everybody BETTER \/OFF |
prosodic re-evaluation off

12. | Get the decisions /\WRONG now |
no change

13. | and we could have A \DOUBLE-DIP | \RECESSION |
no change but two tone groups

14. | And because we believe IN \/FAIRNESS |
no change

15. | as we cut the \deficit | OVER THESE NEXT FEW \YEARS |
no change but two tone groups

16. | we will protect your \police | YOUR NATIONAL \HEALTH SERVICE |
shade

17. | and we will protect YOUR \SCHOOLS |
deshade no change

18. | I know | what this job –INVOLVES |
deshade no change but two tone groups

19. | I look forward to putting my \plan | to \you | THIS \EVENING |
three tone groups and prosodic re-evaluation

Extract 4.2 shows that some of the clausal distributional fields have been broken down into smaller prosodic distribution fields. So for instance, in 19 there are three subfields and within each subfield there are elements, namely *my plan*, *to you*, and *this evening*, which contain the highest CD. Firbas (1992) argues that this is an occasion where the linearity factor comes into its own; the final tonic accent outcompetes the earlier ones, and in this example *this evening* is signalled as the element to which the communication is perspectivized. Firbas (1992) allows one exception: if the final tonic accent is accompanied by a low rising intonation, then the previous falling tonic accent marks the rheme proper. As will be shown in chapter 5, I do not fully agree with this claim. However, as there are no relevant examples in extract 4.2, I will defer discussion of this point until chapter 5.

Overall in seventeen out of the nineteen clauses, there has been no change in the element with the highest CD. The obvious exception is 19 with the element *this evening*, which I had coded as setting, making a diatheme the site of the final tonic accent. It has been prosodically re-evaluated as a further specification. It is the rheme proper and the element to which the communication is perspectivized. In line 16 I had coded *your police | your national health service* as a coordinate unit with the communication perspectivized equally towards both elements. However, the speaker's tonality choice results in the final nominal being assigned the highest CD.

This though is not prosody's only contribution to the assignment of CD. For instance, in 1 there is a case of prosodic intensification. The nominal element *no ordinary times* remains the rheme proper, but within the subfield of the NG the adjectival element *ordinary* is presented as that which has the highest CD within the rheme. Cruttenden (2006), a comparative study of twelve languages, notes that while Given information is de-accented, accented syllables may or may not signal new information. In other words, any element which has been coded on a scale but is not accented is to be re-evaluated as a recoverable (context dependent element) and thus thematic, while elements that were classified as context dependent may need to be reassessed if they are the sites of a pretonic accent. The re-evaluations are presented below.

4.35 | and I \believe | we're moving on a road to prosperity **for \all** |
setting   process   phen   spec further spec
theme   theme   rheme   rheme proper

In 4.35 the process *are moving* has been presented as recoverable information, and hence it no longer functions as a transition between the setting (diatheme) and the rheme. As a recoverable element, the process contributes little to the development of the message and is therefore theme.

4.36 | Now, every promise you \hear | from each of us this \evening
setting   bearer   spec
setting
theme   theme   diatheme
| \depends on one thing | **a strong \economy** |
ascription   quality
theme proper   rheme

In 4.36 the prepositional phrase *on one thing* was coded as a quality and part of the rheme. However, the absence of an accent means that Gordon Brown presented it as recoverable. As the element that contributes the least, it functions as theme proper. The NG *a strong economy* remains the element to which the message is perspectivized, though it has been recoded as quality.

4.37	ǀ Get	the decisions	right	\/**now** ǀ
	~~process~~	phen	spec	further spec
	theme	rheme	rheme proper	

In 4.37 the verbal element *get* is presented as recoverable and hence is theme. In this example because *get* as process was already the element with the lowest CD there is no change to the distribution of CD.

4.38	ǀ we	can have standards of living	**rising** ǀ
		process phen	quality
		mod	
	theme	rheme	rheme proper

In 4.38 the modal *can* is accented. This results in some adjustment to the analysis of CD. From the written text the verbal group had been analysed as recoverable and hence thematic. The speaker's selection of a pretonic accent on *can*, however, means that (1) the process has a higher CD and contributes to the movement of the message, and (2) that within the verbal element the modal carries the highest CD and serves to link the contextually Given setting with the phenomenon. The relationship is not actual but merely possible.

4.39	ǀ as we	cut the \\deficit ǀ	**over these next few \\years** ǀ
		process phen	spec
	theme	rheme	rheme proper

In 4.39 the determiner *these* is accented. As it is already part of the rheme proper and outcompeted by the final tonic accent, there is no prosodic re-evaluation. But within the prepositional phrase it is the element with the second highest CD and outranks the two following adjectives *next* and *few*. This has the effect of signalling the proximity of the time frame to the audience and of personalizing the time frame.

To conclude FSP is a relational theory of informational structure which defines the relative communicative weight of elements within a distributional field. The FSP is determined by the interaction of four factors, one of which, "retrievability," is akin to the SFL concept of recoverability. But it differs in two crucial ways, notably the narrowness of the retrievability span and the fact that retrievability encompasses what I called identifiability. However, when dealing with spoken language, prosody helps to signal which elements are New and which are Given in the SFL sense. Assuming unmarked tonality, the element which receives the tonic accent is signalled as being the element towards which the message is perspectivized. As such, in SFL it represents the focus, or as Halliday (1967a) put it, the burden of the message. In cases of marked tonality, the linearity factor usually determines the rheme proper of the clause. This differs to some extent from Halliday's view that all information units have equal status, though both theories agree that tone groups containing low rises do not contain the main focus. While FSP is a textual and not a psychological theory of communication, the prosodic factor does imply a degree of speaker choice.

In the next part of the chapter, we will consider whether that speaker choice is binary and how informational choices are encoded by the lexicogrammar. In describing speaker choice I will be mindful of Thibault's (2004a, 2004b) observation that the limits of our biological understanding hinder our ability to theorize about and understand language as a system and language as an action.

4.2 Binarity?

In SFL, IS equates to the textual metafunction, which comprises two main components: the systems of Theme and Information. Theme in English, as shown in chapter 2, is realized by syntax with thematic elements preceding rhematic ones. It is a binary system with elements realized either in the Theme or the Rheme. Information, as shown in chapter 3, is realized by prosody and signals a speaker's assumptions of whether or not lexical items are recoverable. Thus, information refers to psychological states which are overtly realized by prosodic choices. As posited by Halliday, such choices are binary: elements are or are not recoverable. There is a general tendency for thematic elements to be Given, and New elements to be found in the Rheme (Fries, 1995). But note, as pointed out in chapter 3, that marked tonality choices may necessitate the presence of New elements in the Theme (see also O'Grady, 2017a, 2024). In this section I will explore whether or not IS is, in fact, binary. In order to do this, we will first consider IS in terms of mental processing before moving on to examine the prosodic and lexicogrammatical coding of IS.

There has to date been some limited work which has explored the relation between information structure and language processing. However, this work has largely emerged from what Newmeyer (2001, p. 3) has dubbed "formal functionalism"; work which, while interested in the uses of language, is predicated on syntactic theories such as minimalism (see for example the individual chapters in Féry & Ishihara, 2016, or Erteschik-Shir, 2007). These scholars assume that language planning and comprehending involves the generation of complex syntactic trees. Each utterance is assumed, at least at an underlying state, to comply with abstract syntactic principles. This way of looking at language production has been sharply criticized by Givón (2017, p. 182), first for neglecting the fact that unplanned speech is produced piecemeal, and second for privileging a *grammatical* analysis over a *pre-grammatical* one where speech is produced as a sequence of subclausal units identified as "constituents falling under their own separate intonation contour" – in other words, tone groups (2017, p. 157). Like me (O'Grady, 2010), he argues that the sequencing of tone groups into larger communicative sequences is tightly governed by the conventions of the language. I will argue that such governance is the result of conventionalized expectations in chapter 5. However, what is important for the present purposes is that the assumption of a grammatical analysis has shifted the research focus away from real speech formed from tone groups and onto constructed language formed out of full clauses, and hence researchers have focused on reading tasks and discourse completion tasks; in other words the focus is on tasks with highly constrained linguistic contexts.

Nonetheless, while this has resulted in the neglect of tone groups/information units, the results in relation to prosodic prominence and Given and New are not to be dismissed. Though one needs to treat the results of such studies on the processing of information structure as suggestive, they do point the way towards an understanding of how information structure is processed online and provide some evidence of what a plausible psychological theory of information structure would look like. We can use these findings to examine how SFL theory measures up in terms of psychological plausibility.

The evidence reviewed in Wagner (2016) supports the view that in English, for the most part, more active and accessible referents are coded earlier in the utterance; less important elements precede more important elements; and in coordinate structure more complex constituents, which are frequently coded as NGs, follow less complex constituents frequently coded as pronominals.[6] These results are hardly

6. This may be a universal or near universal feature of language, as Dryer (2013) reports that out of 1,187 languages with attested dominant word orders, only forty or

surprising since it has long been proposed that people start from the ground of what is Given and proceed to what is New when communicating. Weil (1887/2009) had famously equated the unfolding of sentences with the very movement of the mind itself. More recently Needleman and Van de Koot (2016), building upon the well-known work of Clark and Haviland (1977), have proposed that the ordering of Given before New is likely to reflect the cognitive principle that it is easier to integrate new information if it is grounded by what is already part of the shared common ground (Stalnaker, 1974). Such a view is entirely compatible with the FSP view described above that optimum or unmarked sentence structure is one with increasing CD (Daneš, 1972; Firbas, 1992).

But what is interesting in the work reported by Wagner is what happens when normal expectations are subverted experimentally. For instance, Kaiser (2016, p. 529) reports a reading comprehension experiment where sentences with objects preceding subjects were comprehended more slowly than cognate sentences where the subject preceded the object. Yet in what she describes as a "supportive context," the reading times were almost the same as of those with the subjects preceding the objects. The conclusion is that expectations produced by preceding utterances license non-canonical word orders which reflect the projected information structure. To illustrate using a well-known example from Halliday (1994):

4.40 Bears love to eat honey Honey bears love to eat[7]

The non-canonical order takes longer to process and is perhaps likely to lead to garden pathing with some readers assuming that honey is a modifier which identifies a specific type of bear. But when a suitable context is included the processing difficulty disappears:

3.4 per cent have objects preceding subjects. Thus, as the subject is both more active and likely to carry more active information, it is the ground upon which the object is related.

7. It is also possible that speakers wishing to signal the givenness of honey would produce a sentence with so called left dislocation: *Honey, bears love to eat it*. López (2016) describes such utterances as a hanging dislocation and he argues that the dislocation serves to promote the topic *honey* which is then presented as given. In speech he would predict that the utterance would be produced in two tone groups. This seems to be an analysis akin to Halliday's marked theme, though in *IFG* Halliday presents the sentence without the final preposition. López describes the fronting of the object without a following coreferential pronoun as d dislocation and argues that in such cases the object is both recoverable and contrastive.

4.41 What about honey?
Honey bears like to eat.

Eye-tracking studies have similarly shown that prosody functions as a predictive cue. To illustrate, Dahan et al. (2002) recruited sixteen native speakers of American English and tasked them with moving an object below or above a shape. The objects included pairs of soundalikes which shared the initial syllable and onset of the second syllables, e.g., ˈkæn-d in the words candy /ˈkændiː/ and candle /ˈkændəl/. A follow up utterance contained an accented or de-accented realization which referred to the object mentioned earlier: the soundalike or an unrelated object. The experiment illustrated that the manipulation of accents in relation to cohort pairs presented visually on a screen results in longer gazes at the not-mentioned object when the target word was accented rather than de-accented. Eye fixation to the soundalike showed that hearers interpreted the prominent word as signalling a shift to the soundalike, while non-prominence resulted in fixation on the previously mentioned word. To illustrate, if the previous utterance contained the word *candy*, and in the follow up utterance it was accented, the hearers fixated on the *candle*. Conversely, if the word was unaccented, they fixated on the *candy*. Thus, the perceived prosodic realization of the string ˈkæn-d demonstrated a bias towards treating non-prominence as signalling Givenness. The experiment illustrates the association between non-prominence and Givenness and prominence and the first mention of a referent.

None of this is, of course, a surprise, but as far as I know this is the only experimental evidence that supports the widely held view that New items are signalled in English and in other Germanic languages by prosodic prominence (Baumann & Grice, 2006; Baumann & Schumacher, 2011; Cruttenden, 1997; Ladd, 2008). Newness, defined in terms of non-recoverability, is defined by the influential formal theory of alternative semantic approach associated with scholars such as Krifka (1993), Chierchia (2013), and Rooth (2016) as consisting of alternatives which are based on what is at question.[8] Thus, in the following imagined context – *Who hit whom with what?* – the answer must contain three new items: the actor, the goal, and the means, e.g., *John* hit *Bill* with *a stick*. Such a view would seem to be entirely compatible with Bra-

---

8. As an example of how terminologically confusing the information structure literature is, what we label New items are dubbed foci by scholars such as Rooth. In this book I reserve the label *focus* for the part of the tone group / information unit which contains the tonic accent.

zil (1997), who argued that prosodic prominence signalled a selection from an "existential paradigm": a set of choices available to the speaker at the moment of speaking. The signification of *John* is that he and not any of the other possible candidates committed the act of hitting; Bill and no one else is the victim of the hitting; and the stick and nothing else was the instrument. Or to put it another way, items without prosodic prominence are presented as recoverable.

In an oft-cited and influential paper from the same tradition, Krifka (2008, p. 262) defined "Givenness as a feature X of an expression α iff X indicates whether the denotation of α is present in the CG [common ground] or not, and / or indicates the degree to which it is present in the immediate CG." It is obvious that this is a more expansive definition than that used above; it clearly has a scalar as well as a binary reading.[9] Rochemont (2016) speaks similarly of Givenness connecting a linguistic expression to another if it is mentioned in the discourse or if it has an accessible cognitive status. He uses a well-known example from Chafe (1976) to illustrate.

4.42

The context is	*John and Mary recently went to the beach*
Response	(a) They brought some picnic supplies but they didn't drink the <u>beer</u> because it was warm
	(b) They brought some beer but they didn't drink the beer because it was warm

He argues that the lexical item *beer* is recoverable in 4.42a because it is inferable that beer is a subset of picnic supplies. In the second example, *the beer* is repeated. Rochemont points out that while the first mention of *beer* in 4.42a can be articulated with or without prosodic prominence, in the second example it must be de-accented.[10] He concludes that given items can be accented when inferable but not when previously mentioned. He draws on Stalnaker's (2002) work on common ground and

9. Daneš (1972, 1974) describes FSP in ternary terms: theme, transition, rheme. As there are degrees of CD within theme and rheme it seems possible to reinterpret Firbas's quality, presentation, and combined scales as clines.

10. It will be clarified later that speakers are free to make previously mentioned items prominent. Thus, I argue that Rochemont's claim is too strong and that it would make more sense to argue instead that it would be more unlikely for the second mention of *beer* in (4.42b) to be made prominent. Readers will also recognize that it is the case that only in (4.42b) can the pronoun *it* substitute for the nominal item *the beer*. I will return to this point in examples 4.43 to 4.46.

Krifka's more recent segmentation of common ground into (1) common ground content and (2) common ground management. He equates the former with the updating of shared knowledge and speaker beliefs and the latter with immediate and temporary communicative needs, including the retrieval of inferable items. Thus in 4.42a, while recognizing that the element is Given in the sense of being inferable, the speaker needs to decide how accessible the item *the beer* is at the moment of speaking for the hearer, and depending on his/her judgment he/she will articulate it with or without prominence.

On p. 47 Rochemont provides the following examples:
4.43 If you knock on the door you can ENTER the room
4.44 When the engine died I junked the CAR

He notes that in 4.43 *the room* is de-accented while in 4.44 *the car* is prominent. This, he claims, is evidence that de-accenting can be the result of entailment. I do not find this explanation entirely satisfactory as it seems to me that the speaker in 4.44 could make the verb prominent and the nominal *the car* non-prominent. But Rochemont is clearly correct in that there is something going on here; only the nominal in 4.43 can be elided or substituted by a pronoun. In the circumstances the verbal semantics entails the room. However in 4.44 the final nominal can neither be elided nor substituted by a pronominal.[11] A similar example originally reported in Evans (1977) is the contrast between 4.45 and 4.46:

4.45 John has a wife and she hates him = John has a wife who hates him
4.46 John is married and she hates him = *John is married who hates him

While the former is clearly an acceptable utterance, both Evans (1997) and Wagner (2016) argue that the use of the pronoun *she* is ungrammatical in 4.46. I personally find 4.46 to be awkward but acceptable. However, I agree that the use of the pronoun, which is not an anaphor for an NG, is not as transparent as it could be. In 4.45 the *she* pronoun clearly refers to the recoverable entity *a wife*, while in 4.46 it refers to the inferable fact that *John has a wife*. Note that the utterance *John is married*

11. For me the pronoun *it* would refer solely to the engine, and the sentence would signify that the chassis was maintained.

and his wife/the wife hates him is acceptable, but *John is married and a wife hates him* is not.[12] The paraphrase with the relative pronoun *who* is only acceptable in 4.45, providing further evidence for the recoverability of the pronominal *she* and its referent in 4.45 and the fact that the referent is not (fully) recoverable in 4.46.

The discussion above suggests that there seems to be a binary division between items which are New signalled by prosodic prominence in English and those which are Given. There is, however, also a difference between Given items which are recoverable from the context and those which are inferable. The latter are more likely to be prominent and the former more likely to be substituted by a pronoun. We have also seen that verb semantics plays a role in assigning information status. In chapter 5 I will propose a model of information structure based on expectations to try to account for these facts.

Bonkessel-Schleswsky and Schumacher (2016) is a comprehensive review of work which attempts to relate information structure to neurological states. Their starting point is to argue against searching for specific brain circuits or locations which process information structure. They argue instead that it should be possible to discover manifestations of how information structure is represented neurobiologically. Two main tools are used to investigate neural activity: the electroencephalogram (EEG) and functional magnetic resonance imaging (fMRI). The former measures event brain potentials (ERPs), which are fluctuations in the brain's electrical activity that respond to external sensory stimuli or specific cognitive tasks such as imagining a sad emotion. The latter measures the relative level of blood oxygenated haemoglobin. Increased blood oxygenation is a signal of increased neural processing, and by tracking increases or decreases in blood oxygenation the fMRI is able to measure which brain circuits are active when doing specific tasks. Bonkessel-Schleswsky and Schumacher's focus is on ERPs and the issue of which specific neural circuits are involved remains to be investigated.

Following Krifka (2008), Bonkessel-Schleswsky and Schumacher (2016, p. 582) propose that a neurolinguistic theory of information must be premised on explaining how communication is housed in the brain. They argue that the function of the brain is to allow us to interact with our environment, both physical and semiotic. They base their argument on the perception-action cycle (see Clark, 2016, p. 7), which generates internal models and allows us to make predictions about the way the

12. Or at least in monogamous societies.

world works. Gibson (1979) and, for an SFL-flavoured view, Thibault (2004b) claim that humans, like all organisms, are constrained by our morphology in what we are able to perceive. In the environment there are particular affordances which we perceive as containing information relevant to us, and we perceive the environment in relation to such affordances. The perceptual stimuli (in Gibson's work "visual stimuli") lead to the creation of internal mental models which are updated by further stimuli. Perception in this theory is not passive, and the internal state of the world is generated by the interaction of perception and the subsequent behaviour which influences subsequent perception and so on. An individual's behaviour co-adapts with the predictability produced by the perception/action cycle.

It is obvious that there are too many stimuli in any situation for a human to take in at any one moment, and so expectations and goals, which themselves arise from the relative stability of the situation, guide the person's actions (Barsalou, 1992, pp. 287–8). To illustrate, two friends chatting and having a drink in a bar have no need to attend to noises on the street. But they would clearly be ill-advised to ignore the sound of proximate gun shots. Corbetta and Shulman (2002) described a large-scale network or networks in the brain, the dorsal attention network (DAN), which controls attentional selectivity. And where expectations are met DAN is sufficient. DAN though is supplemented by the ventral attention network (VAN), which is also known as the salience network. Thus, while DAN provides top-down orientation towards an event based on the predictability of the situation or event, VAN allows for a bottom-up reformulation, and for the incorporation of unpredictable but relevant stimuli.

Bonkessel-Schleswsky and Schumacher (2016, p. 592) argue that unexpected linguistic stimuli are detectable through the activation of the VAN network and measurable as disruption to the latency of ERPs in relation to the N400 pattern. They (2016) report that the evidence from previous studies of lexical recall indicate that the N400 pattern in VAN is sensitive to distinctions between lexis which is newly introduced to the context, lexical information which is inferable from the context, and lexical information which has been previously mentioned in the context. Schumacher and Baumann (2010) and Baumann and Schumacher (2011) examined the effect of prosody on the N400 pattern and found that the signal is sensitive to prosodic cues which signal the recoverability of an item.[13] In other words, unexpected prominences resulted

13. This work was conducted on German, but there is every reason to expect that its findings would be replicated for English.

in bottom-up processing in VAN. Thus, it seems that the VAN network may process both lexicogrammatical and prosodic stimuli which is unexpected.

To conclude, it seems that the brain may process information structure as a ternary model, though it may equally process the information as binary with a more delicate distinction between two types of Given information.[14] Accordingly, we will now examine non-binary theories of information while recognizing that the binarity of information remains an open question. While ternary theories of IS are not new (e.g., Daneš, 1972, 1974) perhaps the most influential one in recent years is Princes's (e.g., Prince, 1981, 1992; Ward & Prince, 1991). Her starting point was the recognition that the terms Given and New meant different things to different scholars. She identified three distinct but related meanings: (1) Given: recoverable/predictable, (2) Given: salient, and (3) Given: shared knowledge. While her review is comprehensive, it is simultaneously self-restrictive in that there is no discussion of how the Given/New entities function: are they for instance foci? Nor is there any consideration of propositional meaning. The taxonomy is restricted to the introduction of entities to the discourse. As Prince works with written texts or written transcripts of oral speech, she does not consider prosody.[15] Her taxonomy is grounded in speaker assumptions and is not textual. Furthermore, her conflation of predictability with recoverability is dubious, as the following example of a fictitious football match report illustrates:

4.47 The stadium erupted after Werner put the ball in the net.

The NG *the net* is predictable; after all, where else could the ball have been put? But it does not have to be recoverable. It may not have been previously mentioned. Nor is it co-physically present as the recipient is not in the stadium.

The concept of salience draws from Chafe (1976, 1994, 2018) and refers to lexical items which the speaker can assume that the hearer has in their consciousness at the time of speaking. Lexical items which have

---

14. We need to be somewhat cautious in placing too much weight on current studies which use EEG. Participants will have processed, read-aloud paired sentences in a lab while wearing a magnetic helmet. This is a far cry from engaging in languaging! But nor should such findings be dismissed, as they are to date the only direct evidence we have of what happens inside the head!

15. Her rather disparaging footnote concerning Halliday's view that Given/New is signalled by intonation (1981, p. 227) suggests that she sees IS as being coded by lexicogrammatical choices and that at best prosody may function to signal contrast.

been mentioned become less salient over time as the discussion of recoverability in chapter 3 showed; they gradually fade from consciousness. The third type of Givenness relates to shared knowledge and refers to the lexical items which the speaker can assume that the hearer knows or can infer, even though they are not in consciousness at the time of speaking. Returning to example 4.47, the NG *the net* is inferable. Does this mean though that it is Given, New, or something else?

To answer the prior question, we need to consider the taxonomy in Prince (1981), which is outlined in Figure 4.1.

Figure 4.1: Prince's Non-binary Theory of Information

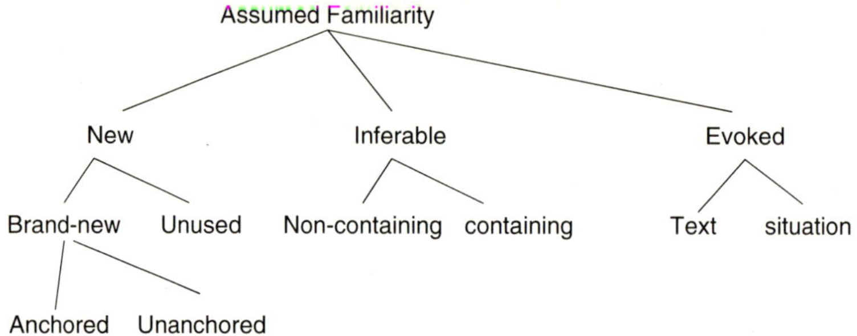

Prince uses the term "assumed familiarity" rather than shared knowledge because her model deals with speaker assumptions at the moment of speaking rather than the totality of shared information; see Lee (2001) for a useful critique of the concept of shared knowledge. As can be seen, there are seven options in total which fall under three headings. The first of these, Evoked, refers to items which the speaker assumes are recoverable from the context or co-text. Lexically Prince notes they are frequently coded by pronouns. Contrasting with Evoked, there is New, which refers to the speaker's assumptions about which items are not available to the hearer. Brand-new items are those which the speaker assumes the hearer is unaware of. Such items may be anchored or unanchored, e.g., *Mr. Kelly, my next door neighbour* versus *A neighbour.* The other class of New items is dubbed "unused" and refers to those for which the speaker assumes the hearer to have a corresponding entry in their mental lexicon. For example, the identity of the UK prime minister may not be recoverable from a discourse, but British people are assumed to be able to name them. It is not entirely clear whether or not the NG *the net* in example 4.47 can be classed as unused. It is true that while it has not been previously mentioned, and that football fans are aware of the presence of nets in goals, it can equally be argued that *the net* in example 4.47 represents an inferable token with the presence of a goal frame entailing the existence of a net. It is not clear how to resolve this issue, and this raises the issue of whether inferables are Given, New, or something else.

Prince (1992) is an attempt to clarify some of the ambiguity in the earlier model. She recognizes that Givenness can be in the speaker's head or alternatively classed as a feature of text regardless of speaker assumption. Thus, we have the following arrangement that a discourse New item may equate with a hearer New or a hearer Given item and a hearer Given item may equate with a discourse Given item.[16] While the introduction of a textual layer of Given/New is welcome, it is still not entirely clear how to code the NG *the net.* As a definite NG it signals that is identifiable and likely Given, but simultaneously it occurs in post-verbal position and thus, according to the principle of end weight (Fries, 1995, Dik, 1978), it would appear not to be straightforwardly Given.

Birner (2006) proposes the following revised taxonomy:

4.48

	Hearer old	Hearer new
Discourse old	Evoked (textual – situations)	Inferable
Discourse new	Unused	Brand new

She describes "inferable" as arising from a situation where elements are discourse Given (she uses the term "old") and hearer New and unused as arising from a blend of discourse New and hearer Given. Her view supports my original thought to code the NG *the net* as unused but does not necessarily help decide whether it is in fact Given, New, or something else. Clarke and Haviland (1977) provide some support for a ternary system of information in that they note inferable items take longer to process than Given ones, but less time to process than new ones; see the discussion of Bonkessel-Schleswsky and Schumacher (2016) above.

16. As all her speakers are "honest," she does not mention the possibility of discourse Given equating with hearer New; see (O'Grady, 2014b).

Kaltenböck (2005) firmly disagrees with the above suggestions. He reinterprets Prince's model of assumed familiarity as one of discourse familiarity, see figure 4.2.

Figure 4.2: Discourse Familiarity with Examples (Based on Kaltenböck, 2005)

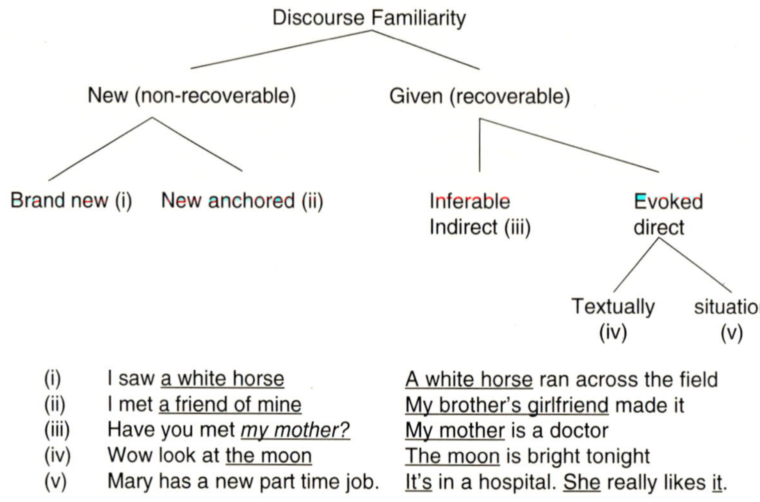

All lexical items introduced by a speaker into a discourse can be identified through a combination of lexicogrammatical realization and recoverability as one of five options. Speaker intention is not a relevant factor, as it presumed that speakers signal their intentions through their lexical choices. While the examples above exemplify Kaltenböck's categories, the examples used may create a false impression that discourse Newness correlates with indefiniteness and discourse Givenness may correlate with definiteness or pronominal use; this is not the case. Definiteness is not defined solely in terms of referential status or uniqueness of specificity (Gundel et al., 2001), e.g.:

4.49 Despina is a moon of Neptune
Despina is one of the fourteen moons of Neptune
Despina is not the largest moon of Neptune

Gundel et al. argue that the defining property of definiteness is that the hearer is able to assign a unique representation to the NG as soon as they have processed it. There is no requirement that the hearer have any prior familiarity with the referent of the NG.[17] In a series of publications, Gundel and her co-workers have developed a Givenness hierarchy. The hierarchy states that Givenness cannot be reduced to whether or not an item is presented as salient. Instead, they argue that their hierarchy recognizes that the lexical coding of NGs and pronouns underdetermines the speaker's intended meaning. For a hearer to comprehend the intended meaning, they need to rely on the speaker's utterance being the most relevant one that the speaker could have produced in the context (Gundel, 2010, p. 150). An example will illustrate:

4.50 The dog chased the cat / the cat was chased by the dog
(a) Luckily it was too fast
(b) Luckily it was too slow

In 4.50a the pronoun *it* refers to the cat and in 4.50b the pronoun *it* refers to the dog despite the fact that both referents are accessible and regardless of the order in which the cat and the dog are presented in the preceding utterance. What does matter though is relevance; hearers will process the first meaning that fulfils a communicative need (Grice, 1975; Sperber & Wilson, 1995). Hearers are aware that it is fortunate that the cat escaped and that it would be very unfortunate if the cat hadn't. The Givenness hierarchy is premised upon the observation that all referring forms encode two kinds of "information." The first is procedural information about whether a referent is part of the common ground or not and the second is "descriptive/conceptual information" – in SFL terms a mixture of experiential and potential interpersonal meaning. Uniquely the Givenness hierarchy does not argue for an exclusivity of status but rather argues that the six identified categories are in a scalar unidirectional relation with the categories to the right being entailed by those to the left.

Figure 4.3: The Givenness Hierarchy (Based on Gundel and Hedberg)

In focus >	Activated>	Familiar	Uniquely identifiable >	Referential >	Type Identifiable
It, she	that, this This NG	that NG	the NG	Indefinite This NG	a N

17. Indeed, I must confess that I was unaware of the existence of any moons around Neptune prior to querying Google.

To illustrate:
In focus. Who ate the sandwich? Mary ate it = associate representation in focus of attention
Activated. Is there any food left? Mary ate that/this = associate representation in working memory
Familiar. You look tired. That dog's barking kept me up all night. = associate representation in memory
Uniquely identifiable. Which one do you want? I'll have the prawn sandwich please = associate unique representation with the NG.
Referential. What did you get up to last night? We saw this/a great new band = associate unique representation.
Type identifiable. Why is John so happy? He exchanged numbers with a very beautiful woman last night.

In O'Grady (2016) I suggested that the In Focus and Activated mapped onto Given, while Referential and Type Identifiable mapped onto New. The other two categories were classed as potentially recoverable.[18] But what I did not fully develop in that paper was the significance of the unidirectional entailment. To illustrate, as a category to the right is entailed by that to the left the speaker has a choice of which lexical expression to use. Consider:

4.51 Did you see anyone interesting last night?
(a) Yeah, I saw her again (In focus)
(b) Yeah, I saw that girl again (Activated or Familiar)
(c) Yeah, I saw the girl we met last week (Uniquely identifiable)
(d) Yeah, I saw this girl (Referential)
(e) Yeah, I saw a girl we met last week (Referential or Type identifiable)

In my contrived example the referent is the same young woman, and the state of shared knowledge between the speaker and the hearer is the same. The speaker, however, has some choice to refer to her using different categories from the hierarchy. For instance, if the *girl* is in focus, he can use any of the terms. If the girl is uniquely identifiable, he can employ utterances (e) to (c). It is only when the information status of the girl is type identifiable that there is no choice. It is also obvious

18. In Gundel et al. (1993, 280–1) the authors note that some of Princes's terms, see Figure 4.1, equate with the terms in the Givenness hierarchy. Unused corresponds with familiar, Containing inferable with uniquely identifiable and Brand new with type identifiable.

that context is required to disambiguate the meanings produced by the choice of the NG in (b) and (e). Thus as with an SFL analysis, an analyst must rely upon a degree of subjectivity when using the Givenness hierarchy to investigate the referential status of NGs. With that caveat in mind, I will attach lexicogrammatical realizations to the choices realized by Kaltenböck's system of discourse familiarity and analyse the text in extract 4.3. Differences in the lexicogrammatical realizations can be attributed to the speaker wishing to provide more explicit experiential or interpersonal information.[19] In agreement with Gundel et al. (1993), while coding I recognized (1) the underspecification of information realized by a potential lexicogrammatical choice, and (2) the one way entailment by which an evoked referent can be coded by any of the lexicogrammatical choices used to code items higher up the scale. Thus while a pronoun can only code an evoked item, the indefinite article NG can code any item on the scale if communicatively appropriate.

Figure 4.4: Entailment According to the Givenness Hierarchy

Brand new items = a NG, | Entailed
New anchored = a NG (+ post modification), this NG,
Inferable = The NG,
Evoked textual, Pro, that, this,
Evoked situation Pro, that, this, ↓

Extract 4.3

1. **These** are **no ordinary times**
   Evoked situation — Inferable / Evoked situation*
2. and **this** is **no ordinary election**
   Evoked situation — Evoked situation
3. **We**'ve just been going through **the biggest global financial crisis in our lives**
   Evoked situation — Inferable
4. and **we**'re moving from r**ecession** to **recovery**
   Evoked situation — Inferable — New anchored
5. and **I** believe **we**'re moving **on a road to prosperity for all**
   Evoked situation — Evoked situation — Inferable

---

19. Gundel et al. (2019) ascribe the different realizations to a speakers' desire not to flout Grice's maxim of quantity. Thus, they produce the referring expression that does not say more than they intend and that they do not say less than they intend.

6. Now, **every promise** **you** hear from **each of us**
BRAND NEW EVOKED SITUATION EVOKED SITUATION
this evening depends on **one thing** **a strong economy**
EVOKED SITUATION BRAND NEW BRAND NEW / INFERABLE*

7. And **this** is **the defining year**
EVOKED SITUATION INFERABLE / EVOKED SITUATION*

8. Get **the decisions** right now
BRAND NEW / INFERABLE*

9. and **we** can have **secure jobs**
EVOKED SITUATION BRAND NEW

10. **we** can have **standards of living rising**
EVOKED SITUATION BRAND NEW / INFERABLE*

11. and **we** can have **everybody** better off
EVOKED SITUATION BRAND NEW / INFERABLE*

12. Get **the decisions** wrong now
INFERABLE / EVOKED TEXTUAL*

13. and **we** could have **a double-dip recession**
EVOKED SITUATION BRAND NEW

14. And because **we** believe in f**airness**
EVOKED SITUATION BRAND NEW* / INFERABLE

15. as **we** cut **the deficit** over **these next few years**
EVOKED SITUATION INFERABLE* / BRAND NEW EVOKED SITUATION

16. **we** will protect **your police** **your National Health Service**
EVOKED SITUATION NEW ANCHORED NEW ANCHORED

17. and **we** will protect **your schools**
EVOKED SITUATION NEW ANCHORED

18. I know what **this job** involves
EVOKED SITUATION INFERABLE

19. **I** look forward to putting **my plan** to **you**
EVOKED SITUATION NEW ANCHORED EVOKED SITUATION
this evening
EVOKED SITUATION

The coding of the extract reveals a number of things. First, as anticipated, the most common coding for a referent is evoked, implying that the speaker anticipated that such a referent would be recoverable and in need of no further description. Second, the asterisk with two coding labels indicates my uncertainty of which code to apply. The asterisk indicates my personal reading, but as lexicogrammar is underspecified it is clearly possible that other recipients may have classed the referents as having a different information status than I did. To illustrate, in line 6 I considered the referent of the NG *a strong economy* to be inferable owing to the prior articulation of the lexical items from the economic field *global financial crisis, recession,* etc. but recognize that others may class the referent as either new anchored or brand new. As there is no way to investigate what was in Gordon Brown's mind when he produced the language, the best we can say is that the lexicogrammatical coding of the referent is ambiguous.

As Brown himself was addressing a dispersed, disparate, and physically distanced audience, he himself could not attempt to gauge how his lexical coding of referents matched individual recipients' understanding of what he assumed to be the common ground. Thus, it is possible that his uncertainty resulted in his coding of referents with forms which had a range of informational states. To illustrate in line 12, Brown produced a second mention of the NG *the decisions.* I have coded this as evoked textually and hence as signifying the same informational value as the pronominal *them* would have done. But Brown's coding is ambiguous and enables the informational status to be classed as inferable. In line 15 I coded the NG *the deficit* as potentially brand new. This is because the determiner does not identify the deficit that is being discussed but rather specifies the uniqueness of the deficit as the national one.

Thus, coding a text in terms of discourse familiarity results in ambiguity. Indeed, Loock (2013) has proposed the existence of structures which he argues are chosen by the speaker to signal indeterminacy, e.g., appositional nouns, appositive relative clauses, and non-restrictive pre-modifiers. However, unlike the work reviewed above, it is clear that Loock is referring to the information status encoded in propositions. Speakers clearly do not introduce referents simply for the sake of it but rather because the referents are themselves part of propositions. In the next chapter we will examine propositional information.

Our claim though is that Given and New information in spoken English is signalled by prosodic means. Table 4.1 lists the referents, their status on the Givenness hierarchy as analysed in extract 4.3, and their prosodic realization as Given, New, or focal. It is immediately obvious that the lexicogrammatical coding of the information status of referents is not a reliable indicator of how speakers present the referents as Given or New. Prior to discussing what Table 4.1 tells us, I will first explain how the table is set out. The first column self-evidentially states which line in extract 4.3 the referent is found in. The second sets out the referent, and it is important to note that the Kaltenböck model of discourse familiarity only classifies the informational status of nominal elements. The SFL model, as illustrated earlier, describes the information management of all lexical elements. The third column lists the results of the

Table 4.1: Congruence between Speaker and Hearer Status in Extract 4.3

Line	Referent	Text Status	Speaker Status	Congruent
1	these	Evoked	Given	Yes
1	no ordinary times	Inferable/Evoked*	Focus –ordinary	No
2	this	Evoked	Given	Yes
2	no ordinary election	Evoked	Focus	No
3	the biggest …	Inferable	Focus	No
3	… global crisis	Inferable	Focus	No
3	in our lives	Inferable	Focus	No
4	we	Evoked	Given	Yes
4	from recession	Evoked	New	No
4	to recovery	Evoked	Focus	No
5	I	Evoked	Given	Yes
5	we	Evoked	Given	Yes
5	on a road to prosperity for all	Inferable	New New Focus	 No …
6	every promise	Brand new	New	Yes
6	you	Given	Given	Yes
6	each of us	Evoked	Focus – each	No
6	this evening	Evoked	Focus	No
6	on one thing	Brand New	Given	No
6	a strong economy	Brand New/Inferable*	Focus	Yes#
7	this			
7	defining year	Inferable/Evoked*	Focus	No
8	the decisions	Brand New/Inferable*	New	Yes#
9	we	Evoked	Given	Yes
9	secure jobs	Brand New	Focus	Yes
10	we	Evoked	Given	Yes
10	standards of living	Brand New/Inferable*	New	Yes#
11	we	Evoked	Given	Yes
11	everybody	Brand New/Inferable*	New	Yes#
12	the decisions	Inferable/Evoked*	Given (Prom)	Yes#
13	we	Evoked	Given	Yes
13	a double-dip …, … re- cession	Brand New Brand New	New New	Yes Yes

Table 4.1: Congruence between Speaker and Hearer Status in Extract 4.3

Line	Referent	Text Status	Speaker Status	Congruent
14	we	Evoked	Given	Yes
14	in fairness	Brand New*/Inferable	Focus	Yes
15	we	Evoked	Given	Yes
15	the deficit	Inferable*/Evoked	Focus	Yes#
15	the next few years	Evoked	Focus	No
16	we	Evoked	Given	Yes
16	your police	New anchored	Focus	Yes
16	your National Health Service	New anchored	Focus	Yes
17	we	Evoked	Given	Yes
17	your schools	New anchored	Focus	Yes
18	I	Evoked	Given	Yes
18	this job	Inferable	Given	Yes
19	I	Evoked	Given	Yes
19	my plan	New anchored	Focus	Yes
19	to you	Evoked	Focus	No
19	this evening	Evoked	Focus	No

analysis set out in extract 4.3. Where, as in line 1, two possible answers are presented the asterisk indicates my preferred answer. The fourth column lists the speaker projection of information status. The division into Given, New, and focus does not imply a ternary division of information but simply indicates that referents have been coded as recoverable, non-recoverable by virtue of being part of the pretonic domain of the New, or focal as signalled by the speaker's tonic choice. Where the final element in the group is not the site of the tonic, this has been indicated. The final column records whether the text status and the speaker projection of the status of the element are in accord. The hash sign indicates congruence with the text status that was not my preferred answer. In line 3 an ellipsis before and between the NG *the biggest global crisis* signals that the element was articulated in two tone groups, with both the adjective and the nominal presented as focal. In line 12 *the decisions* has been coded as Given despite being made prominent because of its recent previous mention.

The issue is what are we to make of the fact that 29 per cent of referents[20] are presented by the speakers in a manner that differs from the information status encoded by the lexicogrammar. Krifka (2008) distinguishes between what he labels common ground content and management. Krifka's view of common ground is influenced by Chafe's view of information packaging. As such he distinguishes speaker intention, temporality, and the current state of speaker attention from the lexicogrammar. While Krifka's work is not concerned with the recoverability of referents,[21] the logic of his argument can be applied to the presentation of lexical items in discourse. As we have seen, the encoding of the lexicogrammar identifies whether or not a hearer is predicted to be able to identify a referent. This is irrespective of whether or not it is presented as recoverable. To illustrate, the referent *this job* in line 18 has been coded as identifiable and also as recoverable by the speaker. By contrast, in line 2 the NG *no ordinary election* is identifiable, but the speaker makes it focal. It is newsworthy and the burden of his message. In other words, both lexicogrammar and prosody combine to signal what, following Firbas, we can label retrievability. But the lexicogrammatical coding signals the identifiability of the referent while tonic choice signals the speaker's projection of the information status of the referent as recoverable or non-recoverable. It is subjective and dependent on the speaker's apprehension of the context as well as the speaker's communicative purpose. As such a speaker is free to project an element as recoverable or non-recoverable regardless of whether the item is available or identifiable. Thus, we would expect the following relations to hold between the discourse familiarity model and the speaker projection of information structure:

---

20. The proportion of incongruent referents would have been 40 per cent had I gone with my preferred answers for the lexicogrammatical encoded information status of the referents.

21. Krifka is not, to put it mildly, a fan of Halliday's view of information. He provides this example (2008, p. 256):

Who stole the cookie? John or Mary?

JOHN stole the cookie

He argues that what is in focus is not New as John has clearly been previously mentioned. Instead, what is new is "the information that John satisfies the description that *x stole the cookie*. But such an argument clearly conflates the information status of lexical elements with that of propositional information. Furthermore, a more congruent answer would have been *John* or *John did* with *John* clearly being the most newsworthy element. In fact, it is the only possible newsworthy element!

Retrievability

Identifiability	Recoverability
Brand New	Tonic or pretonic prominence
New anchored	Tonic or pretonic prominence
Inferable	Non-prominent or pretonic prominence
Evoked textual	Non-prominent
Evoked situation	Non-prominent

The predictions are underspecified for prosodic realization, and actual realizations can only be recognized in context as the moment of speaking. The figure only presents what is likely and not what is possible.

The question posed in the subheading was whether or not information is binary. The studies reviewed above illustrate that the question remains a live one and that there is still no conclusive answer. However, the writing above also illustrates that information can be coded in binary terms and that as there seems to be no compelling reason to code in non-binary terms, I will not do so. At the same time, I have also argued for a superordinate category of retrievability, and it may be the case that patterns of association between identifiable and recoverable information may better be explained in a non-binary model.

4.3 Where Are We Now?

I have introduced three of the four levels of the proposed IS model. By so doing I have disambiguated Theme, identified in English by syntactic position, from topic, which is identified by pragmatic relevance. I have shown that while Theme, topic, and Given frequently co-occur, they should be treated as separate dimensions of the model. Focus has been identified as being signalled by tonicity choices and as the relation between clauses and tone groups is not one-to-one, it can occur anywhere in the clause. Topicality is related to discourse familiarity in that we have seen that topics are usually encoded as identifiable NGs or pronouns, though examples such as 2.40 argue that this is not always the case. Theme is a clausal system and each and every clause must contain a theme. Focus is a prosodic system and mandatory in the tone group / information unit. While tone groups may coincide with clauses, they also frequently diverge. Topic though in SFL terms is a semantic system, and hence not every clause will contain a topic.

In other words, spoken language does not consist of waves found in strings of clauses with a beginning thematic prominence and a final prosodic (tonic) prominence. Instead, it consists of multiple overlapping waves signalling thematic, topic, and focal prominences with the thematic and topical waves often co-occurring. This view may seem to assume that this spoken language is formed out of a sequence of clauses. In fact, as chapter 5 will make clear, this is not my view: I will argue that spoken language consists of a sequence of tone groups which contain lexical elements, the production of which create expectations of the occurrence of following lexical elements, and that this expectation results in the creation of strings of lexical elements in multiple tone groups which form into macro-clause-like structures. I have reserved judgment as to the binarity of information, proposed a superordinate category "retrievability" which encompasses identifiable and recoverable referents, and suggested pairings of prosodic and lexicogrammatical choices.

In the opening chapter, I stated my view that information was Janus-faced in reaching backward and forward. But to date, with the (partial) exception of Theme, which relates and orients clause initial elements to what is to come while at the same time being sensitive to the expectations generated by the co-text, I have only discussed information in terms of reaching backward. Topic signals a matter of standing interest while focus signals newsworthiness or the articulation of an element which is not recoverable from the previous context. In the next chapter, we will consider information in terms of forward-looking expectations and also examine the fourth level, namely that of the proposition. In chapter 6 we will test the model outlined above against a sample of unscripted conversational speech.

5 From Initial to Target State: The Dynamic Unfolding of Propositions

Introduction

In this chapter, I will set out the fourth strand of the proposed IS model: namely that of propositional meaning. It is a truism that speakers do not produce language simply to introduce lexical items as thematic or focal or to signal whether the item is a matter of standing interest. Instead, speakers perform actions by speaking (Austin, 1962; Searle, 1969). Speakers use language to give or demand information or material things,[1] resulting in the speech functions set out in Table 5.1.

Halliday and Matthiessen (2014) claim that there is a congruence between speech function and mood except as indicated by the asterisk for offer (see Table 5.1). Thus, a subject ^ finite order predicts that the speaker intends to produce a statement and produce a wording which will expand the common ground shared between speaker and hearer. In this chapter, we will examine information in terms of expectancies or predictions and see how the incremental chaining of elements results in the creation of utterances which expand the state of speaker/hearer common ground. Expansion of common ground results in the articulation of propositional meaning and in speakers' producing statements, questions, offers, and commands.

In this chapter, I will first examine work on assertion and then move on to a broader discussion of what is meant here by speaker/hearer common ground. Finally I will detail how lexicogrammatical expectations coupled with prosodic realizations unify a series of tone groups/

1. Andersen (2017) is an enlightening discussion which argues that material things are themselves semiotically construed, and thus the distinction between *information* and *goods and services* is not as absolute as table 5.1 presents.

Table 5.1: Speech Functions According to Halliday and Matthiessen (2014)

	Information	Goods and Services
Give	Statement: *I am writing a book*	Offer: *Shall I write a book?**
Demand	Question: *Am I writing a book?*	Command: *Write a book*

information units into propositions which realize speech functions. One major difference between the proposed model and the work discussed in the next section is that I am unconcerned with truth values or indeed with notions such as goodness of fit between utterance and environment. This is because for me, like Halliday, utterances constitute meaning and hence do not fit an external environment. Rather as Hjelmslev (1961) theorized, the flux of experience or purport is formed into meaningful content through semiotic means; we experience and make sense of the world through our ability to semioticize.[2] The philosopher Charles Taylor is quite clear that language does not reflect an external objective reality but rather shapes individual human responses to the world. Such responses are as much emotional as they are experiential (Taylor, 2016). Linguistic meaning is as much feeling as it is thought (see Thibault, 2021). In other words, speakers do not only use language to make a statement, ask a question, make an offer, or issue a command; they also simultaneously signal their attitude towards and evaluation of the utterance they have produced. As a material somatic activity, languaging cannot be divorced from emotion and feeling.[3] Hence it must be remembered that when in the next section I describe assertions in terms of propositional information, I am not telling the complete story. And that on occasion the proposition to be imparted is the speaker's evaluation of information conveyed by the languaging event.

2. This does not of course mean that we can semioticize the world as we wish. We form input into meaningful substance, but we do so with the affordances enabled by the biological capacities of our species, coupled with our social/historical knowledge in the particular spatial and temporal scales we operate in. The world most definitely does not bend to our will.
3. The neuroscientist Antonio Damasio has proposed the "somatic marker hypothesis," which notes that thoughts cannot be divorced from feelings (1994, 1999, 2010, 2021; Bechara & Damasio, 2005). While feelings are clearly grounded in biology and rooted in the soma, emotions are culturally specific and hence at least (partly) conventionalized (Feldman Barrett, 2017). For instance a genuine friendly offer or a genuine apology rather than a half-hearted one imposed on the speaker will be realized differently across language systems and within languages according to tenor variables.

5.1 *Propositional Information and Assertion*

Lambrecht (1994, p. 25) states that the language we produce is the result of the interplay between language-specific conventions and informational structure demands. In English we have seen that there is a tendency for New lexical items to occur towards the end of utterances and Given ones to precede them. However, as English is not a flexible word order language and as it resists the omission of subjects, syntactic conventions may disrupt the informational flow from Given to New. Such a view differs from the SFL Metafunctional view which sees language as having evolved to be as it is because of the functions it has evolved to serve, in that it grants an independent role to typological factors. Regardless, in the typical case, an utterance will be formed out of a combination of Given and New elements and convey something new in the sense that the amount of common ground (Stalnaker, 1974) between speaker and hearer is increased. Utterances, in other words, contain presuppositions and assertions which Lambrecht (1994, p. 52)[4] defines as follows:

5.1 Presupposition: The set of propositions which are lexiogrammatically evoked in a sentence which the speaker assumes the hearer already knows or is ready to take for granted at the time the sentence is uttered.
Assertion: The proposition expressed by the sentence which the hearer is expected to know or take for granted as a result of hearing the sentence uttered.

Lambrecht considers assertions as referring to the speaker's view of the hearer's mental state, and hence assertions are not textual features but instead refer to the speaker's understanding of the common ground.

In order to investigate what the assertion in an utterance is, Erteschik-Shir and Lappin (1979) devised "the lie test." Lambrecht provides the following examples with the underlinings representing the assertions.

5.2 I heard that <u>Jane and Mike got married</u>.
That's a lie = they didn't get married

4. Lambrecht's schema sees information operating at three related levels: (1) activation, which refers to whether an item is active in the speaker's mind, (2) identification, which refers to whether a particular referent is stored in the hearer's mind, and (3) propositional.

The hearer states that the speaker's assertion is inaccurate but does not question that the speaker heard of Jane and Mike's marriage.

5.3 I finally met the woman who moved in downstairs
That's a lie = you didn't meet the woman who moved in downstairs.

The hearer states that the speaker's assertion is inaccurate because while he met someone, it was not the new downstairs neighbour.

Examples 5.1 and 5.2 presuppose the honesty and reliability of the speaker. In contexts where the speaker was known to be a dissembler, the counter-assertion would be as follows:

5.4 I heard that Jane and Mike got married
That's a lie = You didn't hear that

The hearer signals that despite the speaker's intention, the issue of whether Jane and Mike are married or whether the hearer is aware of their marital status is immaterial to the assertion, which is that the first speaker didn't hear a particular thing.

5.5 I finally met the woman who moved in downstairs
That's a lie = you didn't meet the woman who moved in downstairs and you know it.

In this example the hearer treats the original speaker's turn as a single assertion which is denied.

Consider the following example:

5.6 I finally met the woman who moved in downstairs. She is lovely.
That's not true

The first speaker states two propositions. First, that they met somebody, and second, that somebody is lovely. The hearer replies by saying "that's not true." Here it is not clear what is being asserted. Is it that the original speaker is mistaken in the identity? Is it that the first speaker is not being truthful? Is it that the new neighbour is not lovely? Without access to context, it is impossible to know. The implications generated by the lie test seem to be subject to context and to the pre-existing expectations of the interlocutors. In a similar manner to the underspecification of the lexicogrammatical coding of referents, the lexicogrammatical coding of propositions is also underspecified. Hence the state of common ground between the interlocutors prior to the utterance of the assertion constrains the possible meanings produced by the speaker's utterance.

Following Brazil (1995) and O'Grady (2010), I label the state of common ground between the speaker and the hearer as the initial state, and that which has been achieved at the end of the utterance as the target state. As utterances are articulated in time, I will refer to them as increments. In section 5.2.1 I will formalize the syntactic chaining rules which, in combination with prosodic choices, allow us to identify when speakers signal the achievement of target state and hence produce an increment.[5]

5.7

I	met	the woman
Initial state		Target state
Time 0		Time 0+

The speaker first produces the pronominal element *I*, which anticipates the production of the verbal element *met*, which itself anticipates the final nominal element *the woman*. Production of the pronominal and verbal element modifies the initial state, which is equivalent to the common ground between the speaker and the hearer, but it is not until the final nominal element has been produced and target state achieved that the speaker has updated the common ground between speaker and hearer. Following Brazil (1995) I will label elements prior to the realization of target state as realizing an intermediate state.

Let's imagine two scenarios in which 5.6 was uttered. The first is where the hearer has no reason to suspect that the speaker is a fantasist, and the second where the speaker's disregard of the truth is well known to the hearer. While the speaker clearly intends to update the common ground by adding the proposition that *he/she had met an identifiable woman and all that conveys to the interlocutor about the meeting,*[6] it is only in the first scenario that the target state realized the speaker's communicative intention. In the second scenario, the updated common ground can be paraphrased as *The speaker's claim of meeting the identifiable woman and all that conveys to the hearer about the meeting is nonsense;*

---

5. We will see that while I agree with scholars such as Givón that speakers parcel out their message incrementally, I disagree with his claim that spoken language is somehow pre-grammatical.

6. As both the speaker and the hearer are identifiable to the hearer, the hearer will naturally draw inferences about the meeting, its type, and purpose.

the hearer's belief in the speaker's unreliability is further confirmed.[7] Thus, while target state is achieved by the unfolding of lexical items in time, the updated common ground is not necessarily equivalent to the signification of the lexical items added to the existing common ground. Nor is the updated common ground identical for different speakers. Thus, we need to consider the proposition articulated by the chaining of lexical items at two strata: (1) lexicogrammatical and (2) semantic. The terms "initial state" and "target state" will only be used to refer to the lexicogrammatical stratum. In terms of the proposed wave model of information, they are points of prominence at the beginning and the end of "the utterance" which signal the state of common ground before the utterance is articulated and after. The previous sentence suggests a rather static view of discourse and seems to suggest that speakers wait until the completion of the utterance – achievement of target state – before updating the common ground. Nothing could in fact be further from the truth. Each articulated item prior to target state is a member of a syntagm. It is both a contextually appropriate prospection and an element which itself prospects a further element. Thus, the movement from initial state to target state is dynamic, and each articulated element both constrains what follows as well as clarifies/revises what has been said. Thus, interlocutors are constantly updating and revising their understanding of the common ground as they predict target state.

5.7	I finally	met	the woman	who moved in downstairs
	Initial State			Target State
	Time 0			Time 0+

Here the same prospections occur as in 5.6 with the subject nominal prospecting the verbal element which prospects the nominal.[8] However, in 5.7 while the speaker has presented the freshly introduced item *the woman* as identifiable, articulation of the item is not in and of itself in the context sufficient to achieve target state. Thus, a further prospection arises, and the speaker produces a hypotactic clause which functions to identify which of the identifiable women he/she is referring to.

5.8	I finally met the woman who moved in downstairs. She is lovely.	
	Initial State	Target State
	Time 0	Time 0+

7. It is obvious in the second example that the common ground is not really shared or common in any meaningful way. I will develop this argument in section 5.2.3.
8. I am ignoring the contribution of the adverbial element.

Example 5.8 shows us that an increment may expand over more than one independent clause. It is only with the articulation of the adjectival element *lovely* that target state is achieved. The initial clause sets the scene by introducing the Theme and topic of the second clause. After mapping out the chaining rules in sections 5.2.1 and 5.2.2, I will discuss what I mean by common ground and propose a revised version of Stalnaker's claims. This is because the achievement of target state, while formally realized by the combination of syntax and prosody, represents an updating of the common ground.

5.2 *Increments*

Spoken text emerges as a process of negotiated co-construction between interlocutors who share sufficient common ground; the presumed background information shared by the speaker and the hearers (Stalnaker, 2002, p. 701). Interlocutors experience speech as a temporal sequence of words and phrases that conform to their expectations based on their previous experiences of interacting with the language in particular and operating in the individual communicative contexts. Language use has both a synchronic and diachronic reality: it is simultaneously what is spoken in the moment and the result of historical accident. Speakers employ the linguistic resources handed down to them to achieve their communicative purposes, but at the same time their individual purposes can only be achieved by the affordances produced by the linguistic system they and their hearers have access to. Linguistic patterns become conventionalized through use (Hopper, 1987), and a metastable language system emerges. O'Grady and Bartlett (2023) discuss how patterns emerge, and while the system as a dynamic one can never reach stability, it is robust enough for people to fulfil their communicative needs.

While in this chapter my definition of the term increment derives from Brazil (1995), the term is more widely understood in a very different way. In the conversational analysis (CA) and interactional linguistic literature, incrementing is a process where the speaker expands beyond a transition relevance place (TRP). To the best of my knowledge, Schegloff (1996, p. 90)[9] was the first scholar to employ the term "increment" to refer to grammatically structured extensions of the prior talk. To illustrate, scholars such as Ford et al. (2001) classify any grammatical unit if it expands on the prior TRP, regardless of whether it can be integrated into a preceding clause, as an increment. Couper-Kuhlen and Ono (2007, p. 513)

9. Note if I am correct on this point then Brazil (1995) has priority in the use of the term, albeit to refer to the movement from initial to target state.

likewise define increments as grammatical extensions of the prior unit. For Szczepek Reed (2010b, p. 205) increments are stretches of talk which form the building blocks of turns and are theoretically distinct from tone units: they seem to be identical with Brown et al.'s (2015) pause-defined units. While these views and the one presented here are grounded in the fact that speech as a temporal phenomenon emerges in chunks which create expectancies, turn taking is not part of the discussion here, unlike in CA accounts. In addition, the paragraphs below show increments are identified as the realizations of syntactic chains, but expansions are irrelevant. This is because unlike CA approaches and indeed Givón (1995, 2020), the grammar approach presented here posits that speech is fully grammatical and that it can be described in terms of linear chains which form into regular patterns which represent a movement from an initial to a target state. Unlike CA approaches, prosody is a necessary though not sufficient criterion in the identification of the achievement of target state (see section 5.2.2). For now I will set out the three criteria, based on Brazil (1995), needed to identify increments in discourse. An increment is a stretch of speech which fulfils three criteria:

1. The satisfaction of grammatical expectations as formalized by the successful run through of grammatical chaining rules supplemented by a few additional chaining rules – discussed in 5.2.1;
2. The grammatical chain must be coterminous with at least one complete tone group and contain at least one instance of falling tone – discussed in 5.2.2, and;
3. Upon completion of the grammatical chain, the speaker must have updated the speaker/hearer common ground – discussed in 5.3.

The criteria will be illustrated against real data and some modifications will be suggested.

5.2.1 The Grammatical Chaining Rules

Brazil (1995, p. 51) set out seven simple chains which lead to target state in declarative utterances. O'Grady and Bartlett (2019) added an eighth chain (number 7 in table 5.2) for declarative mood utterances realized normally as telling increments.[10] The chains are presented below.

In all examples the initial nominal and verbal elements are mandatory and, as example (1) indicates, on occasion sufficient to complete the chain. If it is not sufficient, the verbal (V) element prospects a further

10. Asking increments would normally commence with a verbal element which would prospect a following nominal element.

Table 5.2: The Simple Chains Illustrated[1]

1	N V	Susan died
2	N V N	Susan kissed Bill
3	N V N A	Susan ate sushi quickly
4	N V N E	Susan likes tea hot
5	N V E	Bill is clever
6	N V P/N	Susan danced in the park
7	N V E A	It was bad as well
8	N V N E A	Bill made Susan sad by accident

[1] A nineth chain, N V A N, e.g., *That depends on one thing a strong economy* will be identified in extract 5.1. A tenth chain, N V E A V, will similarly be identified in example 5.22. The point though is that the exact number of chains is not important. What is important is that such chains can be identified and coded.

nominal (N), adjectival (E), or adverbial (A).[11] Assuming a N element is selected, the chain may be complete, or E or A elements may be prospected. It is immediately clear that the chaining rules presented above cannot account for the workings of the spoken language. For instance, the following examples do not conform to the simple chains.

5.9 Sadly Susan died after an extended illness in the night
5.10 After a few glasses of wine Susan kissed Bill for a joke
5.11 Bill is very clever but also annoying
5.12 It could have been very bad as well
5.13 Susan forgot to buy the wine

Brazil (1995) argued that a number of further formal devices are required to augment the simple chains and account for how elements chain in spoken English. The first of the devices is *suspension*. This refers to the production of an element which does not alter the existing state. For instance, production of the adverbial element *sadly* in 5.09 does not relieve the speaker of the expectation that she will produce an N element which will result in Intermediate State 1, prospect a further V element, and so on. *Suspensive* elements are of informational relevance; the A element asserts the speaker's attitude to the proposition

11. While formally this statement is correct, the verb process plays a role in prospecting which element is chosen. For example, in (2) the material process *kiss* predicts but does not determine that the post verbal element will be N or A, e.g., *Susan kisses John/badly*, while the verbal element in *Susan is pretty/a philosopher* predicts E or N.

in 5.09 or provides a setting for the interpretation of the proposition in 5.10. Suspensions are not restricted to initial position. For instance, the articulation of the A element *very* in 5.11 does not discharge the speaker from their obligation to produce a following E element. While the examples above detail the workings of the chains at group/phrase rank, suspensions also occur within groups, e.g., *a few glasses* contains a suspensive determiner followed by a suspensive E element which do not discharge the obligation to produce the prospected N element. Suspensive elements are coded with lower case letters thus:

5.14 Sadly Susan died
        a   N   V
5.15 Susan bought a few bottles
        N   V   N
                          d e N

The second formal device is reduplication. This, according to Brazil, arises through the production of a second N or A element. Crucially, the production of the repeated element does not exhaust the obligation. Reduplicative elements are notated with a plus sign.

5.16 Sadly Susan died after an extended illness in the night
        a   N   V   A+   A
                           P+   d   e   N+   P d   N

5.17 After a few glasses of wine Susan kissed Bill for a joke
        a   N   V   N   A
        p   d e   n+   p n   P d N

The third formal device is ellipsis, which is the omission of lexical items or clauses that are recoverable from the situation or preceding text (Biber et al., 1999, p. 156). It can occur at the beginning, middle, or end of an utterance (McCarty, 1991, p. 43), though Biber et al. (1999, p. 1104) state that conversationally ellipsis is usually either initial or final. It is classified as either situational or textual. Situational ellipsis is the non-realization of lexical elements which are obvious from the situation context.

5.18 What's the matter
        (I've) Got an awful cold
            Ø V^1 d e   N

In this example the mandatory N V elements have not been produced but are clearly recoverable. The personal pronoun *I*, which is recoverable from the context and the finite V element, have been omitted. I will defer discussion of the coding of *got* for the moment. The Ø symbol notates the ellipsis.

Textual ellipsis is a means of avoiding unnecessary and redundant repetition of items which are predictable and recoverable from the co-text. Textual ellipsis can be divided into the following three categories (Biber et al., 1999):

5.19 In Coordinate Clauses

He squeezed her hand but   met with no response
N V   N   c   Ø V   A
             d N   P   d N

Here the subject *he* of the second clause is predicable, and elided. Brazil (1995) does not code linking elements such as connectors and conjunctions because their presence or absence does not alter the formal obligation to produce a following element. While this is undoubtedly the case, I (O'Grady, 2010, p. 111) argued that on the semantic strata, the connectors signal a change in the speaker's assessment of the predictability of an event occurring. For instance in 5.19 there is no indication that the speaker believed that the unnamed man's squeezing of a woman's hand would be met with no response. Substitution of *but* with *and* would have signalled such an expectation. Accordingly, I code connectors as "c": the lower case signals that the element is suspensive in that it does not alter the pre-existing expectations.

5.20 In Questions and Answers

Have you got an exam on Monday?
     Two   actually
Ø   N   Ø A
     e   Ø

In 5.20 the full non-elided chain is N V N A (I've got two exams on Monday), and the predictable N and V elements are elided. So, too, is the previously mentioned N element *exam*.

5.21 In Comparative Clauses

In my opinion Messi plays better than Ronaldo
a   N   V   E   A   Ø
                                 P   N

In this example the final V element is elided. Had the speaker produced the V element by articulating the element with the substitution *does* or the V element *plays*, they would have completed an N V E A V chain which illustrates that the list of eight chains given above is not complete.

The next formal device is extension. Brazil (1995, p. 57) recognized that there are a number of occasions where speakers have exhausted all the formal possibilities afforded by the chaining rules but have not achieved target state. He provided the example:

5.22 We want to search your car
N V V^1 N

Production of the V element exhausts the N V chain but clearly a target state has not been achieved. Brazil argues that the same formal state is achieved by the articulation of the V element in the example below. The obligation to produce a following N element remains.

5.23 We searched your car
N V N
d N

Brazil (1995) argues that the production of the non-finite V element (V^1) results in a doubling back that allows for the speaker to commence a second run through of the formal rule system: in other words, production of the V^1 element does not alter the expectations generated by the production of the earlier V element.[12] While the V and V^1 coding represent them as formal elements in a chain, extensions code very different types of meaning: modality and verbs in phase. Examples 5.24 and 5.25, reproduced below, illustrate; 5.26 shows how aspect is coded.

5.24 It could have been very bad as well
N V V^1 V^1 a E A
5.25 Susan forgot to buy the wine
N V V^1 N
d N

12. Non-finite verbs are not coded as suspensions because production of the non-finite verbal element may result in the achievement of a target state e.g., *She is sleeping*, *She may go*, *She started writing*, etc.

5.26 I' ve got a very bad cold
N V V^1 N
d a e N

Finally, if a speaker has run through the chaining rules without achieving target state, they may restart the chain, e.g.,

5.27 Bill is very clever but also annoying
N V a E c Ø a E

The production of the E element *clever* satisfies the formal requirements of the chaining rules, i.e., an N V E chain, but in the context it has not achieved target state. Hence, the speaker produces a further run through of the rules.

5.2.1.1 Sample Texts Coded for Increments. In this section I code the same three short texts presented in chapter 3. The achievement of target state is coded with the hash sign. After each increment,[13] I will discuss how the chain accords with the chaining rules and extra formal devices detailed above. The extracts can be considered to represent instances of languaging where 5.1 is the most planned and 5.3 the most spontaneous. Hence if Givón is correct about the pre-grammatical nature of spontaneous talk it should be more difficult to code extract 5.3 than to code 5.1.

Extract 5.1 shows that nineteen clauses form into eight increments indicating that articulation of a clause is not normally sufficient to attain target state.

Extract 5.1

1. These are no ordinary times and this is no ordinary election
N V N c N V N #
d e N d e N

The speaker produces a N V N chain, but this does not result in the achievement of target state. Thus, the speaker produces a suspensive linker followed by a further N V N chain.

13. Though of course these are only potential increments, as without consideration of prosody and context it is not possible to determine if target state has been achieved.

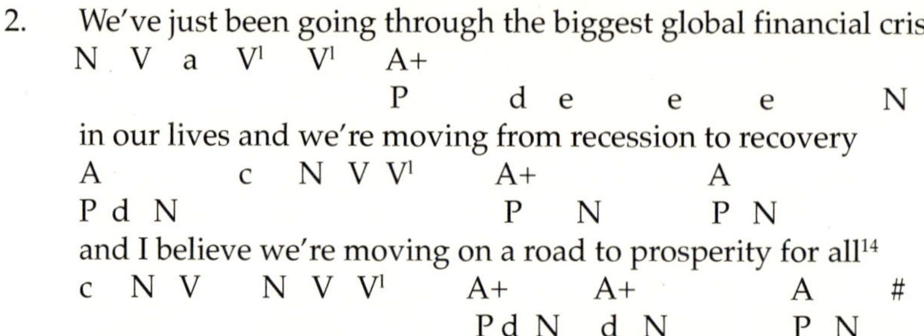

2. We've just been going through the biggest global financial crisis
N V a V^1 V^1 A+
P d e e e N
in our lives and we're moving from recession to recovery
A c N V V^1 A+ A
P d N P N P N
and I believe we're moving on a road to prosperity for all[14]
c N V N V V^1 A+ A+ A #
P d N d N P N

The speaker first produces a N V A chain supplemented by extension and reduplication with a suspensive a element. The two V^1 elements do not discharge the obligation to produce a following N, E, or A element. Neither does the suspensive a element *just* alter the obligation. In order to complete the chain, the speaker produces a reduplicative A element. The production of the linker indicates that target state has not been achieved and the speaker produces a further N V A chain, again supplemented by suspension and reduplication. Once again production of the linker signals that target state has not been achieved. Therefore, the speaker produces a N V chain before doubling back and producing a further N V A chain supplemented by extension and reduplication. This achieves target state.

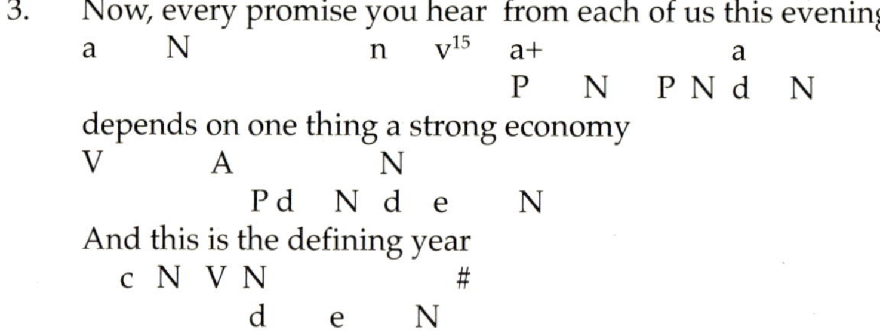

3. Now, every promise you hear from each of us this evening
a N n v[15] a+ a
P N P N d N
depends on one thing a strong economy
V A N
P d N d e N
And this is the defining year
c N V N #
d e N

Increment 3 comprises two chains linked by a connector. The final N V N chain achieves target state. The initial chain comprises an initial suspensive a element followed by an N V A N chain. This was not

14. Note if *I believe* is interpreted as a mental epistemic process, then it signals that the speaker had completed the chain without achieving target state and so restarted a chain. Alternatively, the elements could be coded as a suspensive A elements.
15. The N V chain *you hear* has been coded as suspensive.

a chain identified above, but it is clear that an appositive N element can follow an A element, so the description of eight simple chains needs to be expanded. More significantly is my coding of the N V chain *you hear* as part of a suspensive subchain *you hear from each of us this evening*. I did not code the N elements *promise* and *you* as reduplicative because the nominals do not prospect the same V element. The N V chain *you hear* does not discharge the obligation realized by the previous N element to produce a V element. As the speaker could have produced a similar suspensive chain, *Every promise* heard from each of us this evening *depends*, etc., it is clear that V elements can also suspend even in the absence of overtly realized N elements. This example informs us that while suspensive elements are usually A elements or E elements within NGs, nominal and verbal elements may also suspend.

4. Get[16] the decisions right now and we can have secure jobs[17]
V N E A c N V V^1 N #
d N d^0 e N

I have coded the initial chain as an instance of imperative mood, though I am aware that there was another possible coding available. As an imperative, the chain is V N E A, which conforms to the predictions above, though with the order of the N V elements naturally reversed. The linker signals that target state has not been achieved, and the speaker doubles back and produces a final N V N chain supplemented by an extension. Alternatively, the initial chain *get the decisions right now* could have been coded as commencing with a hypothetical ellipted element, and hence the chain would have been coded as a suspension which set the scene. I chose not to do this for the simple reason that if there is a choice between coding with or without ellipsis, it is more transparent to "trust the text" (Sinclair, 2004).

16. Imperative mood chains which congruently realize commands usually commence with a non-finite V element. They may start with a V element or a V N sequence, e.g., *Play tennis, Do play tennis,* and *let's play tennis.*

17. Following Brazil (1995) I notate the unrealized indefinite determiner as d^0.

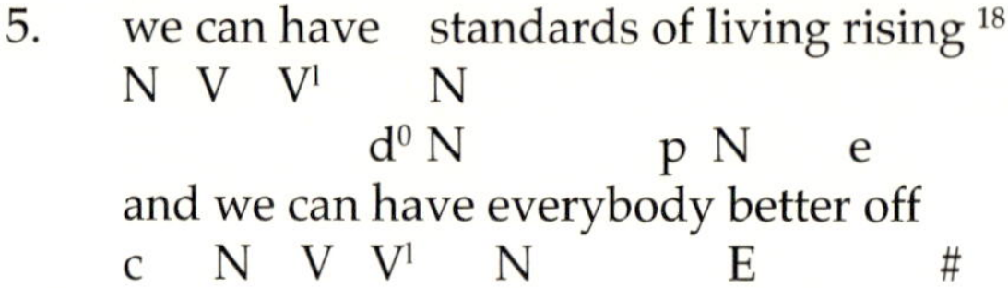
5. we can have standards of living rising[18]
N V V[l] N
d[0] N p N e
and we can have everybody better off
c N V V[l] N E #

Increment five comprises an N V N chain which does not achieve target state, followed by an N V N E chain which does. Both chains are supplemented by suspension. The sole noteworthy feature of this increment is the displacement of the e element *rising* rather than *rising standards of living* (d⁰ e N). However, at group level this does not result in an alternation in coding.

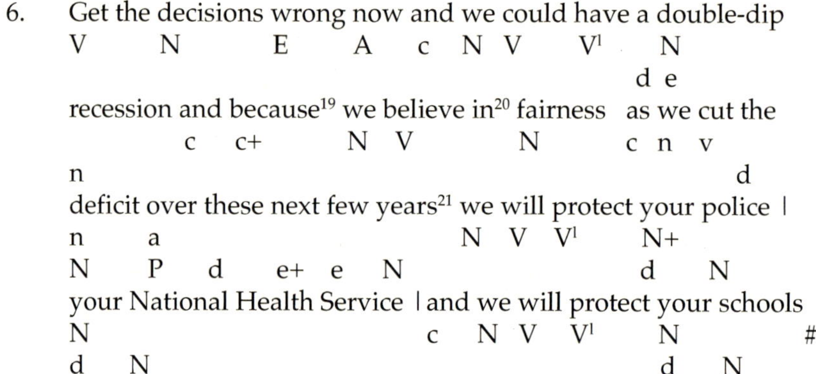
6. Get the decisions wrong now and we could have a double-dip
V N E A c N V V[l] N
d e
recession and because[19] we believe in[20] fairness as we cut the
c c+ N V N c n v
n d
deficit over these next few years[21] we will protect your police |
n a N V V[l] N+
N P d e+ e N d N
your National Health Service | and we will protect your schools
N c N V V[l] N #
d N d N

The opening chains of increment 6 are identical to increment 4. The presence of the linkers and *because* prospect that the target state has not been achieved. Accordingly, the speaker produced further chains; the first is coterminous with a circumstantial clause which enhances the previous N element *fairness* and is coded as suspensive. This is then followed by two N V N type chains connected by a linker.

18. Here the speaker has deviated from the expected word order: *rising standards of living*. In any case the entire element fulfils the expectation of satisfying the obligation to produce an N element. An alternate code would have been standards of living [that are rising] N Ø V[l].
19. Linking elements may also reduplicate.
20. I have coded *believe in* as a V element. See also *look forward* in increment 8.
21. I have coded the circumstantial clause as suspensive in that it did not alter the formal obligations resulting from the production of the previous N element.

7. I know what this job involves
N V N+ N V #
d N

The speaker first produces an N V chain before doubling back and producing a N V chain with a reduplicated element. In a formal grammar, the element *what* would be considered to have moved from the end of the chain this job involves what.[22]

8. I look forward to putting my plan to you this evening
N V V^1 N P/N+ A #
d N

In 8 the speaker produces an increment consisting of an N V N A chain supplemented by an extension and reduplication.

In summary it is clear that, with very minor tinkering, the rules set out earlier are sufficient to identify a semantic unit, the increment, in the extract above. However, as the extract is from a planned monologue, it remains to be seen whether it is as easy to identify increments in spoken extracts where the speaker had not carefully planned out their wording and hence produced wording on the fly. Extracts 5.2 and 5.3 represent more spontaneous speech where the speakers were producing language on the fly. They may know where they want to go, but unlike Gordon Brown in Extract 5.1, they have not mapped out their journey prior to commencing languaging. In order to save space and time, I will only provide a commentary on increments formed from chains which have not been described above.

Extract 5.2

A: 1 | Yeah **I <u>guess</u> what you were <u>say</u>ing about like** | **<u>Port</u>land**
ex N V N+ N V V^1 P N
and stuff | **coz <u>I</u> didn't know <u>where</u> it was** but |
c N c N V V^1 N+ N V c …

Increment incomplete. The speaker produces a basic N V P/N chain which serves as a setting for the remainder of the message. I have not coded it as a suspension because formally there is no suspended expectation. The linker *coz* introduces enhancing information which the

22. In asking increments which are realized as Wh Qs, the Wh element is coded as an open selector (O).

speaker C interprets as an invitation to take the floor, producing increments 2 and 3.

C: 2 | Yeah | **it is in Dorset** | near Weymouth | (overlap)
ex N V P+/N P N
3 | **That's quite bad** |
N V a E

The speaker produces two increments comprising N V P+/N P/N and N V E chains.

A: 1 | but it was ... but then ... **it kind of looked really really bad**
c N V c a N a V a a E
on the video |
P/N

Speaker A returns to the expectations produced by the abandoned increment and produces a basic N V E P/N chain which achieves target state.

C: 4 | Yeah | **but it was only hitting one side of it though** so |
ex c N V a V^{1} d n P/N A c
| **it kind of made it look worse than it actually was** |
N a V N V A c N a V
A: | Yeah | (overlap_)
[ex]
C: | because ... because **the rest of it is sheltered** |
c c N V E

Speaker C produces three chains prior to achieving target state.

5 **it was just only like one** | **portion** |
N V a E d N
| **which obviously is really bad for people that live there** |
N a V a E A N V A
| but | **it probably wasn't as** | **bad** | **as other places** |
c N a V A E a d^{0} e N
| which they | probably didn't **they didn't really show in the clip** |
N+ N a V N V a V^{1} P/N

| whereas there they were like | **this is this inn** | that's been like
a N+ N V a N V N+ N V V^1 a
attacked | **and it's still standing** |
V^1 C N V a V^1

In the absence of prosody, I have coded the entire segment, which comprises of nine run-throughs of the chaining rules, as increment 5. Here we have an example where the achievement of a V^1 element signals the achievement of target state.

6 | this modern road | **it was more like** | **that was more specific**
N+ N V a … N V a E
than | **the other clips** | …
c N
| here **it was just** | **people talking about what they have seen** |
a N V a N Ø V^1 N+ N V V^1
| and **they're sat in their cars** |
c N V V^1 P/N

I have coded one increment above, but it is possible that the first chain represents the achievement of a target state; I will revisit this example when discussing prosody below. But in the meantime, I have analysed the increment as consisting of an abandoned N V chain followed by four run-throughs of the chaining rules.

B: 7 | yeah **it did show you** kind of like | **how** | **the sea front**
Ex N V V^1 N a a N+ N
| **was more protected than inland** | with rivers | with like
V a V a E P/N+ P/N
rivers were just pouring over (unclear overlap)
V a V

A C: | Yeah |
ex
B: | and like **the river banks were just gone** |
c a N V a E
| **and like coming up the paths** | **where as you could see**
c a Ø V P/N N+ a N V V

with the sea | they have like flood | massive barriers[23] **|** yeah |
P/N N V a N ex
that protect that | so I guess it's quite a contrast |
N V N c N V N V a N

A: | Hm | (Minor clause/acknowledgment) (overlap)
Ex

B: **| in that respect |**
P/N

I have coded the entire chunk as one increment; however, as a result of the first overlap I am not confident about the coding because B articulated words that are unclear. However, the following linker suggests that the speaker had not achieved target state. The following N V E chain is also coded as not achieving target state because of the following linker. It is followed by four run-throughs of the chaining rules. Again, because of the presence of the following linker *so*, I have not coded this point of the chain as achieving target state.

The chaining rules and other devices posited to date have proved adequate to code the extract above. However, as expected there are points in the chain immediately preceding linkers where without consideration of prosody it is not clear if target state has been achieved. Since for present purposes I am only interested in seeing whether the chaining rules can potentially code the temporal movement from an initial state to a target state, the fact that there are possible uncoded initial/target states is not important. We have seen that increments, e.g., increment 1 above, may be interrupted and that the expectations generated by previous talk may be returned to and satisfied despite interrupting increments. Or to put it another way, an increment may span a speaker's turn.

The third extract is taken from a conversation in the London Lund 1 corpus (for further details see Bourgoin et al., 2021). As with the previ-

23. Speaker B has clearly departed from the predicted word order, *massive flood barriers*. However, this does not disrupt the expectations at group or indeed word rank. At group rank the V element prospects an N element which the speaker produces. At word rank the expected order is d^0 e N, with the pre-nominal elements suspensive if articulated. Production of the singular N element *flood* informs the hearer of the previous presence of the unrealized indefinite determiner coded as d^0 and anticipates the presence of a further plural N element. This expectation is satisfied by the articulation of the N element *barriers*. The intervening e element *massive* suspends and does not discharge this obligation. The coding is d^0 N+ e N.

ous extract the speakers are languaging on the fly. A difference between the two extracts though is that the speakers A and B disagree about traffic conditions in Reading and adopt a more competitive turn-taking strategy. As in the previous extract, a speaker may complete an increment in more than a single turn.

Extract 5.3

A: 1 | from Marlborough | **she has hit Reading** | at half
a N V V^1 N A
B: | splendid | (overlap)

past eight in the morning |
P/N

In the extract speaker A produces a basic N V N A chain supplemented by extension and suspension.

B: 2 | splendid | agreed | **but you're not** | (incomplete)
e e c N V ...
A: 3 | that is **that is the other side of** Reading |
N V N V N P/N

Speaker B attempts to start an increment but is unable to complete it. Instead A produces a N V N P/N chain.

B: 2 | **going into Reading** |
Ø V^1 P/N

B completes the previous increment coded as N V A with a suspension.

A: 4 | **It will be the other side of Reading** going into Reading |
N V V^1 N P/N Ø V^1 P/N
| **that's where she hit the traffic** |
N V A N V N
| traffic | going in | to Reading | from either side |
N Ø V^1 P/N+ P/N

Speaker A produces four run-throughs of the chaining rules before achieving target state. First A produces an N V N P/N chain, but that is felt to be insufficient. The speaker produces three further chains: the first with an ellipsis specifies the direction of the traffic, the second referring to the location of the traffic jam, and the third repeating the direction of the traffic.

B: 5 | no | **you've missed the point** |
d N V V^1 N

B achieves target state by producing an N V N chain supplemented by an extension.

B: 6 | **the traffic you are worried about** | **is the traffic** | **going**
N+ n v v^1 V N Ø V^1
towards London |
P/N

Increments 5 and 6 further illustrate that increments and turns are distinct with the turn comprising two increments. The subchain *you are worried about* has been coded as suspensive – see increment 3, extract 5.1 for reasoning.

A: 7 | no Petey | at half past eight in the morning | ... (abandoned)
voc p/n+ p/n
B: 8 | **there is not a mysterious line** | which divides traffic going
N V a N+ N V N Ø V^1
to London | immediately at Reading |
P+/N A P/N

Speaker A's attempt to articulate increment 7 is outcompeted by B's articulation of increment 8, which comprises a chain with reduplicated elements and ellipsis.

A: 7 | no | **but there is traffic** |
c N V N

Here speaker A returns to the increment 7 I have coded the N V N element as achieving target state, but in the absence of prosody I have no way of knowing whether the speaker achieved target state or not.

A: 9 | **there is a traffic rush hour at Reading** | when traffic piles
N V N+ N P/N N+ N V

into Reading | **and it is about eight thirty** | that my mother
P/N c N V a A N+ N
has gotten stuck | in traffic trying to get into Reading |
V V¹ V¹ p/n V¹ V¹ P/N

Increment 10 comprises two run-throughs of the chaining rules connected by the linker *and.*

B: 10 | **most of it** | **is going to London** |
N V V¹ P/N

Increment 11 comprises a single run through of the chaining rules.

A: 11 | what from the other side of Reading | (ellipsis)
Ex Ø P/N+ P/N
B: Yes
Ex Ø

I have interpreted increment 11 as an asking increment which requires input from both interlocutors. Speaker A's contribution has been reconstructed as containing an ellipted N V sequence *the traffic is/is the traffic* (in whatever order). B's contribution similarly comprises an ellipted N V sequence.

A: 12 | yes | **that may well be true**
ex N V a V¹ E

A produces increment 12 which is realized as a single run through of the chaining rules. This increment resolves the argument by signalling A's partial acceptance of B's point of view.[24]

To conclude, as in the previous two extracts the chaining rules are sufficiently powerful to capture the achievement of potential target states. In the next section after a brief discussion of prosody grounded in studies such as O'Grady (2010, 2021) and O'Grady & Bartlett (2019), I will re-examine extract 5.3 and discuss the combination of prosodic and lexicogrammatical choices in order to see if the potential increments identified above need to be revised.

---

24. Increments 15 and 16 combine to form an exchange with A producing the inform and feedback moves while likely assuming a secondary knower (K2) role rather than a primary knower (dK1) role. See Berry (2016).

5.2.2 Prosody

In English there is widespread agreement that there are five primary tones: fall \, rise /, fall-rise \/, rise-fall /\, and level – (Brazil, 1997; Cruttenden, 1997; Halliday, 1967a, 1970a; Halliday & Greaves, 2008; O'Grady, 2010; Tench, 1996, 2003; etc.). There is slightly less agreement as to what the functions of these tones are. The paragraphs below set out the differing views. Once I have done so I will provide a short critique in order to arrive at a synthesis.

Halliday argues that falling tones project speaker certainty while rising tones signal speaker uncertainty. Thus, he argues that statements are normally realized by falling tone while polar interrogatives are signalled by rising tone. Fall-rises and rise-falls signal a blend of certainty and uncertainty. A fall-rise signals that a speaker's wording seems certain but is not so. A rise-fall signals that while the speaker may have seemed uncertain, they are in fact certain. A level tone[25] signals that the speaker is opting out from the choice between certainty and uncertainty, perhaps because they are uncommitted in the sense that they are (1) signalling contingent agreement with something stated or implied by their interlocutor, (2) uninterested in the content of their own message, or (3) are struggling to find the lexical content needed to realize the intended speech function. Cruttenden (1997), however, argues that tones function to signal speaker relations, with falling tones being centred on the speaker and rising ones directed towards the hearers. Thus a rise or a fall-rise signals the speaker is seeking something: a function naturally realized by a question.

Brazil (1997) similarly argues that the function of tone is to signal the speaker's projection of the state of understanding existing between the speaker and the hearer. This results in what he labels speakers adopting either a direct or oblique orientation. Oblique orientation is signalled by the choice of level tone and projects that the speaker is opting out of engaged communication. This may be because the communication is routine, or they are struggling to form their message and instead focusing on their wording choices. In direct orientation the choice of either falling and

25. Halliday and Greaves (2008) label this tone as level rising. In their classification they eschew descriptive labels and employ numerical ones. Thus, their system is Tone 1 (falling), Tone 2 (high rising), Tone 3 (level rising), Tone 4 (fall-rising), and Tone 5 (rise-falling). There are two further compound tones, 1 + 3 and 5 + 3, where they argue that that the two tones are fused with a major focus followed by a minor one. For reasons set out in O'Grady (2010) and Tench (1996) I reject this analysis.

rise-falling tone projects the speaker's assumption that their words are expanding the state of convergence existing between speaker and hearer while fall-rising and rising tone signals that they are not expanding the state of convergence. Fall and fall-rise are considered the unmarked choices with rise-fall and rise signalling that the speaker is more committed. Thus, an offer produced with a rise is projected as more insistent and possibly more genuine.

Tench, in a series of works (1990, 1996, 1997, 2003), argues that the chief function of tone is to signal what he labels "information." In a manner akin to Brazil and Halliday, the choice of level tone functions to signal a routine or a formula. Falling tone along with its more committed rise-fall variant signals that the content of a tone unit is a chunk of major information, while rising tone, if followed by falling tone, signals that the chunk of information is incomplete. If the rising tone follows the falling tone, it signals that the information is minor in the sense that it glosses or quantifies the previous information. This view is not dissimilar to Halliday's tones 1+3 and 5+3, where the second focus is a minor one. Halliday and Greaves (2008, p. 131), in their discussion of tactic relations in spoken English, note that the sequence of rising tone followed by a falling tone signals that the content of the first tone group is incomplete and dependent on the following tone group even if the initial tone group encodes a paratactic clause.

Despite the differences between the descriptions above, it is clear that all of the above scholars agree that in the management of information, statements, or tellings are associated with falling tones. Without a falling tone, the sequence of tone groups does not contain a piece of major information; it is dependent on a following information chunk and cannot signal speaker certainty or project an expansion of the shared understanding. A sequence which does not contain a falling tone is therefore either preliminary to an act of telling or seeks hearer intervention. A sequence which contains a falling tone but is completed by a rise may signal (1) that the speaker seeks the hearer's intervention to achieve target state or (2) seeks hearer acknowledgment that a target state has been achieved – see 12 in extract 5.3 below – or (3) provides a gloss on the earlier information.

Below I provide an analysis of extract 5.3 which incorporates prosody. This analysis enables us to see how the speakers formed increments out of the temporal flow of information units. Above I identified the extract as being formed from twelve possible increments. As can be seen the twelve increments contained thirty-seven tone groups with one tone group not forming part of an increment.

Table 5.3. The Number of Tone Groups in Extract 5.3 by Speaker

Speaker	Within Increment		Not within Increment
A	22	Tone #	0
		\ 18	
		/ 4	
B	15	Tone #	1
		\ 15	
		/0	
All	37	Tone #	1
		\33	
		/4	

The extract itself comprises a tonal inventory of mostly falls and rises. There are no fall-rises, rise-falls, or level tones, and speaker B only produces falls signalling that the content of each of his tone groups/information units is expected to expand the common ground he shares with speaker A. Similarly speaker A only produces rises on four occasions, signalling his confidence that the content of his tone groups/information units were expanding the common ground. As noted above, rises preliminary to falls may indicate speakers' signalling that they have not yet completed their message, while at the end of the increment a rise may occur after an act of telling and function to involve the hearer as a co-constructor of the achieved target state by seeking acknowledgment that the hearer is in agreement that a target state has been achieved.

In the extract below consideration of prosody does not result in any change to the suggested increment boundary unless explicitly stated.

Extract 5.3 (reworked to include prosody)

A: 1 | \from Marlborough | she has hit \Reading | at half
a N V V N A
B: splendid | (overlap)

A: past eight in the \morning |
P/N

Target state is achieved by the chaining of three pieces of information, all of which are signalled as adding to the common ground.

B: 2 | \splendid | \agreed | but you're \not | (incomplete)
e e c N V ...

The increment is incomplete and achievement of target state is interrupted.

A: 3 | \that is that is the other side of Reading |
N V N V N

The increment consists of a single tone group.

B: 2 | \going into Reading |
Ø V P/N

The speaker's production of a fourth tone group achieves target state. The increment comprises four chunks of information, each of which is signalled as expanding the common ground.

A: 4 | \It will be the other side of Reading going into Reading |
N V V^1 N P/N Ø V P/N
| \that's where she hit the traffic |
N V A N V N+
| /traffic | / going in | \ to Reading | \ from either side |
N Ø N P/N+ P/N

The increment contains six chunks of information of which two are signalled as not expanding the common ground. The speaker repeats information that has been previously mentioned. Target state is not achieved until speaker A clarifies that the traffic comes from both directions.

B: 5 | \no | \you've missed the point |
d N V V^1 N

The increment consists of two chunks of information: the first which signals disagreement and the second which elaborates the point.

6 | \the traffic you are worried about | \ is the traffic | \going towards London |
N+ n v v V N Ø V^1 P/N

Increment 6 consists of three chunks of information which are all signalled as expanding the common ground.

A: 7 | no \Petey |\ at half past eight in the morning | ... (abandoned)
voc p/n+ p/n

Increment 7 is interrupted after two chunks of information aimed at expanding the common ground while at the same time the lexicogrammatical elements signal a suspension prior to initial state.

B: 8 |\ there is not a mysterious line | \which divides traffic going
N V a N+ N V N Ø V^1
to London | \immediately at Reading |
P/N A P/N

Increment 8, which interrupts the previous one, comprises three chunks, all of which are signalled as expanding the common ground.

A: 7 |\no | /but there is traffic |
c N V N
| \there is a traffic rush hour at Reading | \when traffic piles
N V N+ N P/N N+ N V
into Reading |
P/N

The speaker continues the interrupted increment 7. Consideration of prosody here leads to a change in the coding of where in the sequence target state has been achieved. The rising tone on the fourth tone group signals that the speaker is not adding to the common ground, and hence as the preceding tone units were coterminous with suspensive lexical items target state cannot have been achieved. It is only achieved by the production of two further tone groups, both of which expand the common ground.

A: 9 | \and it is about eight thirty | \that my mother has gotten
c N V a A N+ N V V^1
stuck | \in traffic trying to get into Reading |
V^1 p/n V V^1 P/N

Speaker A expands the target state achieved in increment 9 by producing three tone groups all signalled as expanding the state of common ground.

B: 10 | \most of it | \ is going to London |
N V V^1 P/N

Speaker B achieves target state by producing two tone groups.

A: 11 | \what from the other side of Reading |
Ex Ø P/N+ P/N
B: | \yes |
Ex Ø

As noted above I have notated both speakers contributions as realizing an asking increment. B's use of falling tone signals that his contribution indicates that his answer adds to the common ground.

A: 12 | \hm that may | / well be true |
Ex N V a V^1 E

I have notated the final two tone groups as representing an increment, though one where the final tone group does not signal an expansion of common ground. Rather, the earlier tone group satisfies the requirement that an increment contain a falling tone. The final rising tone functions to seek acknowledgment from B of the softening of A's certainty that the troublesome traffic was Reading bound and his partial acceptance of the fact that it was actually London bound. A signals that the target state achieved is at best contingent and that he may well revisit the issue in the future.

While tone signals how the hearer is to receive the proposition the speaker has imparted, the system of key signals how the speaker predicts the hearer will react to what will be said (Brazil, 1997). Brazil states that speakers have the option of producing high, mid, or low key. A high key signals to the hearer that the speaker will articulate a proposition which contrasts with the expectations created by the previous discourse. This may be because the high key signals the introduction of a new, unexpected topic or because the speaker intends to develop the discourse in an unexpected way. A low key signals that the speaker projects that the following discourse is equivalent to the previously created expectations. Selection of mid key carries no such implications. To illustrate in a televised election debate in 2010, the incumbent UK prime minister Gordon Brown said in the reference to his rival David Cameron, "David is wrong to mislead people about his cap." As his utterance conformed to the chaining rules and was formed out of two-tone groups containing falling tone, it represents an act of telling: Brown's words are projected to update the state of convergence between him and the televised audience.[26]

5.28a | HDavid is \wrong | to mislead people about his \cap |
5.28b* | David is \wrong | to mislead people about his \cap |
5.28c* | LDavid is \wrong | to mislead people about his \cap |

Brown produced the utterance with high key on the onset syllable *Da* signalling his expectation that his audience would find Cameron's "wrongful actions" to be contrary to their expectations. Had he chosen a low key, the message would signal that the wrongfulness of Cameron's actions were entirely predictable and that the audience would have expected no less. A mid key would have signalled that Brown did not predict that his audience would find Cameron's wrongfulness either contrastive to prior expectations or in line with their previous expectations. The speaker has the additional choice of choosing to pitch the tonic syllable as higher or lower than the preceding onset. Following Brazil (1997) we describe such choices as high termination, mid termination, and low termination. A high termination signals that the speaker anticipates the hearer will adjudicate the proposition. A mid termination anticipates hearer concurrence with the proposition, while a low termination projects no expectations and signals closure. Example 5.29 glosses the meanings.

5.29a* | David is \wrong | to mislead people about his H\cap | = (Do you or do you not agree)
5.29b* | David is \wrong | to mislead people about his \cap | = (And I'm sure you agree with me)
5.29c* | David is \wrong | to mislead people about his L\cap | = (And that is all I have to say about it)

To conclude, the combination of choices from the prosodic systems of key, termination, and tone signal both the speaker's assumption of how the hearer will receive the utterance to be produced and also signal whether the utterance is projected as expanding the state of convergence existing between speaker and hearer. In the next section I will review the notion of common ground in order to revise the concept of "telling" by showing that communication is not grounded in assump-

26. This example is discussed in detail in O'Grady (2014b, p. 694). The asterisks signify the choices Brown did not make.

tions of shared or expanded states of convergence existing between speaker and hearer but rather in speakers' assessments of who has access to knowledge.

5.2.3 Common Ground Revised

In previous work (O'Grady, 2010, 2021; O'Grady & Bartlett, 2023), I pointed out some issues with the notion of a common ground built upon shared experience. The first of which is the "mutual knowledge paradox," which recognizes the fact that for knowledge to be shared and for speakers to converge towards it, it must be known to be shared. Such knowledge of sharing leads to an infinite regress of knowledge which cannot be processed in a finite time. In other words, shared knowledge could not be the ground upon which communication occurs but would be an impediment blocking its fulfilment. This obviously cannot be the case. A number of fixes to this paradox have been proposed. The first accepts that there is "an infinite regress of knowledge" but posits a mechanism for inferring mutual knowledge in real-time languaging. For instance Clark (1992) argues that speakers rely on extra-linguistic evidence such as the physical context, community membership, and assumptions based upon the human biological, physical, and mental faculties to infer mutual knowledge. Thus, interlocutors are able to circumvent the mutual knowledge paradox. A second solution is to argue that the mutuality of knowledge can normally be established by a limited number of regressive steps. For example Bach and Harnish (1979) argue that mutual knowledge can normally be established if the speaker knows that the hearer knows that the speaker knows that the hearer knows that the speaker knows X.[27]

Sperber and Wilson (1995) argue that communication is not grounded in the mutuality of knowledge but rather on what they label the speaker's "cognitive environment" – the sum of a speaker's prior experiences with the language system, context, genre, etc. Recognition that a speaker has produced an ostensive and contextually appropriate signal is sufficient for hearers to recognize that that the speaker intends to communicate something which is relevant to speaker and hearer. The common ground is formed out of individual cognitive environments and hence no mutuality of knowledge is required.

I concur with Sperber and Wilson's view that there is no need for interlocutors to share knowledge, and so like them I argue that the com-

27. Both fixes recognize the imperfect nature of linguistic communication; speakers can never be certain that hearers share common ground with them.

mon ground is not formed out of mutuality. However, I do not follow their view that the common ground between speakers is the overlap in their cognitive environments. Instead, I follow and build upon Muntigl's (2009)[28] view that what is shared is not knowledge but access to knowledge. While knowledge is distributed across a community, access to it is unequal. Nor is it the case that the speaker imparts knowledge to the hearer: see Grosz and Sidner (1990, p. 421) for an apt criticism of what they label the master slave assumption, where the active speaker is the master who transfers knowledge to the passive hearer. Knowledge is not a transferrable resource. Instead, it is a resource held in common to which speakers in their interactions may contest by claiming higher, lower, or indeed no access to on a moment-by-moment basis through their linguistic choices. Furthermore, it recognizes the imperfect nature of linguistic communication as interlocutors recognize their similar communicative/mental abilities grounded in their shared biological heritage but may incorrectly estimate access to the relevant knowledge.[29]

Muntigl's work is itself grounded in conversation analysis (e.g., Heritage & Raymond, 2005, and Raymond & Heritage, 2006, who themselves have been influenced by work in social epistemology,[30] e.g., Hutchins, 1995). Such scholars argue that *epistemological* claims involve (1) the degree to which speakers can access knowledge, (2) a speaker's rights to make a knowledge claim, and (3) the linguistic means through which speakers display their alignment to having or not having knowledge. This view is summed up by Heritage and Raymond (2005, p. 16), who claim that "the distribution of rights and responsibilities regarding what participants can accountably know, how they know it, whether

28. Readers will note that Muntigl refers to knowledge and not information. In SFL theory (Berry, 2016; Martin, 1992, 2000), such work is traditionally classed as part of the interpersonal metafunction as it involves negotiations between interlocutors as to who lays claim to being the primary knower in a conversational exchange. However, I have included it within my IS model because the achievement of target state is informative in that it revises the common ground by resetting the interlocutors' claims of access to knowledge.

29. The following paragraphs are based upon an article I published in the journal *Lingua* in 2021.

30. I of course am totally uninterested in the central tenet of social epistemology: namely explicating how people can best discover the truth with the help or hindrance of others. But I am obviously keenly interested in how people access and lay claim to knowledge with the help or hindrance of other social actors and have no interest in whether that knowledge can be assessed in relation to truth.

they have rights to describe it and in what terms is directly implicated in the organized practices of speaking."

Muntigl (2009, p. 260–1) states that "epistemic rights – includes (1) a speaker's degree of accessibility to knowledge (to what degree is someone expected to know?); (2) the right to make a claim to knowledge; (3) a speaker's interest in ensuring that the proposition gets accepted." In other words, when producing increments which modify common ground by updating who has access to common ground, speakers project their understanding of their and their interlocutors access to the required knowledge. Production of an increment asserts their own or their interlocutor's claim to access the knowledge and warrants that the target state achieved is relevant to the speaker's communicative intention. Prosody is obviously not the sole way speakers signal their claim to knowledge. Before discussing how speakers use prosody to assume knowledge roles or to be assigned them, I first need to describe how languaging is a dynamic event with utterances revising common ground and increasing or decreasing the probability of future utterances. Speakers alternate in their assumption of or their nomination to the roles of primary (K1) and secondary (K2) knowers after the completion of each move. The examples below from O'Grady (2021) illustrate.

5.30	A:	I don't like concrete either	I	K1
	B:	Uh no	R	K2
	A:	N/A	F	K1f

Speaker A produced an initiating move and presents himself as having privileged access to knowledge. He occupies the KI slot, and B acknowledges this with her reply. A did not but could have produced a further follow up (K1f) move acknowledging B's response. In the same conversation the following exchange occurred later.

5.31	A:	Is it Venice that is sinking	I	K2
	B:	Ya	R	K1
	A:	N/A	F	K2f

In this extract, A assumes the K2 role and assigns the K1 role to B, whose response indicates her willingness to accept the role. Speaker A again does not produce a further follow up move. In a different context such as an oral exam, the distribution of assumed knowledge roles would be different.

5.32	A:	Is it Venice that is sinking	I	dKI

B:	Ya	R	K2
A:	Yes	F	K1

Speaker A assumes the primary knower role and consigns B to the role of secondary knower. At the same time though he signals that his assumption of the K1 role is deferred until after B has spoken.

Muntigl recognized that in addition to assuming a knowledge role, speakers lay claim to their access to the knowledge. Thus, they may position themselves with more or less access to the knowledge through their linguistic choices. For instance, in 5.32 had B replied by saying *probably,* she would have lowered her claim to knowledge while remaining the primary knower. Table 5.4 summarizes Muntigl's (2009) view of the of the linguistic means by which speakers contest and promote their own and other speakers' epistemic positioning. Up arrows signal a raising of a speaker's epistemic rights while down arrows signal the converse.

Muntigl's careful taxonomy is however incomplete. A speaker's intonation choices signal their certainty or lack of certainty towards the information contained in a tone group (Halliday, 1967a; Halliday & Greaves, 2008). Thus, they interact with lexicogrammatical resources to position the speaker or hearer epistemically. To illustrate, I will incorporate intonation into the description and re-examine example 5.32.

5.33			A	B
A:	| Is <u>it</u> <u>Ve</u>nice that's \\<u>sink</u>ing |	I	↑K2	K1
B:	| \\Ya |	R	↑K2	K1

Speaker A positions himself as the secondary knower, but his selection of falling tone positions him as projecting an expectancy that B will confirm the truth of his proposition that *the place that is sinking is Venice.* His initiating move positions both conversational partners as being responsible for the proposition that *Venice is sinking.* Had B wished to contest A's presumption, politeness would have dictated that more than a minimal response was required. In other words, the secondary knower does not require the primary knower to transfer any knowledge. Instead, what seems to be at stake is that A wishes to check that he and his hearer are on the same page. Rather than tell B that *it is Venice that is the location of the sinking,* he prioritizes social relations by not presuming to tell B something which B is likely to know. Example 5.33 is relatively straightforward in that A's initiating move is realized in a tone group. The example below is more complicated.

5.34

			A	B
A:	I I guess cause the British climate is \relatively I	I	↓K1	K2f
	I sort of \unextreme I		K1	K2f
	I we kind of got away for however long /building I		↓K1	↑K2f
	I pretty /bad buildings I		↓K1	↑K2f
B:	I \/ya I	R		↓K2f

Speaker A produces a completed proposition which is supported by B's K2f move. A's completed proposition is formed out of four tone groups: three of which signal A's lowering of his own epistemic rights. He is the primary knower but not a confident one. Similarly, B's selection of a non-falling tone suggests she is downplaying her role as secondary knower. Thus, her support of the completed proposition is signalled as no more than signalling that she has no reason to contradict A's proposition and is prepared to accept it. She does not claim independent knowledge of the standards of British building. We see that speakers engaged in languaging are not transferring knowledge but rather signalling their access to knowledge.

Now that we have considered knowledge not in terms of a resource which is passed like a parcel between speakers but rather as a resource which speakers can assume and assign responsibility for, it is time to reconsider example 5.30 reprinted as 5.35.

5.35

			A	B
A:	I I don't like \/concrete either I	I	↓K1	↑K2f
B:	I uh \/no I	R	↓K1	↑K2f

Speaker A assumes the role of primary knower, but his intonation choice downplays his epistemic responsibility. He does not expand the common knowledge he shares with B by telling her that like her he is not a fan of concrete, but instead he suggests that they both have prior access to knowledge of the other's likes. B as secondary knower in the K2f move similarly signals that she did not have to be told of his non-liking of concrete. And by so doing she signals that she too is primarily interested in maintaining and developing the interlocutors' social relationship. There is no transmission or negotiation of a new proposition. Instead, A and B signal their affiliation by lowering their own claims to knowledge and thus boosting their hearer's responsibility for knowledge. Hence while there is no exchange of knowledge or action, there is an exchange of affiliation, and we can tentatively label this exchange a complete affiliative exchange. Such a move has consequences for the earlier definition of increment and the stipulation that

Table 5.4: The Linguistic Realization of Epistemic Positioning in Exchanges

Move	Slot	Epistemic Position	Linguistic Realization
Initiate	K1	↓ [+k], [self]	modality, evidentials, declarative + tag
		↑ [-k], [other]	declarative +tag
Initiate	K2	↑ [-k], [self]	factive predicate
		↓ [+k], [other]	modality, restrictive y/n question
Respond	K1	↓ [+k], [self]	modality
		↑ [-k], [other]	accessing the KI slot though an embedded query
Respond	K2f	↑ [-k], [self]	contradiction, oh-preface
		↓ [+k], [self]	counterclaim, agreement token
Respond	K1	[-k], [self]	deny knowledge
		[+k], [other]	seek confirmation from third party source
Respond	K2f	[+k], [self]	account, counterclaim
		[-k], [other]	contradiction

an increment that results in the achievement of target state must contain a falling tone.

Target state was defined above as the state assumed by the speaker after the completion of the increment, and one of the three criteria was the presence of a falling tone which signalled that an act of telling has occurred. Yet as our discussion has illustrated, knowledge is better considered in terms of a resource which people lay claim to rather than as a transferable commodity. Furthermore, our evaluation of our own access to knowledge is not invariant but rather partly depends on our previous social and physical interactions (Nagel, 2014). And while the definition of knowledge or information remains highly contestable within the epistemological literature,[31] it clearly relates in some manner to individual beliefs of what conversational partners think. Thus, I propose the following redefinitions.

31. To illustrate, Plato's classical definition of knowledge stated that for knowledge to exist it must be true, believed and justified. However, Gettier (1963) famously challenged the classical definition by providing counterexamples to the argument that true justified belief always amounts to knowledge. Needless to say, Gettier's counterexamples have divided opinion and have been accepted by some and resisted by others. In summary it is hard to disagree with Nagel (2014, p. 56), who wryly writes that "trying to get a clear definition of knowledge out of the conflicting ways we intuitively speak of it is like trying to identify the make and model of a car composed of assorted scrap parts."

Initial State: The degree of accessibility to knowledge and the right to make a claim to that knowledge as positioned by a speaker. Initial state exists prior to the commencement of the increment.
Target State: The degree of accessibility to the updated knowledge and the right to make a claim to that knowledge. Target state is achieved after the satisfaction of an increment. In discourse each target state feeds into the following initial state.
An increment: A stretch of speech which fulfils three criteria:

(1)The satisfaction of grammatical expectations; the grammatical chain must be able to form an utterance which can stand on its own;

(2)The grammatical chain must contain and be finished by a fully formed tone group;

(3)In the context in which it was produced, it must represent an acknowledgment that both speakers have claims on the updated knowledge resource.

Using these redefined terms, we can see that example (5.35) above fulfils the criteria to be classed as an increment. The target state reached is joint interlocutor access to the knowledge that they share the same view of concrete.

We have now added the fourth level of IS to the three levels presented earlier (see summary at the end of chapter 4), and in the final chapter we will test how the four overlapping informational waves operate to manage information expectancies in an extended and unscripted text.

6 Information Structure in the Wild

Introduction

In this final chapter, we will examine the four overlapping informational waves in the wild. Our data consists of a short conversation between three young women who discuss recent winter flooding in the UK. The three young women were acquaintances studying the same university course. Prior to the start of the conversation, they had watched a short YouTube video on the floods – see O'Grady (2016) for full details. In the next section I will provide a short increment by increment description of the conversation[1] in order to illustrate the dynamism of the interplay of the four waves in weaving speakers' narratives into a unified, coherent text. Readers who are more interested in how the coupling and uncoupling of the patterned selections of Theme, topic, and focus signal the IS are invited to move to section 6.2. I will end the book by reflecting on the strengths and weaknesses of the proposed model.

6.1 A Description of a Conversation in Terms of Information Waves

A:

```
1.   | Yeah I Hguess what you were \saying about like | (.67)
       con a        w    n    v    v'       p     a |
       \/Portland and stuff |
          n+        c n
```

This is an incomplete chain which does not achieve a target state on its own. The entire chain is thematic, but the speaker fails to produce

1. Because of space restrictions I will discuss the first five increments in more detail.

the expected finite verbal element and following rhematic information. The topic is the anaphoric element *what you were saying*. I have coded the element *I guess* as an interpersonal modal element. The focal element *saying* is both thematic and part of the topic. The focal element *Portland* is presented as thematic but as hearer New. As this is the opening of the discourse, it is discourse New; however, the speaker's words show that *Portland* had been mentioned prior to the start of the recording.

| coz I didn't know L/where it was but | (.68)
c N V V[I] W N V c

Speaker A produces a complete chain but one that is not coterminous with a tone group. The rising tone signals that the speaker has not yet achieved target state. The Theme is textual ^ topical with the topical Theme *I* also being the topic. The focal element *where* is rhematic and it is discourse New.

C:
| \Yeah | it is in ... (.77) \Dorset | (.27)
c N V P N (#[x])
| near \Weymouth | (1.33)
P N #

Speaker C interprets A's contribution as a K2 move in an asking exchange and provides a KI move in two tone groups. The first tone group is coterminous with a falling tone group. But despite achieving a potential target state, C decides that her utterance does not achieve target state. Speaker A does not yet have sufficient access to common knowledge. Consequently, she produces a reduplicative P/N element which enhances the prior intermediate state and achieves target state. The topical Theme and the topic are coterminous and realized by the pronominal element, *it* which refers to the previously mentioned *Portland*. The two foci in the chain are rhematic and discourse New.

A:
2. | That's quite \bad that it was ... | (.49)
N V A E [c] [N] [V]

Speaker A reassumes the speaker role. She produces a tone group with falling tone which contains a compete chain plus some extra material. By so doing she signals that she has not achieved a target state.

The topical Theme and the topic are coterminous with the anaphoric pronoun *that*, which refers to *the flooding*. The focus is discourse New.

but then ... it Hkind of looked really really \bad
c a N a V A A E (#)
on the /video | (.91)
P d N ... #ˣ

The hesitation pauses and the repetition signal that A is struggling to articulate the words she needs to achieve target state. She produces a chain articulated with falling tone which achieves a potential target state. However, as this is followed by a reduplicative P/N element which enhances the prior intermediate state, it is clear that she feels that the initial state did not achieve a target state. The rising tone signals that the final tone group encodes information which provides a gloss on what has gone before. The effect is to realize a target state where A signals her uncertainty and distance from the assumed common knowledge. The topical Theme is the dummy pronoun *it*. There is no topic encoded in this chain. The two foci are classed as discourse Given as the first one has been previously mentioned in the previous tone group. The second one has not been mentioned in the discourse, but all the speakers are aware that the wider discourse context includes the knowledge that all three of the interlocutors have had the shared experience of watching the video prior to their conversation.

C:
3. | \Yeah | but it Hwas only hitting one side of it /\though so | (.41)
con c N V a Vˡ d N PN A c (#)⁼

C reassumes the speaker role and articulates a tone group with rise-falling tone followed by a conjunction. Consequently, she signals that she has not achieved a target state. Her selection of initial high key suggests that she presumes that her interlocutors (or perhaps only A) will find the shared access to common ground achieved after the realization of her intended target state to contrast with their(her?) current assumptions. The topical Theme and the topic are both coterminous and realized by the pronominal *it*, which refers to *the storm*. Her selection of rise-falling tone signals her heightened commitment to the proposition expressed by her words. The focal element is the adverbial *though*, which further highlights the contrast with prior expectations.

| it Hkind of made it look \worse than it actually was |
N a V NV^{l} E c N a V #^{x}

C achieves a target state through two run-throughs of the chaining rules signalled by the conjunction *than*. The topical Theme and the topic are coterminous and realized by the pronoun *it*, which refers to the video. The focus is in the rheme and is discourse New.

A:
| \Yeah |
A produces a supportive follow up move signalling her agreement.
C:
4. | because ... because the Hrest of it is \/sheltered | (.38)
[c] c d N+ P N V E

The target state achieved by increment 3 is extended by the following chain which is articulated in a single tone group with fall-rise. The topical Theme and topic are realized by the definite NG *the rest of it*. The focal element is in the Rheme and is discourse New. The fall-rise signals that C has not yet updated access to the common knowledge and requires her to produce a further chain.

| it was only like –one | (.74) \portion |
N V a a num N+ Ø (#$^{+}$)

The next run-through of the chain is articulated in two tone groups. The first of which contains level tone which signals C's deliberation in choosing the elements which will achieve target state and allow her to successfully update access to knowledge for all speakers. The focal element is the NG *one portion*, which unusually is articulated in two tone groups separated by an extended pause. Both the numeral and noun are made tonic. The topical Theme is the dummy element *it*. Consequently, the NG *one portion* functions as ftopic; the hearers are instructed to make a new filing card as what is introduced becomes the matter of standing interest. It is also the focal element which is rhematic and discourse New. Despite C having formally articulated a chain with falling tone, it is clear that she has not updated access to the common ground, and so she produces a further chain which achieves target state by enhancing the prior intermediate state.

| which obviously is really bad for \people that live there | (.41)
N a V A E P d^{0} N+ N V A #^{x}

The topical Theme is *which,* but as this is not a matter of standing interest, there is no topic. The focal element is the indefinite NG *people that live there.* It is discourse New.

5. | \but | (.72) it \ /probably wasn't as (.93) | L\bad | as L/other
c N a V A E A d^0 e N+
places |
($\#^+$)

C articulates a chain in four tone groups. The final one contains a rising tone signalling that, despite the presence of the earlier falling tone, she has not completed her proposition. The topical Theme is the dummy element *it,* and consequently there is no topic. There are four foci. The first is the textual Theme *but,* which foregrounds that the speaker is about to articulate a proposition which contrasts with what has been said. C could have signalled the contrast by selecting high key, illustrating the redundancy inherent in the language system. The remaining foci are rhematic. The first is the modal element *probably,* which presents as New the speaker's assessment of her knowledge. The third is the discourse Given *bad.* The final focus is the discourse Given indefinite NG *other places.* The low key signals that the content of the tone group is equivalent to the previously generated expectations, thus little would have been lost had the speaker ellipted the overt contrast.

| which –they | (.26) probably didn't they didn't really L\ /show in the
N [N] a [V] N V a V$^{|}$ P d
clip | (.21)
N $\#^x$

C achieves target state by producing a further chain, albeit one containing repeated lexical items. The level tone in the initial tone group signals her difficulty in navigating her attitude towards her target state. The modal element *probably* is replaced by the salient adverb *really* signalling a greater commitment to her words. I have coded *which* as topical Theme, but the topic is the pronoun *they,* referring to the inferable makers of the video. There are two foci. The first is the topic *they,* but this likely to be the unintended result of processing difficulties. The second focus is the predicator *show,* which seems to be an illustration of what Ladd (2008) labelled a default accent. Had C made the discourse Given element *the clip* or the adverbial *really* tonic, she would have focused either on the clip as being news or signalled that her attitude to the truth of her proposition was the news.

6. | where as L/where they were like |
   a+ a+ a n v a
   | this is this L\inn | that's been like at\tacked |
   N V p N+ N V $V^{|}$+ a $V^{|}$ $\#^{+}$

Target state is achieved by the articulation of three tone groups. The first contains a setting which projects the video makers' verbiage. The verbiage is articulated in two falling tone units. Each tone unit contains a run-through of the chaining riles. The first run-through presents an NG and the second achieves target state by stating what happened to it. There are two Themes. The first is the cataphoric element *this*, and the second is the anaphoric element *that*, which refers to *a specific inn that was shown on the video*. The cataphoric Theme cannot be a topic. Instead, its articulation prospects that the ftopic *this inn* will be introduced and the hearers instructed to make a new filing card.[2] The foci are both rhematic and discourse New with the first one being realized on the ftopic.

7. | and it's Lstill L\standing | (.45)
   c N V a $V^{|}$ $\#^{+}$

Increment 7 extends the previous target state. It is realized as a single chain in a single tone group with falling tone. The topical Theme and the topic are coterminous and realized by the anaphoric element *it* referring to the inn. The focus is the verbal element *standing*, which is discourse Given owing to the expectations created by the conjunction *and* plus the adverb *still*.[3] The combination of low key and low termination present the target state as one that is in accord with the previously generated expectations.

8. | this \/one road | it was H\more like | (.31)
   d e N+ N V a a …
   | that was more H\specific than |
   N V a e N^{+}
   | the other \clips | (.59)
   d e N+ $\#^{x}$

Target state is achieved by the articulation of four tone groups which realize an abandoned chain followed by a reduplicated chain. The ini-

2. As all speakers had watched the same video, it could be argued that *this inn* was identifiable if not recoverable.
3. At the very least, the occurrence of the semantic content coded by *standing* is predictable.

tial topical theme and *topic* is *this one road,* but C does not comment on it and it is not clear if it is coreferential with the following pronoun.[4] The Theme of the second chain is *that,* which seems to refer to *the particular video clip* and therefore functions as topic. There are two foci in the non-abandoned chain. The first is the adjective *specific* and the other is the inferable and hence discourse Given item *the other clips.* The high termination invites her audience to adjudicate her statement. A and B do not verbally respond, their silence presumably signalling their acceptance.

9. | L\/where it was just | (.81)
a N V a
| people talking about what they have \seen |
d^{0} N Ø V| P W N V V| (#^{x})
| and they're Hsat in their \/cars |
c N V V| P d N #$^{+}$

Increment 9 extends the previously achieved target state by first specifying what was not specific about the other clips. The target state which is achieved by the articulation of three tone groups though the tonality division is unusual in the first two. The nominal element *people* would have been predicted to have occurred in the initial tone group as it is part of the value in the cleft structure. In Halliday's terminology, it is a predicated Theme and thus two foci: the textual theme *where* and the indefinite NG *people* are thematic and focal. The topic is the value. The second chain contains the pronoun *they* in the Theme, which is itself topic. The focal element is the discourse New *seen.* The speaker has achieved a potential target state, but as it is followed by a tone group with fall-rise tone which is coterminous with an extensive chain, the realization of target state is deferred until the articulation of that chain.

The final chain in the increment adds information that speaker C presents as contrary to expectations: we could not ordinarily expect *people to sit in their cars while in the proximity of a flood!* However, her selection of fall-rise signals that she is uncertain that the final chain is information that needs to be added to the common ground. As all three speak-

4. It may be the case that *this one road* is a gloss on the previous increment and is not thematic. Were this the case, the topical Theme would be the dummy element *it,* and there would be no topic. However, to my listening, this appears less likely owing to the preceding pause and the prosodic integration of the tone group with the following material.

ers had seen the video, this was information they all had access to, but what they did not have access to was C's presentation of this information as contrary to expectations. The topical theme and the topic is *they*, referring to the recoverable NG *people*. The focus is the discourse Given *cars*.

10.
B: | Hyeah it did show you \kind of like | –how | (.59)
con N V V^{I} N a a W
| the \sea ... (.43) front | was more protected than /inland |
d N+ N V a V^{I} A E ($\#^{x}$)
| with H/rivers | with like rivers were just \pouring over |
[P] [d^{0}] [N] P a d^{0} N Ø V a V^{I} P Ø $\#^{+}$
A C:
| \Yeah |

Speaker B assumes the speaker role and produces a potential target state by two run-throughs of the chaining rules articulated in four tone groups. The topical Theme is realized by the pronoun *it*, which refers to the previously mentioned video clip. As this is the matter of standing interest, it functions as the topic. There are six foci of which the first two are the result of the speaker attempting to choose the lexical items required to achieve target state. The initial high key signals that the increment is projected as being contrary to the previously created expectations. The other foci are *the sea front* and *inland*, the first of which is discourse New with *inland* being inferable. Overt realization of the comparison is redundant and the accompanying rising tone suggests that B has not yet achieved target state, though she has formally satisfied the requirements. She produces one further reduplicative subchain with some repetition. This results in an updated access to common ground where all speakers are aware of the consequences of the lower standard of inland flood protection. The generic NG *the sea front* is found in the Rheme, but it is a topic. B introduces it into her discourse and then comments on it. Speaker A and C signal their support for B.

11.
B: | and like the river banks were just \/gone |
c a d N+ N V a V # (.60)
| and like coming up the \paths |
c **Ø a** V^{I} P d N $\#^{+}$

In increment 11 the target state is realized by the articulation of two chains connected by a conjunction. Each of the chains is articulated by a single tone group. The topical Theme and topic is realized by the definite NG *the river banks*. In the second chain the Theme and the finite are elided. The two foci are both rhematic and discourse New. The opening chain cannot achieve a potential target state as the fall-rise tone signals that B is not certain she has provided sufficient knowledge to update her interlocutors' access to common ground.[5] Target state is achieved by the articulation of the second chain, which contains elided subject nominal and finite elements.

12. | whereas ... you could see with the \sea | they have like \flood
    c n v v^l p d n N V a [d^0] [N]
    | (.39) | massive \barriers |
    e N+ ($\#^+$)
    | \yeah | that /protect that | (.32) $\#^+$
    Con N V N

Increment 12 extends the prior target state by further detailing the contrast between sea and river defences. Target state is achieved by the production of three run-throughs of the chaining rules, which are articulated in five tone groups. The first chain is a setting and is a marked Theme. The pronoun *they* is not referential and cannot function as topic. The plural indefinite NG *flood massive barriers* functions as ftopic. There are three foci. The first *the sea* is part of the Theme and is discourse Given. The second and the third refer to the same referent *flood barriers* and are rhematic, discourse Given, and ftopic. The chain realizes a potential target state, but B's production of the immediately following chain signals her understanding that she has not achieved target state. The final subchain is produced with a rising tone signalling that it glosses the previous target state by adding the purpose of *the flood barriers*.

13. | so I guess it's quite a \contrast |
    c a N V a d N+ (#)
A: | \Hm |
| in that /respect |
p d N $\#^x$

5. Had the chain been spoken in isolation, the fall-rise would have signalled an updating of the affiliative common ground – see example 5.36.

Increment 13 enhances the prior target state by explicitly stating the existence of the contrast between the two types of defence. Target state is realized by the production of a reduplicative chain articulated in two tone groups. The first is itself a complete chain and realizes a potential target state though one that is subsequently itself enhanced by the reduplicative P/N element. The topical Theme is the dummy element *it*. I have coded *I guess* as an interpersonal modal Theme rather than as a separate projecting clause because for me that natural mood tag for the utterance is *isn't it* rather than *don't I*. There is no topic and therefore *a contrast* is the ftopic. *A contrast*, which is discourse Given by being clearly inferable, is nonetheless focal. The rising tone on the second chain both signals that it modifies the previous information and acknowledges that B seeks input from her interlocutors.

A: …

14. | yeah cause that's a \problem with | (.4)

con c n v d n p …

| where I Llive at home it's – Llike | (.61)

w n v p n … n v a …

| the river LTest always L\floods |

d N N a V #$^{+}$

Speaker A reassumes the speaker role. She achieves a target state through the production of two chains. The first chain is articulated across two tone groups, but as the second tone group is incomplete I have coded it as a suspensive chain. It contains a focus on the indefinite NG *a problem*, which is rhematic. The topical Theme is the anaphoric pronoun *that*, which refers to the *poor state of river defences*. The suspensive subchain *where I live at home* is a marked Theme and signals the physical setting in which the message is grounded. The second tone unit is completed by an n v a suspensive chain articulated with a level tone. It is the production of the following chain which updates the common ground. The speaker selects the NG *the river Test* as topic. It is a discourse New element but it is not made focal. The focal element is the discourse Given *floods*.

15. L/and | (.75) they don't really do anything to /stop it |

c N V a V$^{|}$+N V$^{|}$ N

| cause (clears throat) (.47) it Hdoesn't happen that /often |

c N V V$^{|}$ A+ A

so like …. I guess (overlap unclear) (.43)

c a a

B: | /Yeah |
C: | they just Hdon't see it as … \powerful |
N a V V' N A E
| as the /sea doing it |
A d N V' N #+

Speaker A attempts by the production of increment 15 to add to the previous target state. However, after producing two chains coterminous with tone groups containing rising tone and thus signalling that she has not achieved target state, her contribution is interrupted. The first topical Theme and topic is the pronoun *they,* which refers to the discourse Given *the relevant authorities.* The second topical Theme and topic is the element *it,* which refers to the discourse Given *flooding.* The two foci are the discourse Given verbal element *stop* and the discourse New adverbial element *often.* C takes the floor and completes increment 15 by producing a single chain realized as two tone groups. The second tone group contains a rising tone. It is a minor gloss which overtly realizes comparative knowledge already available to the interlocutors. The first chain is articulated with high key which signals C's projection that her interlocutors will find her proposition contrary to expectations; a reasonable authority would not compare the destructive potential of river flooding with that of sea flooding. The topical Theme and topic is the pronoun *they,* referring to the discourse Given *authorities.* There are two foci: the first, the adjective *powerful,* is discourse New. The second, the definite NG *the sea,* is discourse Given.

16. | oh it's just a H\little river |
ex N V a d e N #
AB: | \yeah |

Increment 16 extends the previous common access to knowledge. The speaker produces a single chain articulated in a single tone group with a falling tone. Her selection of high termination invites A and B to adjudicate the reasonableness of the target state which conveys her assumption of the authorities' view. The topical Theme is the cataphoric pronoun *it,* which refers to *a little river,* which itself functions as ftopic. The focal attributive element *a little river* is rhematic and discourse New.

17.
C: | It'll be /\alright |
N V V' E #+

C assumes the role of speaker by seemingly ironically roleplaying the voice of the authorities. Target state is achieved by a simple chain articulated in a single tone group. Selection of rise-fall tone signals her projection of the authorities' commitment to the achieved target state; *what they are saying may seem uncertain but in fact it is certain.* The topical Theme is the dummy element *it*. Hence there is no overtly coded topic. The focus is rhematic and discourse New.

18. | and when it does \happen they're like | (coughs)
c w n v v^{I} N V A
| oh yeah well there wasn't any … \flood defence | (unclear overlap)
con a N+ V d N+ N #
| \yeah |
CON

C continues in the speaker role. Target state is achieved by the articulation of two tone groups with falling tones. I have coded the first tone group as being formed out of a preliminary suspensive chain and a following chain which contains a projecting verbal process. The second chain is a projected clause. The Theme is the suspensive elements *and when it does happen*. The topic is the anaphoric pronoun *they,* referring to the discourse and hearer Given authorities. There are two foci, and despite the first one, the predicator *happen,* being part of the Theme, it is both hearer New and discourse New. The second focus, the NG *the flood defences,* is *ftopic* and hearer New but is clearly discourse Given.

19.
B: | Didn't they Hsay they \spent it on | (.95)
V^{I} N V^{I} Ø N V N P
| like … /\wildlife or something |
a d^{0} N+ c N #

Speaker B produces an interrogative mood chain. Because of the negative polarity of the initial finite and the absence of rising tone, I interpret the increment as realizing a telling and not a questioning. Target state is achieved by the articulation of two tone groups. The first contains both the projecting and projected verbal processes. The second chain is a reduplicated NG *wildlife or something*. The increment consists of two chains, the first is a V N V^{I} chain which projects the verbiage, and the second, which is found across the two tone groups, is a N V N

P/N c N chain. There are two Themes: *didn't they* and *they.* The element *they,* referring to the government, functions as topic. The focal elements are found in the Rheme and are both discourse New and hearer New. The rise-fall in the second tone group demonstrates B's commitment to her belief that all speakers have access to the shared information after the utterance of increment 19.

20. | there was like a \budget for it | (.59)
N V a d N P N #+

B extends the previous target state by adding access to the proposition. She achieves a target state through the production of a single chain articulated within a falling tone group. The Theme is the existential element *there.* There is no overt topic though the indefinite NG *a budget* is introduced as the ftopic, which the hearers are advised to open a filing card on. The NG *a budget* is also the focus and is both hearer New and discourse New.[6]

21. | and they spend it on something \else | (.56)
c N V N P N A #=
A C: (laughs) …

B enhances the target state achieved in increment 20. A target state is achieved by a single chain articulated in a falling tone group. The topic *they,* which refers to the relevant authorities, is contained within the Theme *and they.* The focal element *something else* is in the Rheme and is discourse New and hearer New.

22. | And that's ʟwhy everyone was blaming the \government | (.47)
c n v w N V V' d N #x

Increment 22 enhances the achieved target state, though the low onset signals that the achieved target state is in line with the previously created expectations. The target state is achieved by the articulation of a falling tone group which contains a preliminary suspensive subchain followed by an extended NVN chain. The Theme is the suspensive

6. It is arguable that the previous mention of the verbal element *spend* means that the nominal *a budget* is inferable and therefore discourse given. However, I have coded it as new as *budget* adds the information that money had been explicitly set aside for a specific purpose rather than there simply being a general pot of money which could be tapped into.

subchain *and that's why*. The topic is the indefinite noun *everyone*, and it is located in the Rheme. The lack of prominence signals that B projects the item as hearer Given. The focal element is the NG *the government*, which is projected as hearer New despite being discourse Given.

23. | because they ... because they are supposed to \spend | they
[c] [N] c N V V^{I}+ V^{I} ... N
were going to spend it on like (.23) \flood defences |
V V^{I}+ V^{I} N P a d^{0} N+ N ($\#^{x}$)
| in \towns and things |
P d^{0} N c N ($\#^{x}$)
| for L\rivers |
P d^{0} N $\#^{x}$

Increment 23, which enhances the previous target state by stating the reason why people *blame the government*, commences with an abandoned chain. The verbal process *are supposed to* is replaced by the verbal process *were going to* after the articulation of the first tone group. A potential target state is achieved in the second tone group. However, B feels that in order for all the interlocutors to have access to the common ground, she needs to tack on the P/N elements in tone groups 3 and 4. The Theme comprises the elements *because they* with the pronominal *they* functioning as topic and referring to the discourse Given and hearer Given *authorities*. There are four foci and *spend, flood defences* and *rivers* are discourse Given. Only the nominal *towns* is discourse New. The final low termination signals that B has completed her message.

24. | and then they L\spent it on | (.68)
c a N V N P ...
| I think it's something to do with like (.21)
a N V N V^{I} P a d^{0}
bird H/endangerment |
N+ N $\#^{+}$

However, she continues in increment 24 to occupy the speaker role and achieves a further target state through the articulation of two tone groups. The first one contains an abandoned chain as B chooses to downgrade her certainty as to what the money was spent on. The initial low onset signals that the extended target state will be equivalent to that reached prior to the production of the increment. There are two Themes: the first in the abandoned chain is *and then they* with the pronominal *they* functioning as topic. In the second chain, I have coded

I think as a modal element rather than a projecting clause and hence the Theme is *I think it.*[7] As the pronoun *it* is not referential, it does not function as topic. Hence *bird endangerment* is an ftopic. There are two foci: the first, *spend,* is discourse Given. The second, *bird endangerment,* is inferable owing to the prior mention of *wildlife* in increment 19. B's choice of a rising tone coupled with a high termination projects that she anticipates hearer adjudication, in the sense that the hearers will find the expanded common ground to be somewhat ludicrous.

25. | and people were like (.51) H/what |
c d^{0} N V a ex
| that doesn't make H\sense | (Laugh)
N V $V^{|}$ N #

In increment 25, B produces two tone groups. The first contains a projecting clause and the second the verbiage. As in increment 24, the target state is presented as worthy of adjudication; the common knowledge is not only "the nonsensical spending choices" but also a shared reaction to that decision. The target state is achieved by the production of two chains. The first Theme is *and people.* The plural indefinite NG *people* is the matter of standing interest and hence functions as topic. It is discourse Given, and hence there is no need for the hearers to open up a new filing card because of its co-referentiality with *everyone* in increment 22. The second Theme is the pronoun *that.* There are two foci. The first one, the exclamative *what,* projects *the general surprise* as hearer New and discourse New. The second one, the predicator *make sense,* is arguably inferable and so is discourse Given but projected as hearer New.

26.
A: | Hwhy is that so /important |
W V N A E

Speaker A produces the opening move in an asking exchange. However, B does not produce a relevant answer addressing the importance of protecting birds. As a result, I coded A's contribution as incomplete.

7. I have done so owing to the absence of an intonational prominence and the non-articulation of the relative pronoun *that.* See O'Grady (2017b) for further details.

27.
B: | yeah (.23) I did H\hear um | that they um … they (.29) \put like | (.45)
con N V $V^{|}$ ex c [N] ex N V a …
| I don't know L\what it was |
n v $v^{|}$ w n v
| but they \/somehow | (.51) tried to \stop the river | (.31)
c N a V $V^{|}$ d N ($\#^{x}$)
| like (.41) flooding up the / H Thames | ($\#^{x}$)
A $V^{|}$ P d N
| like stopping \/London being flooded |
A $V^{|}$ N $V^{|}$+ $V^{|}$ ($\#^{x}$)
| so they pushed it /Hdown | (.43)
c N V N A $\#^{x}$

Here it is clear that B has some difficulty in achieving target state. She produces eight tone groups of which the first three state her lack of knowledge of the means by which the authorities attempted to stop linked waterways and tributaries flooding the Thames.[8] The chain articulated in the fourth and fifth tone groups realizes a potential target state. But B feels that she needs to produce two further tone groups containing rising and fall-rising tones which enhance the prior potential target state and themselves realize potential target states. The high termination in the sixth tone group anticipates adjudication of *what a flooded Thames* would entail. The fall-rise tone in the seventh tone group signals a contrast between *London and other places being flooded* and implies that other communities were sacrificed in order to prevent *London being flooded.* The final tone group contains a further run-through of the chaining rules, but owing to the presence of the rising tone it cannot be an independent increment. Instead, it realizes the target state. The rising tone coupled with the high termination anticipates hearer adjudication of the morality / wisdom of the government's actions. Increment 27 contains four Themes which contain the topics *I* and *they*, referring to the *speaker* and the *government.* There are eight foci and all of them are Rhematic and discourse New.

28. | so like that's L/why | (.30) a Llot of the \/south | (.35)
c a n v w **ø d** n+ p d n+

8. B has previously discussed flooding in her local river the Test. But as the Test is not a tributary of the Thames, she is either discussing Thames tributaries in general or is mistaken about the Test.

| like with \ /rivers and stuff | it \overflowed so much |
a p d^0 n c n N V A+ A #^{x}

The target state achieved enhances the previous target state by overtly stating her perception as why *the south flooded.* The target state is articulated in four tone groups; the final one of which contains a falling tone. I have coded the chain in the first three tone groups as preliminary and suspensive. The suspensive subchain is Theme, but as it is the setting it cannot include the topic. I have coded the pronominal element *it* as a dummy element, and hence there is no topic in increment 28.[9]

29. | because they didn't want L / \London to get | /flooded |
c N V $V^{|}$+ N $V^{|}$+ $V^{|}$ #^{x}

The target state in increment 29 is realized by a single run-through of an extended chain. It is articulated in two tone groups. The low onset signals that the enhanced target state will be equivalent to the prior expectations. The presence of the final rising tone signals that B defers to the shared access to the common knowledge. The Theme is *because they* and the anaphoric pronoun *they* functions as topic. There are two foci and both are discourse Given.

30.
C: | Did you Hsee some of the \photos of people's like | (.65)
v n $v^{|}$ d p d n p d^0 n+ [a]
| really like L\fancy houses |
a+ a e n
| just like … (.36) \ /marooned |
a+ a e
ABC: (laughs) …
| and they are just like moats around them |
c N V a+ a d^0 N p N
(intonation unclear) (.63)
(#$^{+}$) ?
| and they Ljust like – Lkind of | stood there … just one little
c N a+ a+ a V A a num e
L\house | and the L–rest of it was just like |
N c d N+ P N V a+ a
| Lcovered in \ /water |
$V^{|}$ P d^0 N #

9. Had I coded *it* as referring to *rivers* it would have functioned as topic but I do not do so owing to the lack of number agreement.

Speaker C takes over the role of speaker in increment 30. This increment though is difficult to code, and it may well be that a target state was realized by the articulation of the fourth tone group. The speaker initially produces an asking increment articulated in three tone groups. As she does not seemingly require an overt response from her interlocutors, I have coded the chain as a suspensive scene setting prior to the telling. The chain in tone group 4 realizes a potential increment which extends the prior target state. However, as I am unable to determine the intonation, I do not know whether the tone group contains a falling tone.[10] The remainder of the increment comprises four tone groups coterminous with two chains. The first one is realized by a sequence of level tone followed by falling tone and the second by level tone followed by fall-rising tone. The presence of the three low key choices signal that the additions to the potential target state realized after tone group 4 are equivalent to what had been realized. In a sense, inferable knowledge is conveyed. Within the increment there are four Themes: *did you*, *and they*, *and they*, and *and the rest of it*. Two of the Themes contain the topics which are discourse Given: *you* is situationally present and *the rest of it* is inferable. The Themes realized by the cataphoric pronoun *they* point to the discourse New ftopics *moats around them* and *one little house*. I have coded seven foci of which one, *the rest of it*, is Theme and topic; thus, the Theme and the topic are projected as being hearer New. The focus in the final tone group *water* is discourse Given.

31.

B: | /hm | (.48) /yeah | and I Hguess it didn't really \show the
ex con c N V N V a V' d
like | (.89) | like extent of the after H/aftermath |
[a] a N+ p d [N] N #

In increment 31, speaker B once again assumes the speaker role. She achieves target state by the production of a single chain articulated

10. More accurately, I do not know for certain that the stretch of speech contains a tonic syllable, though I suspect *moats* is focal. The amount of intrusive background noise though means that it is impossible to say anything about the prosodic nature of the stretch of speech I have coded as the fourth tone group in increment 30.

by two tone groups.[11] The high termination signals her anticipation of her interlocutors' adjudication and signals her intent to move the discussion on from *the floods* to *the effect of the flooding*. The Theme is *and I guess I*.[12] The high key on *guess* projects that her target state realized by the increment will be contrary to expectations; she introduces a new proposition, *the effect of the flooding*. The pronominal *it*, which refers to the video the interlocutors watched together, functions as topic. There are two foci, both of which are in the Rheme and discourse New.

32. | like ... (.79) it H\\took ages | to get everything back where
a ... N V d⁰ N V' N A W
my –friend | (.26) | she supposed to\\ work | (.44)
d N N Ø V'+ V' (#)
| like (.24) the \\/week after Christmas | (.53)
a d N P N #ˣ

Increment 32 comprises four tone groups and two run-throughs of the chaining rules. Both chains are extensive. As the first chain is completed by a mid-level tone group which includes material signifying a further run-through of the chaining rules, it cannot realize a potential target state. A potential target state is realized by the articulation of the third tone group in the increment, but B feels the need to add an enhancing nominal element specifying the time. The pronominal element *it* is Thematic and a dummy element, and hence *ages* functions as ftopic. There are four foci of which three are found in the Rheme and all three are discourse New. The remaining focal element *where my friend* is simultaneously discourse New and topic.

33. | and L/um | she works in \\Debenhams |
c ex N V P+ N (#⁺)
| in L/town | (.29)
P N #ˣ

11. I do not include the filler *hm* and the continuative *yeah* as part of the increment structure.
12. Despite the prominence on *guess* I have not coded it as a projecting verbal process. I have done so because (1) of the absence of the relative pronoun that, (2) my interpretation that the grammatical subject is the pronoun *it*, and (3) the presence of an independent high key choice which required that a syllable be made prominent.

Increment 33 consists of a single chain articulated by two tone groups. The chain in the first tone group realizes a potential target state, but B signals that target state is not achieved until she has enhanced it by specifying the location. The pronominal element *she* is both Theme and topic. There are two foci and both are discourse New.

34. | it's literally on the /Hriver bank |[13] (.43)
N V A P d N+ N
| so – Llike | the river goes /behind it | (.33)
c a d N V P N
| so when it H\overflooded | the /whole of Debenhams |
c W N V d N+ P N
| like the whole like \floor | (.31) was just L\completely | (.49)
a d N+ a N V a+ a
\/ ruined | like all the stock and /stuff | $\#^{=}$
$V^{|}$ $(\#^{+})$ a d d N c N

Increment 34 consists of three chains articulated in nine tone groups. The first chain is coterminous with the first tone group. The chain realizes a potential target state, but as it is accompanied by rising tone and a high termination, speaker B signals that the extension to the prior target state is a setting which the speaker anticipates adjudication of. She signals that the location of the shop is of vital importance for the unfolding of her message. The second chain is coterminous with the following two tone groups, but it does not realize a target state because of the absence of a falling tone. The intermediate state achieved elaborates on the previous potential target state. The third chain commences with the fourth tone group and reaches a potential target state through the unfolding of the extended chain in tone groups four to eight. Yet for her own reasons, B did not feel she had successfully updated access to common knowledge, so she produces an elaborating tone group containing a nominal element. Within the increment there are three Themes, *it*, *so like the river*, and *so when it overflowed.* The first two Themes contain the topics *it*, referring to *Debenhams*, and *the river.* The third topic, *the whole of Debenhams*, is found in the Rheme and is discourse New.[14] There are

13. It is debatable whether the first tone group of increment 34 is actually the final tone group of increment 33. If this is the case, it would signal that the speaker expects that for a target state to be achieved, her hearers need to adjudicate the impact of the location of the department store, Debenhams.
14. While *Debenhams* is discourse Given, the *whole of it* is not.

nine foci. Seven of them are found in the Rheme and of one of them, the definite NG *the river bank,* is discourse Given. The focal verbal element *overflooded* is Theme and discourse Given.[15] The focal element, *the whole of Debenhams,* functions as topic.

35. | so she had to \go in | (.50)
c N V $V^{|}$ P Ø ($\#^{x}$)
and literally just help /clean | (.57)
c a Ø a $V^{|}$+ $V^{|}$ Ø $\#^{+}$

Increment 35 consists of two chains with each chain being coterminous with a tone group. The final rising tone signals that while she has extended the prior target state there is more to say. The Themes are *so she* and *and literally with an elided subject.*[16] The pronoun *she* functions as a topic and refers to *the friend.* The two foci are in the Rheme and discourse Given though *clean* is potentially inferable.

36. and it was just really \bad like | (.52)
c N V A+ A E A $\#^{+}$

Increment 36 comprises a single chain produced in a single tone group. The achieved target state extends the prior one. The theme is *and it* with the pronoun *it* referring to *the mess caused by the flooding,* and it functions as topic. The focus is *bad,* which is Rhematic and discourse New.

37. | there was a cin \cinema next to it | (.29)
N V d [n] N A P N (#)
| and they can L\open | (.25)
c N V $V^{|}$ Ø $\#^{+}$

Increment 37 also consists of two chains produced in two tone groups. The first chain formally realizes a target state, but in the context I interpret the telling of the fact that a cinema existed as not fulfilling the need to update the common ground. The Theme of the first chain is the dummy existential element *there.* There is no overt topic, though the focal and discourse New element the indefinite NG *a cinema* functions

15. I do not discuss the tonic adverbial element *like* as it does not project the element as hearer New.
16. The verbal element *had to* has also been elided.

as an ftopic. In the second chain the Theme and *topic* is the anaphoric pronoun *they,* referring to the *cinema (management).* The focal element *open* is found in the Rheme and is discourse New. The presence of the low termination suggests that B has completed her utterance, though as increments 38 and 39 indicate, she has not.[17] The presence of a mid key signals that her following contribution will not be contrary to or equivalent to previous expectations.

38. | and like me and my friends went to the \cinema |
c a N c d N V P d N (#$^{+}$)
| like a L/week after | #^{x} (.48)
a d N A

The target state realized in increment 38 consists of a single chain produced in two tone groups. The first tone group extends the previous target state and is itself enhanced by the second one. The low termination followed by a mid key functions as in increment 37. The rising tone defers to the hearers and signals, that despite the low termination, B has more to say. The Theme is *and like me and my friends* with the NG functioning as topic. There are two foci: the first one, the definite NG *the cinema,* is discourse Given while the second one, the indefinite NG *a week after,* is discourse New.

39. | and –um | (.19) you could just smell /Hdamp | \/everywhere |
c ex N V a V^{I} E A
| cause like they couldn't properly \clean it |
c a N V a V N #^{x}

Increment 39 contains two chains which are produced in three tone groups.[18] As the first chain does not contain a tone group with falling tone it cannot realize a target state. Target state is achieved by the production of the second chain which enhances the telling by explaining why *the cinema smelt of damp*. There are two Themes *you* and *cause like they.* As the pronoun *you* is not referential it cannot function as topic; the adjectival element *damp* is ftopic and presented as focal despite being discourse Given. The pronoun *they* functions as topic and refers to

17. Had there been no low termination I would have coded increments 37 and 38 as a single increment.

18. I have not included the initial tone group, which I interpret as B's signalling that she is assembling her message.

B's friend and co-workers. There are three foci: *damp* discussed above and *everywhere* and *clean* both of which are discourse New.

40. | cause they Lwanted it to get it L/open | (.51)
c N V N V' N E
C: | to get \money | #=
Ø V d^0 N
B: | \yeah | (.96)
CON

Increment 40 is unusual in that it is co-constructed by B and C.[19] There are two chains produced in two tone groups.[20] The first cannot realize a target state because of the absence of a falling tone. The presence of the low termination signals the exhaustion of the topic despite the absence of target state. The rising tone defers to the hearers and C supplies the chain that achieves target state by elaborating on the prior intermediate state. The Theme is *cause they* with the pronoun *they* functioning as topic. The two foci *open* and *money* are Rhematic and discourse Given.

41.
A: | \yeah | yeah it's H\not (.51) | yeah H\because like |
[con] con N V NEG ... con c a
| what you were \saying about | (.29)
w n v v' p
| it Lbeing ... (.29) –Lreally like |
N Ø V' a+ [a]
| like (.30) \affecting | (.89) |
a E' #+

In increment 41 speaker A assumes the floor. She is clearly struggling to compose her message, and it is really difficult to code and discuss her words in terms of a target state. There do not appear to be any topics within the increment. The core of the utterance seems to be a pseudo-cleft *What you were saying about it is affecting*. However, A ellipts the finite *is*. If my analysis is correct, the Theme is *yeah because like what*

19. It is also possible to code C's contribution as a minor elaborating clause occurring after B has completed the increment. I have not coded this way because C introduces material that, while inferable, was not overtly said. In this case increments 39 and 40 would be a single increment.

20. I have not included B's final acknowledging contribution.

you were saying about it.[21] The focal elements *saying* and *affecting* are discourse New with the former found in the Theme.

42. | I haven't really and I think you just need to \hear like | (.93)
N V a c N V N a V V^{I} a ...
| it's kind of a bit more interesting to watch \video |
N V a d N A E V^{I} d^{0} N (#)
| where you L\hear about \people |
W N V P d^{0} N ($\#^{+}$)
| and like people in their L\homes and that |
c a d^{0} N P d N c N $\#^{+}$
C: | L\yeah |
B: | \yeah |

In increment 42 there are four tone groups of which the first one represents an abandoned chain. The remaining tone groups contain two run-throughs of the chaining rules. A potential target state is achieved after the production of the nominal *video*, but it is clear in the context that A has not updated access to common knowledge. The following tone group extends the access to common knowledge and is itself extended by the following tone group. The Theme and topic of the abandoned chain is *I*. The Theme of the other chain is the dummy element *it*, which cannot function as the matter of standing interest. The focal elements are Rhematic and discourse New.

43.
C: | there was a H\program wasn't there | (.43)
N V d N V N ($\#^{+}$)
| on Channel \4 about it |
P N P N $\#^{x}$
B: | \yeah | (.56)
CON

I have coded increment 43 as having achieved target state, though it could potentially have been coded as a preliminary telling or setting. It contains a single chain which is realized in two groups. The second of which enhances the first by specifying the location of *the program*. The

---

21. An alternate analysis would be to argue that the increment is incomplete/abandoned and encodes the following *What you were saying about it being affecting*: the value is not realized.

Theme is *there,* and it introduces as ftopic the indefinite NG *a program.* The ftopic is discourse New and focal. The remaining focus is *channel 4* which is also discourse New.

44.
C: | and it was L\people in their houses |
c NV d^0 N P d N $(\#^+)$
| and they were just ... you could just see that they just like ...
c N V a ... N V a V^{I} N+ N a+ a
left \everything | (.39)
V N $\#^+$

C achieves target state through the production of two complete chains with an intervening abandoned NV chain articulated in two tone groups. The first chain, which is coterminous with the first tone group, realizes a potential target state which extends the prior access to common knowledge. However, in the context in which it was uttered, it does not achieve a telling. The second chain is required to tell us about *the people.* The low key signals that the upcoming content will be in accord with the expectations generated by the previous discourse. In her effort to achieve target state, she reformulates her wording and produces an extensive subchain which contains a projecting and projected clause. There are four Themes in the utterance. The first is *and it.* As *it* does not refer to anything, it cannot function as topic. The plural indefinite NG *people in their houses* functions as ftopic. In the abandoned subchain the Theme is *and they* with the anaphoric pronoun functioning as topic. The Theme of the projecting clause is the generic pronoun *you* and that of the projected clause is *they,* which refers back to *the people in their houses* and is topic. There are two foci. The first is the ftopic *people* and it is discourse New. The second is the indefinite pronoun *everything,* which is discourse New.

45. | and L\everything had just like | (.54)
c N V a a ...
| it was just L\ruined |
N V A V^{I} $\#^+$

Speaker C extends the target state by the production of an abandoned chain followed by a chain which achieves target state. The Themes are *and everything* and *it.* The first Theme functions as topic, and assuming *it* is coreferential with *everything,* the second one does too. The low key signals that the achieved target state will not be contrary to the previous discourse expectations while the low termination signals the closure of the topic. The foci are *everything* and *ruined*. The former is Theme, topic, and discourse Given. The latter is Rheme and discourse New though it is arguably inferable.

46.
B: | \/yeah | (.26)
CON
| and Hpeople trying to \drive |
c d^0 N Ø V^{I}+ V^{I} ($\#^{x}$)
| just people \still | just L\driving |
a d^0 N Ø a+ a V^{I}
| in a like (unclear all giggle) yeah … this is like \/coming
P d a con … N V a V^{I}
up now | (.61)
P A #

In increment 46, B assumes the speaker role. The increment is extremely difficult to parse owing to the non-overt realization of finites, the giggling, and the unclear reference of the pronoun *this*. It is unclear whether 46 achieves a target state or whether it forms part of a larger increment including what I have coded as 47 and 48. The Themes are *and people, just people,* and *this*. The indefinite plural NG *people* functions as topic. It is not clear if the pronominal *this* is topic. All the foci are rhematic with *drive* and *coming* being discourse New while *driving* is discourse Given.

47.
C: | now my L\car will protect me | (2.05)
con d N V V^{I} N #
ABC: (laughs) …

Speaker C achieves target state by the production of an extended chain articulated in a single tone group. The low key signals that the achieved target state will be equivalent to the previously created discourse expectations.[22] The Theme is *now my car* with the discourse Given NG *my car* functioning as topic. The Theme, topic, and focus are coterminous; *my car* is projected as hearer New. It is the most newsworthy item, consideration of which is essential for the comprehension of

22. Owing to my difficulty in parsing increment 46, I am unsure if this is the case. The wider point being that those outside the discourse are not always able to explicate the context in which the interlocutors operate.

the target state. The post-focal items, while grammatically required to complete the chain, are projected as semantically redundant.

48.

A: | and then Lpeople just L\ /giving up |
c a d^0 N Ø a VPHR$^{|}$
| and Lgoing on \boats |
c Ø V$^{|}$ P d^0 N #$^{+}$

Speaker A reassumes the speaker's role in increment 48 and achieves target state through the production of two chains; each of which is articulated in a single tone group. As above, finites are ellipted and the low key signals that the achieved target state is equivalent to previous discourse expectations. The first chain cannot achieve target state because of the absence of a falling tone. The low termination choice signals that A projects the extended intermediate state as neither anticipating speaker adjudication nor concurrence with the content of the tone group. The second chain achieves target state and extends access to common knowledge which the low key anticipates will be in accord with prior expectations. The Theme in the first chain is *and then people* with *people* functioning as topic. Neither Theme nor topic is overtly realized in the second chain, though we can infer that it is *people.* There are two foci, *giving up* and *boats,* both of which are discourse New.

49.

B: | I H/guess | (.51) uh … like … it did come out a /bad time like
N V ex a N V V$^{|}$ A d e N A
| H /Christmas like | (.69)
N A

C: | \ /yeah |
con

B: | It was like \probably | (.51) ruined a lot of \people's | (.39)
N (V) a+ a … V d N P d^0 N+
Christmas \spirit |
N+ N #$^{+}$

In increment 49, B achieves target state by producing an extended chain followed by a second chain which includes an abandoned finite. B revised the wording needed to achieve target state and produced a new finite. The first chain functions as setting for the second one. The Theme of the setting chain is *I guess it* and that of the second chain is *it.* As I interpret the pronoun *it* to refer to *the flooding and attendant damage,* the pronoun functions as topic. The foci are all rhematic, with the exception of the interpersonal element *guess,* which presents the speaker's view of the likelihood of the achieved target state occurring as hearer New. She emphasizes her view of the likelihood of the occurrence by making *probably* focal and hence hearer New. While the foci *a bad time* and *Christmas* are discourse New, the two final foci, *people's* and *Christmas spirit,* are discourse Given. B unusually projects a single NG as two focal items.

50. | but then at the \same time | –it's kind of | (.75)
c a p d e n … N V a
| if it's going to H\happen | (.29) it it's (.35) a Hgood time in a
c n v $v^{|}$+ $v^{|}$ [N] NV d e N P d
–sense | that everyone's –there like | (.81) \rather than | (.31)
N+ N N+ A+ A A …
| cause they don't have L/work | and \stuff |
c N V $V^{|}$ d^0 N c d^0 N $\#^x$
A: | \yeah |
CON

Speaker B's wording in increment 50 signals that she had some processing difficulty in finding the wording required to achieve target state. In the opening three tone groups, she produces two preliminary chains which set the scene for the telling. These chains are separated by the abandoned chain found in the second tone group. The chain articulated in the fourth and fifth tone groups does not contain a falling tone and so does not realize a potential target state. The initial high key signals that the achieved target state will be contrary to the previously generated expectations. After a relatively long pause, B produces a reduplicative A element and restarts her chain by introducing a contrast. She however abandons her chain and instead starts another one that enhances the previous access to common ground. There are a number of Themes in the increment. The first one is *but then at the same time,* which contains the focal and discourse New item *at the same time*. The Theme *if it is going to happen* contains the pronoun *it,* which refers to flooding and functions as topic. The Theme contains the focal element *happen.* The final two foci, *work* and *stuff,* are both Rheme and discourse New.

51.
B: | and usually people have L/time off |
c a d^0 N V N
| so like … (.46) they Lcan … (.22) L\help get it back |
c a N V $V^{|}$+ $V^{|}$ N A #

| \/yeah | (1.38)
CON ... ?

Increment 51 is produced by two chains, each of which is coterminous with a tone group. The initial chain does not contain a falling tone and so cannot achieve target state. The second chain extends access to common knowledge. The low key signals that the achieved target state will be equivalent to the previously created discourse expectations. It is obvious that people will have time to help remedy flood damage if they are not at work. The Themes are *and usually people* and *so like they*. The topic is contained in the Theme and is realized by the indefinite plural NG *people* and the coreferential pronoun *they*. The foci are both Rheme and discourse New.

52.

A: | L/yeah | I think was just –like | (1.41) it's just a bit of a –strange | (.49)
con a Ø V [a] a ... N V a d N+ P d e
| \video in general | (.97)
N P N #
| \like |[23]

B: | /yeah |
con

Speaker A assumes the speaker role and achieves target state by producing a single chain which is preceded by an abandoned chain and is itself articulated in two tone groups. The presence of the extended pause suggests that the speaker reset her means of achieving target state. As such the Theme is the dummy element *it*, which cannot function as topic. Instead the focal element *a strange video* is ftopic and discourse Given. A choses to make both the adjective and noun focal, signalling that the quality of the video is of equal newsworthiness as is the existence of the video.

53.

A: | it kind of makes you L\/see it and you're like woo |
N a V N V N c N V A EX
| it's L\quite like | (.78) it was /crazy but | (1.43)
N V a a ... N V E c

23. I did not code the tonic element *like* as being part of the increment structure.

B: | yeah a H\lot of people in it |
con d N+ P N P N
| were like more interested in \/videoing |
V a A E P $V^{|}$
| the like L/\rising water |
d a d^0 e N #

Increment 53 is jointly completed by A and B. A produces two chains articulated in three tone groups. Her contribution is interrupted, and the contrast signalled by the conjunction *but* is unsaid. A's contribution sets the scene for the achieved target state by continuing to describe her reaction to the content of the video. There are four Themes: three of which are the dummy element *it*, the other is the non-referential generic pronoun *you*. There is therefore no topic in A's contribution. There are three foci found in the Rheme and all are discourse New. B's contribution may or may not realize A's signalled contrast. The high key signals that the achieved target state is anticipated to be contrary to the previously generated expectations. She produces a chain which realizes a potential chain articulated in three tone groups. The Theme and topic are *a lot of people*. The focus occurs within the Theme and topic, signalling that a discourse Given element which is the matter of standing interest is projected as newsworthy. The other two focal elements are in the Rheme, with the first one being discourse New and the second discourse Given. The low termination signals the completion of the topic.

54.
C: | like H\running away from it | (All laugh)
a Ø $V^{|}$ A P N $\#^{=}$.

In increment 53, C elaborates on the previous target by stating what the people did not do. Her selection of high key signals that their actions are contrary to anticipated expectations. There is no overt Theme or element functioning as topic, though we can infer that *a lot of people* fulfils these roles. The focus is found in the Rheme and is discourse New.

55.
A: | yeah (unclear) | and some \people are like |
ex c d N V a
| \skim boarding | $\#^{+}$ (.55)
$V^{|}$ #

The initial part of increment 54 is unclear owing to background noise. But A extends access to common knowledge by producing a chain articulated within two tone groups. The Theme is *and some people* with the NG functioning as a discourse Given topic. The NG *some people* is focal and thus projected as hearer New and newsworthy. The other focus *skim boarding* is Rheme and discourse Given.

56. | this looks /fun | like (unclear intonation overlap with laughing) (1.08)
N V A a
| L /yeah | (.43)
CON …

Increment 56 is incomplete as while the first tone group contains a complete chain, there is an absence of an observed falling tone. Hence A's contribution adds to the existing common ground by realizing an intermediate state which serves to signal the speaker's affiliation with her hearers. She projects that they all regard skim boarding as enjoyable.

57.
C: | It's \different type of like | to a natural to \disaster in that uh | (.58)
n v d e [n] [p] a … p d n [p] n p n ex
| \other things | people tend to … L\run away from it |
d⁰ e N+ N V V' A P N #⁺

Speaker C achieves target state by producing two chains articulated in two tone groups. The first chain is itself comprised of abandoned elements, and I have reconstructed it as *It's different to a natural disaster in that*. It serves as a setting for the second chain, which achieves target state. The low termination signals the closure of the topic. There are two Themes. The first is the dummy element *it* which cannot function as topic. Instead, the indefinite NG *a natural disaster* is ftopic. The ftopic is focal and is therefore both hearer New and discourse New. The second Theme is the marked NG *other things*, and the remaining three foci are Rheme and discourse New.

58.
| Lwhereas they are like |
c N V a …
B: | /yeah | (.41)
con

| L<u>part</u> of the L/<u>slow</u>ness of water | (All laugh)
d⁰ n p d n p d⁰ n
C: | H \<u>Let' s</u> video |
V N V' #

Increment 58 is fragmented between B and C. C produces two chains in two tone groups. The first projects and the second is a verbal projection. The Theme of the chain is *whereas they*, with the pronoun which refers to the discourse Given *some people* which functions as topic. The focus is on the fused V N element *let's* presumably because C recognizes that *video* is discourse Given. B produces an interrupting fragmented chain consisting of an NG. As it does not contain a N V sequence, it cannot lead to the attainment of target state. Rather it functions as a suspension, which provides a reason for the people's lack of fear of the water.

6.1.1 Reflections on the Conversation

As I was not party to the conversation, at times my analysis is informed guesswork, and as the footnotes indicate there are occasions where more than one interpretation is possible. Despite that, there were few issues with identifying Theme or focus; though in the case of increments with abandoned openings, it was not always clear whether to include earlier material in the Theme. Topic, which by definition is identified as the matter of standing interest, proved more challenging. For instance, in increment 28 the pronominal *it* in the chain *it overflowed so much* may be coreferential with the recoverable element *river.* Had I interpreted it as such, rather than as a dummy element, I would have coded it as topic.

The major difficulty in the analysis was identifying increment boundaries. This was for a number of reasons: (1) overlapping speech meant that it was not always possible to identify all intonational tone movements, (2) the fragmented nature of speech meant that I as analyst had to reconstruct the ellipted elements, and (3) as I was not part of the context my judgment in whether a stretch of speech that fulfilled the intonational and grammatical criteria also fulfilled the semantic criteria is necessarily subjective.

To illustrate as part of her contribution, B tells a story about her friend. I have coded her narrative into five increments (32–6). But as I am outside the conversation, I cannot be entirely confident that the telling achieved by increment 33 is in the context sufficient to achieve target state. It may be that the B feels the name of the workplace is needed to achieve target state. However, as increment 33 represents a formal run-through of the chaining rules, contains a falling tone, and

Table 6.1: The Information Waves in the Conversation

Theme = 99					Topic = 38		Focus		Increment		
Top	Int	Text	Mkt	Abd	topic	ftopic	mess	org	Sing	Joint	Abd
99	12	70	8	4	38	18	172	30	53	4	1

is separated from increment 34 by an extended pause, I have coded an achieved target state. Similarly, it may be that for speaker B increments 34 and 35 achieve a single target state, though again the combination of a successful run-through of a chain coupled with falling tone and extended pause resulted in my coding of the stretch of speech as two increments. In other words, while we can be sure that speakers have negotiated updated access to the common ground, we cannot know precisely how many tellings a speaker's contribution contains.

With these necessary caveats in place, table 6.1 summarizes the data. It is immediately noticeable that there are many more topical Themes than there are topics. Hence while the unmarked realization of a topical Theme and of a topic is a subject, it is clear that the two functions are not always identical. In section 6.2, I will examine divergences between topical Theme and topic in regard to discourse function. Almost half of the topics are ftopics. As table 6.1 makes clear, there are 202 foci contained within the fifty-eight increments, which following Sinclair and Mauranen (2006), I have classed as either message foci or organizational foci. The former conveys experiential news which pushes the message forward, while the later organizes the message to enable the speakers to expand access to common ground.[24] In section 6.3 I will examine the relation between the two types of focus, Theme, and topic in order to explicate the meaning-making potential of coupling and decoupling the various functions. Finally, I will propose a hierarchy of foci within increments and then consider how speakers project the convergence of access to common ground through their key and termination selections.

6.2 *Topical Theme and Topic Revisited*

In this section I will examine the relation between the topical Theme or first experiential element in the clause and the topic or the matter of

24. In Sinclair and Mauranen's schema there are two types of organizing elements: those that function to manage the interaction and those that function to organize the message into a coherent text.

Table 6.2: The Correspondence between Topical Theme and Topic

Theme/topic	Grammatical function
Yes = 62	Pronoun = 47
	Indefinite Pro = 1
	Relative Pro = 1
	Definite NG = 6
	Indefinite NG = 6
	Possessive NG = 1
No = 37	Dummy Element = 18
	Cataphoric Pro = 5
	Indefinite Pro = 2
	Relative Pro = 1
	Interrogative Pro = 1
	PP = 1
	Indefinite NG = 1
	Clause = 9

standing or current interest. As noted in chapter 2, we would expect a correspondence between topical Theme, topic, and subject. We would further expect all three to be realized by discourse Given elements. There are, however, two exceptions. The first of which is the presence of dummy elements[25] in clause initial position, and the second is in relation to marked Theme.

Table 6.2 shows that on sixty-two occasions the topical Theme and the topic were realized by the same element. However, this was not the case on thirty-seven occasions. On forty-seven (75.8 per cent) occasions where the topical Theme and topic corresponded, the grammatical function was realized by a pronoun. On one further occasion the topical Theme and topic were realized by the indefinite pronoun *everything*. Finally, the relative pronoun *which* was the topical Theme once, and as it referred back to the immediately previous ftopic *one portion*, it functioned as topic. In all cases discussed above the pronouns functioned as subject and were discourse Given.

On thirteen occasions (20.9 per cent) the topical Theme and topic were realized by an NG. There are six instances of definite NGs (9.7 per cent) realizing topical Themes and topics which functioned as subject,

25. Though note as discussed in chapter 2 dummy elements are themselves semiotically meaningful (Bolinger, 1973, etc.).

e.g., *the rest of it* or *the river banks.* All bar one exception were discourse Given. The sole exception is the extraposed Theme *this one road,* which is subject but not present in the prior discourse. However, it is the topical Theme/topic of an abandoned increment (also see fn 3 for further discussion). It does not play a role in achieving target state. There are six instances of an indefinite plural NG functioning as subject, topical Theme, and topic, all of which reference *people.* As such I interpret these NGs as a generic NGs and thus as discourse Given. The remaining topical Theme, topic, and subject is the possessive NG *my car,* which is inferable from the preceding discourse and thus discourse Given. To conclude, sixty-one of the sixty-two examples predictably conflate topical Theme, topic, subject, and discourse Givenness.

However, there are also thirty-seven (37.4 per cent) instances where topical Theme did not encode the topic. On eighteen (48.6 per cent) occasions, the Theme was a dummy element, either *there* or *it,* and on another five occasions (13.5 per cent) it was a cataphoric pronoun. The Theme, in other words, pointed towards the introduction or presentation of an element. On fifteen occasions the element introduced in the discourse is an ftopic, e.g., *a cinema, a strange video, a program, a contrast, any flood defence,* etc. All of the ftopics are discourse New. On the remaining eight occasions, there was no overly coded topic; the elements presented were adjectival, e.g., *bad, alright, interesting,* etc. In other words, the speaker perceived that the topic, i.e., matter of standing interest, did not need to be overtly coded. For instance the topic described by the adjective *bad* is obviously *storm* or a synonym of such. In other words, while all English clauses encode starting points, the matter of standing interest is not necessarily encoded in all clauses. There are two indefinite pronouns realized by the element *you* which do not encode topic. In one case, *you can just smell the damp,* the clause introduces an ftopic, the inferable discourse Given NG *the damp.* The other example, *you're like woo it quite like ... it was crazy,* does not contain a topic. There is a further example where a pronominal theme does not encode the topic. It is the interrogative pronoun in the clause *why is that so important?* The topic is the anaphoric pronoun *that,* which refers to the protection of wildlife which is the matter of standing interest and discourse Given.

On ten occasions the Theme is realized by a PP (2.7 per cent) or a clause (24.3 per cent). On eight of the ten occasions the initial PP or hypotactic clause functions as a marked Theme and is immediately followed by the subject. Table 6.3 lists all examples of Themes realized by clauses or PPs.

Table 6.3: Clausal and Marked Theme and Topic in the Conversation

Theme	Topic	Subject
*What you were saying about Portland and stuff	x	What you were saying about Portland and stuff
You could see with the sea	they	they
Where I live at home	The river Test	The river Test
When it does happen	they	they
And that's why	everyone	everyone
That's why a lot of the South with rivers and stuff	it	it
When it overflowed	The whole of Debenhams	The whole of Debenhams
*What you were saying about it	x	What you were saying about it
If it's going to happen	A good time	A good time
At the same time	x?	it

There are two distinct patterns illustrated in table 6.3. In the first, the Theme is a Thematic equative where the Theme equals Rheme.[26] The asterisk diacritic indicates that these are unmarked Themes (Halliday & Matthiessen, 2014, p. 95). The remaining eight examples are all marked Themes and in each case the Theme functions as a setting for what follows by orienting the clause temporally, geographically, conditionally, etc. And what follows is usually the topic/subject. The marked Theme *At the same time* is found in the abandoned increment *but then at the same time it's kind of.* While we cannot know the speaker's intention, it seems likely that the subject pronoun *it* represents a dummy element and thus it cannot be topic. Three of the topics – *river Test, the whole of Debenhams,* and *a good time* – are not discourse Given.

To conclude this section, we have noted that in the conversation there is a tendency for topical Theme, topic, and subject to correspond with one another and to be realized by discourse Given items, but this is not always the case. In the next section, we will examine the relation of focus (hearer New elements) with Theme, topic, subject, and discourse newness.

26. In non-SFL literature the equative Theme here would be described as the variable with the Rheme being the value.

Table 6.4: The Distributions of Focal Elements

Message = 170						Organising = 32						Total = 202					
Theme			top	dn		Theme			top	dn		Theme			top	dn	
T	In	To		Y	N	T	In	To		Y	N	T	In	To		Y	N
1	1	18	23	45	43	8	0	0	0	0	0	9	1	18	23	45	43

6.3 *A Focus on Focus*

Focus, which is signalled by the placement of the tonic accent, projects the lexical item it occurs in as the "burden of the message." It typically occurs at the end of the tone group/information unit. As such we would expect that focal elements will typically (1) occur in the Rheme, (2) not be topic, and (3) coincide with discourse New elements. Table 6.4 sketches the distribution of the 202 focal elements in the conversation.

Table 6.4 illustrates that the majority of thematic elements were not selected as foci. Out of the sixty-seven textual Themes in the conversation, only nine (13.4 per cent) were focal. There were only twelve interpersonal Themes in the conversation with one (8.4 per cent) being focal. There were ninety-nine topical Themes and eighteen (18.2 per cent) were focal. Hence it is clear that the unmarked option for a Theme is not to be articulated by a tonic prominence. But it also clear that speakers have the option of making a Theme tonic if it suits their communicative needs. The focal elements in the conversation have been classed as occurring in either tone groups/information units which contributed to the message or in others, which I have classed as organizing.

Of the two hundred and two foci located in the conversation thirty-two of them have been classed as being in organizing tone groups which do not form part of increment structure. On eight occasions speakers made the organizing textual Theme focal, e.g.,

6.1 | \yeah | it is in ... (.77) \Dorset |

Here the focal element *yeah* does not signal a polarity choice but rather projects the speaker's need to organize her thoughts to allow her to achieve target state. The sole occasion where a textual Theme was made focal in a message tone group is:

6.2 | yeah H\because like | what you were \saying about |

Table 6.5: Topical Thematic Foci

Theme	Marked	Subject	Topic	Dis New
/Where*	yes	they	they	N/A
This \/one road*	no	this one road	this one road	yes
\/Where	yes	it	people**	N/A
You could see with the \sea*	yes	they	they	no
And when it does \happen*	yes	they	they	N/A
/Why	yes	it	it	N/A
a lot of the \/South	yes	it	it	yes
\/rivers[1]	yes	it	it	no
The –rest of it	no	The rest of it	The rest of it	no
When it \overflooded	yes	it	it	N/A
What you were \saying about it***	no	What you were saying about it	N/A	N/A
\Everything *	no	everything	everything	no
At the \same time*	yes	it	N/A	yes
My \car	no	My car	My car	no
If it's going to happen	yes	it	a good time**	N/A
A lot of \people in it	no	A lot of people in it	A lot of people in it	no
\people	no	people	people	no
\let's	no	N/A	N/A	N/A

The diacritic * signals that the Theme occurred in an abandoned chain. ** signals that the topic is an ftopic. *** signals an equative Theme. The underlined element is the tonic syllable.

[1]The nominal element *rivers* is part of the marked Theme *so like that's why a lot of the South with rivers and stuff*, which contains three foci.

Here the speaker focuses on the news that the following clause is oriented to supplying a reason for the previous target state. In addition the presence of the high key signals that the reason will be contrary to the previously generated expectations.

The speakers made an interpersonal Theme focal on one occasion.

6.3. | I H/guess | (.51) uh ... like ... it did come out a /bad time like |

In 6.3 the interpersonal element *guess* is made focal; the tentativeness of the speaker's prospected target state is foregrounded. She signals her uncertainty of her own access to the common ground achieved by the articulation of her utterance. Despite this tentativeness, her selection of high key signals that she anticipates what she is about to say will be contrary to her hearers' expectations. Example 6.3 is in contradistinction to the other four instances where the speakers produces the modal metaphor *I guess* as an interpersonal theme; on three occasions it is prominent but not tonic, and on the other it is not prominent. Thus, we see confirmation of the rareness of interpersonal Theme being selected as focal.

In the conversation, eighteen topical Themes were projected as focal, or in other words 10.5 per cent of the foci corresponded to topical Themes.[27] I have listed the eighteen topical Theme foci in table 6.5.

It is noticeable that a third of the focal topical Themes correspond with abandoned chains. This suggest that the speakers, in pursuit of their communicative goals, were not certain of the syntactic choices required to achieve target state. It is further noticeable that more than half of the focal Thematic elements were found in marked Themes or in an equative Theme; the speakers projected that the orientation for the telling contained a newsworthy element. In order to achieve target state, the speaker projected that she could not assume that her hearers did not need to pay attention to the setting and orientation of her message.

There were five instances in non-abandoned chains where the focal topical Theme was unmarked. In three of these cases, e.g., *the* rest *of it* and *a* lot *of people,* the speaker projected that the amount or quantity was newsworthy. In the case of *some* *people,* the quantity is not projected as newsworthy; rather the speaker signals the oddity of those *skimboarding in a flood* as newsworthy. The topical Theme *my* *car* is discourse Given, but the speaker projects it as if it were news in order to convey the ridiculousness of the belief in the protective power of one's car when faced with potential flooded roads. The final instance is an unmarked imperative Theme, and it is likely that as *video* is discourse Given, the speaker made the Theme focal to avoid presenting *video* as focus. To conclude, unmarked topical Themes may be focal, and if they are it seems that the speaker is focusing on either a quantity or quality, or projecting an unspoken conversational implicature.

In the next paragraph I will examine the relation between focus and topic. Table 6.6 summarizes the relationship between foci and topic, including ftopic.

---

27. Overall, in the message tone groups/information units twenty foci (11.6%) were thematic. If one includes all tone groups/information units, the percentage of foci found in the theme matter is 13.9 per cent.

Table 6.6: The Correspondence between Focus and Topic

Focus		Topic	Ftopic	All Topic	Discourse New		
					Ftopic	All	
Org	32	0	0		0	0	0
Mess	170	7 (4.1%)	17 (10%)	24 (14.1%)	2 (1.2%)	12 (7.1%)	13 (7.6%)
All	202	7 (3.5%)	17 (8.4%)	24 (11.9%)	2 (1%)	12 (5.9%)	13 (6.4%)

Table 6.6 shows that seventeen focal tone groups/information units were coded as part of an ftopic. The ftopics *one portion* and *strange video* were articulated as two tone groups with a focus on both the adjective and noun. Fifteen ftopics contained one or two focal elements. The four foci which coded the three discourse Given ftopics are flood *defence, some* people, and *a* strange video. Despite these elements being present in the discourse, the speakers selected them as focal to suit their communicative needs. The refocusing and reintroductions of *flood defence* and *some people* convey the speaker's incredulity of the absence of the former and, as discussed above, a negative appraisal of the conduct of the skimboarders. Similarly, the articulation of *a strange video* with two foci foregrounds the speaker's negative appreciation of the video she has seen. In other words, reintroducing an element as a matter of standing interest and concurrently as newsworthy enables speakers to convey implications and appraisals. Focus is not simply a textual device for projecting New information. Instead, it present elements within tone groups/information units in relational terms as the most newsworthy elements irrespective of their status as non-recoverable or recoverable.

The remaining seven focal topics were also unmarked theme. Only two of them, *the* rest *of it* and *this* one *road,* were discourse New. One topic was pronominal, i.e., *they* in increment 5. As it is articulated by a level tone, its selection as focus may be the inadvertent result of processing problems. In the conversation as whole, there are eighty-four topics, including the fifteen ftopics of which sixty-two are thematic. Only twenty-one (25 per cent) of the topics contained a focus. Sixty-five of them were discourse Given. To conclude, typically focus and topic do not, with the exception of ftopic, co-occur, and when they do co-occur, they typically encode discourse Given elements and signal that the focal topic is the most newsworthy element in the tone group.

Speakers in pursuit of their communicative goals are free to project discourse Given elements as hearer New. Table 6.7 describes the relation between focus and discourse New elements in the conversation.

Table 6.7: The Relationship between Focus and Discourse Newness

	Focus	Discourse New	Discourse Given	Other
Organizing	32	0	0	32 (100%)
Message	170	45 (26.5%)	42 (24.7%)	83 (48.8%)
All	202	45 (22.3%)	42 (20.8%)	115 (56.9%)

Table 6.7 illustrates that slightly more than half of the foci occurred on elements which were neither discourse New or Given. Indeed, only 22.3 per cent of focal elements occurred on lexical referents which were newly introduced to the discourse. Speakers were not primarily making elements focal to introduce or reintroduce participants into the discourse. Instead they were signalling the newsworthiness of circumstances, locations, evaluations, comparisons, quantities, and purposes, etc. Information structure is Janus-faced in that it refers back while simultaneously prospecting forward. Speakers engaged in managing information may select linkers as focal in order to manage their hearer's expectations by conveying how the following words relate to what has gone before (see example 6.2). Almost half of the non-referential foci were predicators, which along with one mass noun *slowness*, projected the process as newsworthy. The focus is on the process that is unfolding rather than on the participants who are doing/undergoing the actions. The conversation is less a listing of participants than a focusing in/out of the unfolding processes, attitudes, and angles which allow the interlocutors to create an emerging shared access to common ground.

6.4 A Hierarchy of Information Units?

Increments are formed from one or more tone groups. Consequently, they frequently contain more than one information unit. This raises the issue of which quanta of information the hearer needs to pay more or less attention to in the movement from initial to target state. For instance, in example 6.4 (Increment 34 in 6.1 above) there are nine tone groups/information units of which the second information unit is an organizational one.

6.4 | it's literally on the /Hriver bank | (.43) | so – Llike | the river goes /behind it | (.33)
| so when it H\overflooded | the /whole of Debenhams | like the whole like \floor | (.31) was just L\completely | (.49) \/ruined | like all the stock and /stuff |

Table 6.8: A Hierarchy of Information Units (Example 6.4)

<table>
<tr><td>| so when it H\overflooded |</td><td>Most Informative</td></tr>
<tr><td>| like the whole like \floor |</td><td></td></tr>
<tr><td>| was just L\completely |</td><td></td></tr>
<tr><td>| its literally on the /Hriver bank |</td><td></td></tr>
<tr><td>| like all the stock and /stuff |</td><td></td></tr>
<tr><td>| V ruined |</td><td></td></tr>
<tr><td>| the /whole of Debenhams |</td><td></td></tr>
<tr><td>| the river goes /behind it |</td><td></td></tr>
<tr><td>| so – Llike |</td><td>Least Informative</td></tr>
</table>

Of the eight message information units, four contain rising tone, one contains fall-rising tone, and three contain falling tone. Esser (1988) has proposed a hierarchy of information units with those containing falling tone outranking those with rising tone, which themselves outrank those with level tone. Where the information units contain the same tone choice, units with high termination[28] outrank those with mid termination, which outrank those with low termination. I pointed out (O'Grady, 2010, 2016) that initial key and final termination choices functioned to signal the speaker's expectation of how the hearer would receive the upcoming target state or react to the freshly introduced target state. A high termination final tone group may not necessarily be more significant than an earlier tone group. I (2016) also pointed out that a weakness of Esser's system was that as he did not specify a domain in which adjoining information units are projected as being more or less significant, and I proposed the increment as the appropriate domain. I further noted that when two information units were of equal rank in Esser's system, the latter one took precedence. In table 6.8 I present the hierarchy of information in example 6.4.

The most informative part of the increment concerns the reality of the flooding and its extent. This was the information which the speaker articulated in order to ensure that all three interlocutors had the right to access it. She presented the location of the shop and the resultant damage as common ground which was already accessible to the hearers.

28. Esser described the high, mid, and low as key choices, but his transcriptions make it clear that he is referring to the pitch level of the tonic syllable, i.e., what is called termination here.

Once the fact of the flood and its spread was established, the extent of the damage to the previously named shop and its contents was predictable. The increment final information unit contains a rising tone which signals that, despite achieving a target state, there is more to say.

In extract 6.1 above, there are fifty-eight increments. One of the increments was incomplete. In twenty-four (42.1 per cent) out of the remaining fifty-seven increments, the most informative information unit was not found in final position. Thus, in the interactive dynamic weave of conversation, the achievement of target state does not necessarily correspond with the articulation of the most informative information unit as in 6.4 above. Speakers balance hearers' informational needs on a moment by moment basis with their own desire to achieve target state.

6.5 A Brief Wrap Up

In this book I have proposed a view of information structure that builds upon the notion that clauses consist of thematic (Given) elements followed by New (focal) elements. I have done this by first showing that, contra Givón (2020), ordinary conversational English is not pre-grammatical. It is, however, as Givón (2017, 2020), Halliday (1967a), Chafe (2018), Cruttenden (1997), etc. noted, formed from a string of tone groups / information units. But as Brazil (1995) and O'Grady (2010) argued, these chains of tone groups / information units form into grammatical increments which achieve target state. Though a target state itself is not a final state but merely a stage in the dynamic process of the unfolding emergence of the conversational interaction. In the running commentary section 6.1, I have indicated how the target states relate logically. I have, however, pointed out that at times marking increment boundaries is, to put it kindly, subjective.

We have also seen that with while topical Theme and topic (and indeed subject) frequently co-occur, this is not always the case. First, in relation to marked Themes, the Theme is the setting for subject and for a possible topic. Second, dummy elements are thematic but not topic. Third, cataphoric pronouns are not topic though both dummy elements and cataphoric pronouns may present an ftopic. Finally, while paratactic clauses have to have themes (even if elided), there are clauses without topics. Focus is a property of the tone group / information unit, and as clauses and tone groups are not always coterminous, a focus may occur anywhere within the clause. We have noted a tendency for marked Themes to contain foci. More significantly we have seen that speakers' selection of foci is about more than the introduction and presentation of participants. Foci may convey implicatures about the newsworthiness of processes, circumstances, and linkers. In short, foci prospect forward as much as they refer back. They signal referential and relational meaning.

To conclude, the speech signal does not consist of two prominences – one at the beginning of the clause and one at the end. Rather it consists of overlapping waves of prominences which occur throughout the speech signal. These do not merely present starting points and introduce/present participants. A full understanding of IS in spoken English must recognize that as a spoken English interaction emerges temporally between contextually grounded participants, the prospection of what will come is as important for the updating of access to the common ground as is the signalling of the referential status of participants as they are (re)introduced into the discourse. With that in mind, there are a number of major omissions from the theory presented here. The first refers to the speech signal itself. I have not accounted for the informational value of pretonic prosodic prominences, and the systems of key and termination have been alluded to but not fully discussed. More seriously, I have not accounted for rhythm (Auer et al., 1999; Couper-Kuhlen, 1993; Martinec, 2000; Van Leeuwen, 2011; etc.) and how rhythmic waves overlap with the other informational waves.

The second issue is that I have assumed an equality of access to the distributed common ground. But this is not likely to be case (Fairclough, 2015). Certain speakers in specific situations may wish to obfuscate and control access to the knowledge and present ground as common though it is not. A fuller model of IS would need to consider genres where speakers will actively try to restrict access to knowledge and others will contest their right to do so.[29] Finally, the model proposed assumes that the interlocutors share a commonality of cultural assumptions. This is unlikely to be the case in many interactions in our increasingly globalized world.

Nonetheless the IS model proposed in this book illustrates how the overlapping of the various informational waves function to assist speakers in managing a coherent and cohesive conversational interaction. Interlocutors tune into the prominences in the speech signal in order to align with one another in their joint management of the interaction on a moment-by-moment basis. By coupling and decoupling expected matches such as Theme/topic, speakers signal contextually appropriate meanings which help to realize their message.

29. Increasingly studies of communication and indeed the evolution of communicative practice have started to pay attention to agonistic communication as a shaper of grammatical practice underlying our conversational interactions, see Ferretti (2025).

Bibliography

Adam, M. (2007). *A handbook of functional sentence perspective: FSP in theory and practice*. Masarykova univerzita. https://www.researchgate.net/publication/40343873_A_handbook_of_functional_sentence_perspective_FSP_in_theory_and_practice_with_key

Aijmer, K. (1989). Themes and tails: The discourse functions of dislocated elements. *Nordssic Journal of Linguistics, 12*(2), 137–54. https://doi.org/10.1017/S033258650000202X

Andersen, T. (2017). Interpersonal meaning and the clause. In T. Bartlett & G. O'Grady. *The Routledge handbook of Systemic Functional Linguistics* (pp. 115–30) Routledge.

Arús-Hita, J. (2022). Theme as a point of departure in English and Spanish conversation: A contrastive study. *Language Context and Text*, 4(2), 197–226. http://dx.doi.org/10.1075/langct.21009.aru

Auer, P., Couper-Kuhlen, E., & Muller, F. (1999). *Language in time: The rhythm and tempo of spoken interaction*. Oxford University Press.

Austin, J. (1962). *How to do things with words*. Harvard University Press.

Bach, K., & Harnish, R. (1979). *Linguistic communication and speech acts*. MIT Press.

Bäcklund, I. (1992). Theme in English telephone conversation. *Language Sciences 14*(4), 544–64. https://doi.org/10.1016/0388-0001(92)90029-E

Baddeley, A. (2010). Working memory. *Current Biology, 20*(4), R136–R140. https://doi.org/10.1016/j.cub.2009.12.014

Bakthin, M. (1986). *Speech genres and other late essays* (C. Emerson & M Holquist, Trans.). University of Texas Press.

Barnes, K.T. (1977). Aristotle on identity and its problems. *Phronesis, 22*(1), 48–62. https://doi.org/10.1163/156852877X00173

Barsalou, L.W. (1992). *Cognitive psychology: An overview for cognitive scientists*. Lawrence Erlbaum Associates.

Barth-Weingarten, D. (2016). *Studies in language and social interaction: Vol. 29. Intonation units revisited: Cesuras in talk-in-interaction*. John Benjamins.

Bartlett, T., & O'Grady, G. (2019). Language characterology and textual dynamics: A cross linguistic exploration in English and Scottish Gaelic. *Acta Linguistica Hafniensia, 51*(2), 124–59. https://doi.org/10.1080/03740463.2019.1650607

Baumann, S., & Grice, M. (2006). The intonation of accessibility. *Journal of Pragmatics, 38*(10), 1636–57. https://doi.org/10.1016/j.pragma.2005.03.017

Baumann, S., & Schumacher, P.B. (2011). (De)Accentuation and the processing of information status: Evidence from event related brain potentials. *Language and Speech, 55*(3), 361–81. https://doi.org/10.1177/0023830911422184

Bechara, A., & Damasio, A. (2005). The somatic marker hypothesis: A neural theory of economic decision. *Games and Economic Behavior, 52*(2), 336–72. https://doi.org/10.1016/j.geb.2004.06.010

Berry, M. (1995). Thematic options and success in writing. In M. Ghadessy (Ed.), *Thematic development of English texts* (pp. 55–84). Bloomsbury.

–. (1996). What is theme? A(nother) personal view. In R. Fawcett, M. Berry, C. Butler & G. Huang (Eds.), *Meaning and form: Systemic functional interpretations* (pp. 1–64). Ablex.

–. (2016). Dynamism in exchange structure. *English Text Construction, 9*(1), 33–55. http://dx.doi.org/10.1075/etc.9.1.03ber

–. (2020). On choosing the subject theme. In G. Tucker, G. Huang, L. Fontaine & E. McDonald (Eds.), *Approaches to systemic functional grammar: Convergence and divergence* (pp. 235–51). Equinox.

–. (2021a). Inequalities in status: How do they show in discourse and what can be done about them? *Lingua*, (261), 102294.

–. (2021b). "Actually given" versus "presented as given" and "actually new" versus "presented as new": What happens when the "presented as" gets out of step with the "actually"? *English Text Construction, 14*(1), 1–24. https://doi.org/10.1075/etc.00041.ber

Biber, D., Johansson, S., Leech, G., Conrad, S., & Finnegan, E. (1999). *Longman grammar of spoken and written English*. Longman.

Birner, B.J. (2006). Semantic and pragmatic contributions to information status. *Acta Linguistica Hafniensia, 38*(1), 14–32. http://dx.doi.org/10.1080/03740463.2006.10412201

Bolinger, D. (1972). Accent is predictable (if you're a mind-reader). *Language, 48*(3), 633–44. https://doi.org/10.2307/412039

–. (1973). Ambient *it* is meaningful too. *Journal of Linguistics, 9*(2), 261–70. https://doi.org/10.1017/S0022226700003789

–. (1977). *Meaning and form*. Longman.

–. (1986). *Intonation and its parts: Melody in spoken English*. Stanford University Press.

Bonkessel-Schleswsky, I., & Schumacher, P. (2016). Towards a neurobiology of information structure. In C. Féry & S. Ishihara (Eds), *The Oxford handbook of information structure* (pp. 581–98). Oxford University Press.

Boomer, D.S., & Laver, J.D. (1968). Slips of the tongue. *British Journal of Disorders of Communication, 3*(1), 2–12. https://doi.org/10.3109/13682826809011435

Bourgoin, C., O'Grady, G., & Davidse, K. (2021). Managing information flow through prosody in it-clefts. *English Language and Linguistics, 25*(3), 485–511. https://doi.org/10.1017/S1360674321000216

Brazil, D. (1984). The intonation of sentences read aloud. In *Intonation, accent and rhythm: Studies in discourse phonology* (pp. 46–66). De Gruyter.

–. (1995). *A grammar of speech.* Oxford University Press.

–. (1997). *The communicative function of intonation.* Cambridge University Press.

Brown, G., Currie, K., & Kenworthy, J. (2015). *Questions of intonation.* Routledge.

Büring, D. (2016). (Contrastive) topic. In C. Féry & S. Ishihara (Eds.), *The Oxford handbook of information structure* (pp. 64–85). Oxford University Press.

Chafe, W. (1974). Language and consciousness. *Language, 50*(1), 111–33. https://doi.org/10.2307/412014

–. (1976). Givenness, contractiveness, definiteness, subjects, topics and points of view. In C.N. Li (Ed.), *Subject and topic* (pp. 25–55). Academic Press.

–. (1994). *Discourse consciousness and time: The flow and displacement of conscious experience in speech and writing.* University of Chicago Press.

–. (2018). *Thought-based linguistics: How languages turn thoughts into sounds.* Cambridge University Press.

Chamonikolasová, J. (2018). *Intonation in English and Czech dialogues.* Masaryk University Press.

Chierchia, G. (2013). *Logic in grammar: Polarity, free choice, and intervention.* Oxford University Press.

Choe, W.K., & Redford, M.A. (2012). The distribution of speech errors in multi-word prosodic units. *Laboratory Phonology, 3*(1), 5–26. https://doi.org/10.1515/lp-2012-0002

Chun, D. (2002). *Discourse intonation in L2: From theory and research to practice.* John Benjamins.

Clark, A. (2016). *Surfing uncertainty: Prediction, action, and the embodied mind.* Oxford University Press.

Clark, H.H. (1992). *Arenas of language use.* University of Chicago Press.

Clark, H.H., & Haviland, S.E. (1977). Comprehension and the given-new contract. In R.O. Feedle (Ed.), *Discourse production and comprehension* (pp. 1–40). Ablex.

Coffin, C., & Derewianka B. (2008). Multimodal layout in school history books: The texturing of historical interpretation. In G. Forey & G. Thompson (Eds.), *Text type and texture* (pp. 191–215). Equinox.

Collins, P. (2015). *Clefts and pseudo-cleft constructions in English*. Routledge. (Original work published 1991)

Corbetta, M., & Shulman, G.L. (2002). Control of goal-directed and stimulus-driven attention in the brain. *Nature Reviews Neuroscience, 3*(3), 201–15. https://doi.org/10.1038/nrn755

Couper-Kuhlen, E. (1993). *English speech rhythm*. John Benjamins.

Couper-Kuhlen, E., & Ono, T. (2007). "Incrementing" in conversation. A comparison of practices in English, German and Japanese. *Pragmatics, 17*(4), 513–52. https://doi.org/10.1075/prag.17.4.02cou

Cowley, S.J. (2011). *Distributed language*. John Benjamins.

Croft, W. (1995). Intonation units and grammatical structure. *Linguistics, 33*(5), 832–89. https://doi.org/10.1515/ling.1995.33.5.839

–. (2007). Intonation units and grammatical structure in Wardaman and in cross-linguistic perspective. *Australian Journal of Linguistics, 27*(1), 1–39. https://doi.org/10.1080/07268600601172934

Croot, K., Au, C., & Harper, A. (2010). Prosodic structure and tongue twister errors. *Papers in Laboratory Phonology, 10*, 433–59.

Cruttenden, A. (1997). *Intonation* (2nd ed.). Cambridge University Press.

–. (2006). The de-accenting of given information: A cognitive universal? In G. Bernini & M.L. Schwartz (Eds.), *Pragmatic organization of discourse in the languages of Europe* (pp. 311–56). Mouton de Gruyter.

Crystal, D., & Davy, D. (1975). *Advanced conversational English*. Longman.

Cutler, A., Dahan, D., & Van Donselaar, W. (1997). Prosody in the comprehension of spoken language: A literature review. *Language and Speech, 40*(2), 141–201. https://doi.org/10.1177/002383099704000203

Dahan, D., Tanenhaus, M.K., & Chambers, C.G. (2002). Accent and reference resolution in spoken-language comprehension. *Journal of Memory and Language, 47*(2), 292–314. https://psycnet.apa.org/doi/10.1016/S0749-596X(02)00001-3

Damasio, A. (1994). *Descartes' error: Emotion, reason, and the human brain*. G.P. Putnam.

–. (1999). *The feeling of what happens: Body and emotion in the making of consciousness*. Harcourt Brace.

–. (2010). *Self comes to mind: Constructing the conscious brain*. William Heinemann.

–. (2021). *Feeling and knowing: Making minds conscious*. Pantheon.

Daneš, F. (1970). One instance of Prague School methodology. Functional analysis of utterance and text. In P. Garvin (Ed.), *Theory and method in linguistics* (pp. 132–46). Mouton.

–. (1972). Order of elements and sentence intonation. In D. Bolinger (Ed.), *Intonation* (pp. 216–32). Penguin.

–. (1974). Functional sentence perspective and the organisation of text. In F. Daneš (Ed.), *Papers on functional sentence perspective* (pp. 106–28). Mouton.

Davidse, K. (1987). M.A.K. Halliday's functional grammar and the Prague School. In R. Dirven & V. Fried (Eds.), *Functionalism in linguistics* (pp. 39–79). John Benjamins.

–. (2000). A constructional approach to clefts. *Linguistics, 38*(6), 1101–31. http://dx.doi.org/10.1515/ling.2000.022

Davidse, K., & Kimps, D. (2016). Specificational there-clefts: Functional structure and information structure. *English Text Construction, 9*(1), 115–42. https://doi.org/10.1075/etc.9.1.07dav

Davidse, K., & Njende, N.M. (2019). Enumerative there-clauses and there-clefts: Specification and information structure. *Acta Linguistica Hafniensia, 52*(2), 160–91. https://doi.org/10.1080/03740463.2019.1677136

Davidse, K., Njende, N.M., & O'Grady, G. (2023). *Putting specificational and presentational there-clefts on the map: Coupling meaning to grammar and prosody*. Palgrave.

Davies, M. (1989). Prosodic and non-prosodic cohesion in speech and writing. *Word, 40*(1–2), 255–62. https://doi.org/10.1080/00437956.1989.11435807

–. (1992). Prosodic cohesion in a systemic perspective: Philip Larkin reading "Toads Revisited." In P. Tench (Ed.), *Studies in systemic phonology* (pp. 206–30). Bloomsbury.

–. (1994). "I'm sorry, I'll read that again": Information structure in writing. In S. Čmejrkova & F. Štícha (Eds.), *The syntax of sentence and text: A festschrift for František Daneš* (pp. 75–89). John Benjamins.

Declerck, R. (1988). *Studies on copular sentences, clefts and pseudo-clefts*. Leuven University Press.

Dik, S.C. (1978). *Functional grammar.* North Holland Linguistic Series.

–. (1989). *The theory of functional grammar. Part 1: The structure of the clause.* Mouton de Gruyter.

Downing, A. (1991). An alternative approach to theme. *Word, 42*(2), 119–43. https://doi.org/10.1080/00437956.1991.11435835

Drápela, M. (2011). *Aspects of functional sentence perspective in contemporary English news and academic prose*. Masaryk University Press.

Dryer, M.S. (2013). On the six-way word order typology, again. *Studies in Language. International Journal Sponsored by the Foundation "Foundations of Language"*, 37(2), 267–301. https://doi.org/10.1075/SL.37.2.02DRY

Durham, M. (2011). Right dislocation in Northern England: Frequency and use – perception meets reality. *English World-Wide, 32*(3), 257–79. https://doi.org/10.1075/eww.32.3.01dur

Erteschik-Shir, N. (2007). *Information structure: The syntax-discourse interface.* Oxford University Press.

Erteschik-Shir, N., & Lappin, S. (1979). Dominance and the functional explanation of the island phenomena. *Theoretical Linguistics* 6(1–3), 41–86. http://dx.doi.org/10.1515/thli.1979.6.1-3.41

Esser, J. (1988). *Comparing reading and speaking intonation*. Rodopi.

Evans, G. (1977). Pronouns, quantifiers and relative clauses (I). *Canadian Journal of Philosophy* 7(3), 467–536. https://doi.org/10.1080/00455091.1977.10717030

Evans, V. (2015). *The crucible of language: How language and mind create meaning*. Cambridge University Press.

Fairclough, N. (2015). *Language and power* (Rev. 3rd ed.). Routledge.

Fawcett, R.P. (2000). *A theory of syntax for Systemic Functional Linguistics*. John Benjamins.

Feldman Barrett, L. (2017). *How emotions are made: The secret life of the brain*. Macmillan.

Ferretti, F. (2025). Agonistic communication: A cognitive-interactive perspective on the origin of grammar. In I. Adornetti & F. Ferretti (Eds.), *Introducing evolutionary pragmatics: How language emerges from use* (pp. 124–49). Routledge.

Féry, C., & Ishihara, S. (2016). *The Oxford handbook of information structure*. Oxford University Press.

Firbas, J. (1964). From comparative word order studies: Thoughts on V Mathesius' conception of the word order system on Czech compared with that in Czech. *Brno Studies in English, 4*(1), 111–28. http://hdl.handle.net/11222.digilib/118010

–. (1987). On the delimitation of the theme in functional sentence perspective. In R. Dirven & V. Fried. (Eds.), *Functionalism in linguistics* (pp. 137–56). John Benjamins.

–. (1992). *Functional sentence perspective in written and spoken communication*. Cambridge University Press.

–. (1995). Retrievability span in functional sentence perspective. *Brno Studies in English, 21*(1), 17–45. https://hdl.handle.net/11222.digilib/104106

Flohr, H. (1991). Brain processes and phenomenal consciousness: A new and specific hypothesis. *Theory & Psychology, 1*(2), 245–62. https://doi.org/10.1177/0959354391012006

Ford, V., Fox, B., & Thompson, S.A. (2001). Constituency and the grammar of turn increments. In C. Ford, B. Fox & S.A. Thompson (Eds.), *The language of turn and sequence* (pp. 14–38). Oxford University Press.

Forey, G., & Sampson, N. (2017). Textual metafunction and theme: What's "it" about? In T. Bartlett & G. O'Grady (Eds.), *The Routledge handbook of Systemic Functional Linguistics* (pp. 131–45). Routledg.

Frazier, L., Clifton, C., Jr., & Carlson, K. (2004). Don't break, or do: Prosodic boundary preferences. *Lingua, 114*(1), 3–27. https://doi.org/10.1016/S0024-3841(03)00044-5

Fries, P.H. (1981). On the status of theme in English: Arguments from discourse. *Forum Linguisticum, 6*(1), 1–38.

–. (1995). Themes, methods of development, and texts. In R. Hasan & P.H. Fries (Eds.), *On subject and theme: A discourse functional perspective* (pp. 317–59). John Benjamins.

–. (1997). Theme and new in written English. In T. Miller (Ed.), *Functional approaches to written text: Classroom discourse*. USIS. https://www.tesol-france.org/uploaded_files/files/TESOL%20Vol%202%201996%205%20Theme%20and%20New.pdf

Geluykens, R. (1989). Information structure in English conversation: The given-new distinction revisited. *Occasional Papers in Systemic Linguistics, 3*, 129–47.

–. (1991). Information flow in English conversation: A new approach to the given–new distinction. In E. Ventola (Ed.), *Functional and systemic linguistics*. Mouton de Gruyter.

Gettier, E. (1963). Is justified true belief knowledge? *Analysis, 23*(6), 121–3. https://doi.org/10.1093/analys/23.6.121

Gibson, J.J. (1979). *The ecological approach to visual perception.* Houghton Mifflin.

–. (1983). Topic continuity in discourse: An introduction. In T. Givon (Eds), *Topic continuity in discourse: A quantitative cross language study* (pp. 1–41). John Benjamins.

–. (1993). *English grammar: A function-based introduction* (Vol. 2). John Benjamins.

Givón, T. (1995). Coherence in text versus coherence in the mind. In M.A. Gernsbacher & T. Givón. (Eds.), *Coherence in spoken texts* (pp. 59–115). John Benjamins.

–. (2017). *The story of zero.* John Benjamins.

–. (2020). *Coherence.* John Benjamins.

Gleick, J. (2011). *The information: A history, a theory, a flood*. Fourth Estate.

Gómez González, M.A. (2001). *The theme-topic interface: Evidence from English.* John Benjamins.

Greaves, W.S. (2007). Intonation in systemic functional linguistics. In R. Hasan, C.M.I.M. Matthiessen, & J.J. Webster (Eds.), *Continuing discourse on language: A functional perspective* (Vol. 2, pp. 979–1025). Equinox.

Grice, H.P. (1975). "Logic and conversation." In P. Cole & J. Morgan (Eds.), *Syntax and semantics* (Vol. 3, pp. 41–58). Academic Press.

Grosz, B.J., & Sidner, C.L. (1990). Plans for discourse. In P.R. Cohen, J. Morgan & M. E. Pollack (Eds.), *Intentions in communication* (pp. 417–45). MIT Press.

Gundel, J.K. (1985). "Shared knowledge" and topicality. *Journal of Pragmatics* 9(1), 83–107. https://doi.org/10.1016/0378-2166(85)90049-9

–. (2010). Reference and accessibility from a givenness hierarchy perspective. *International Review of Pragmatics, 2*(2), 148–68. https://doi.org/10.1163/187731010X528322

Gundel, J., Hedberg, N., & Borthen, K. (2019). Different senses of reference. In J. Gundel & B. Abbot (Eds.), *The Oxford handbook of reference* (pp. 100–16). Oxford University Press.

Gundel, J.K., Hedberg, N., & Zacharski, R. (1993). Cognitive status and the form of referring expressions in discourse. *Language, 69*(2), 274–307. https://doi.org/10.2307/416535

Gundel, J.K., Hedberg, N., & Zacharski, R. (2001). Definite descriptions and cognitive status in English: Why accommodation is unnecessary. *English Language & Linguistics, 5*(2), 273–95. https://doi.org/10.1017/S1360674301000247

Gussenhoven, C. (1984). *On the grammar and semantics of sentence accents.* De Gruyter Mouton.

–. (2004). *The phonology of tone and intonation.* Cambridge University Press.

Halliday, M.A.K. (1967a). *Intonation and grammar in British English.* Mouton.

–. (1967b). Notes on transitivity and theme in English: Part 1. *Journal of Linguistics, 3*(1), 37–81. https://www.jstor.org/stable/4174950

–. (1968). Notes on transitivity and theme in English: Part 2. *Journal of Linguistics, 3*(2), 199–244. https://doi.org/10.1017/S0022226700016613

–. (1970a). *A course in spoken English: Intonation.* Oxford University Press.

–. (1970b). Language structure and language function. In J. Lyons (Ed.), *New horizons in linguistics* (pp. 140–65). Penguin.

–. (1975). *Learning to mean: Explorations in the development of language.* Edward Arnold.

–. (1978). *Language as a social semiotic: The social interpretation of language and meaning.* Edward Arnold.

–. (1985). *An introduction to functional grammar* (1st ed.). Edward Arnold.

–. (1994). *An introduction to functional grammar* (2nd ed.). Edward Arnold.

–. (2002). *On Grammar* (Vol. 1). Continuum.

Halliday, M.A.K., & Greaves, W.S. (2008). *Intonation in the grammar of English.* Equinox.

Halliday, M.A.K., & Hasan, R. (1976). *Cohesion in English.* Longman.

Halliday, M.A.K., & Martin, J.R. (1993). *Writing science. Literacy and discursive power.* The Falmer Press.

Halliday, M.A.K., & Matthiessen, C.M.I.M. (1999). *Construing experience through meaning: A language-based approach to cognition.* Cassell.

–. (2004). *An Introduction to functional grammar* (3rd ed.). Routledge.

–. (2014). *Halliday's introduction to functional grammar* (4th ed.). Routledge.

Hasan, R., & Fries, P. (1995). *On subject and theme: From the perspective of functions in discourse.* John Benjamins.

Hebb, D.O. (1949). *The organization of behavior: A neuropsychological theory.* Psychology Press.

Hengeveld, K., & Mackenzie, J.L. (2008). *Functional discourse grammar. A typologically-based theory of language structure.* Oxford University Press.

Heritage, J., & Raymond, G. (2005). The terms of agreement: Indexing epistemic authority and subordination in talk-in-interaction. *Social Psychology Quarterly, 68*(1), 15–38. https://doi.org/10.1177/019027250506800103

Hjelmslev, L. (1961). *Prolegomena to a theory of language.* University of Wisconsin Press.

Hopper, P. (1987). Emergent grammar. In J. Aske, N. Beery, L. Michaelis, & H. Filip (Eds.), *Proceedings of the thirteenth annual meeting of the Berkeley Linguistics Society* (pp. 139–57). Berkeley Linguistics Society.

Huang, G. (2017). Theme in the Cardiff grammar. In T. Bartlett & G. O'Grady (Eds.), *The Routledge handbook of Systemic Functional Linguistics* (pp. 163–77). Routledge.

Huddleston, R., & Pullum, G.K. (2002). *The Cambridge grammar of the English language.* Cambridge University Press.

Hutchins, E. (1995). *Cognition in the wild.* MIT Press.

Kaiser, E. (2016). Information structure and language comprehension: Insights from psycholinguistics. In C. Féry & S. Ishihara (Eds), *The Oxford handbook of information structure* (pp. 523–40). Oxford University Press.

Kaltenböck, G. (2005). It-extraposition in English: A functional view. *International Journal of Corpus Linguistics, 10*(2), 119–59. https://doi.org/10.1075/ijcl.10.2.02kal

Kempe, V., Schaeffler, S., & Thoresen, J.C. (2010). Prosodic disambiguation in child-directed speech. *Journal of Memory and Language, 62*(2), 204–25. https://doi.org/10.1016/j.jml.2009.11.006

Kohler, K.J. (2009). Rhythm in speech and language: A new research paradigm. *Phonetica, 66*(1–2), 29–45. https://doi.org/10.1159/000208929

Kuroda, S.Y. (1972). The categorical and the thetic judgement: Evidence from Japanese syntax. *Foundations in Language, 9*(2), 153–85. https://www.jstor.org/stable/25000656

Krifka, M. (1993). Focus and presupposition in dynamic interpretation. *Journal of Semantics, 10*(4), 269–300. https://doi.org/10.1093/jos/10.4.269

–. (2008). Basic notions of information structure. *Acta Linguistica Hungarica, 55*(3–4), 243–76. https://doi.org/10.1556/aling.55.2008.3-4.2

Ladd, D.R. (1980). *Study of intonational meaning: Evidence from English.* Indiana University Press.

–. (2008). *Intonational phonology* (2nd ed.). Cambridge University Press.

Lambrecht, K. (1994). *Information structure and sentence form: Topic focus and the mental representations of discourse referents.* Cambridge University Press.

–. (2001). A framework for the analysis of cleft constructions. *Linguistics 39*(3), 463–516. https://doi.org/10.1515/ling.2001.021

Langacker, R.W. (1991). *Foundations of cognitive grammar. Vol. 2: Descriptive application.* Stanford University Press.

Laver, J. (1970). The production of speech. In J. Laver & J. Lyons (Eds.), *New horizons in linguistics* (pp. 53–75). Penguin.

Lee, B.P.H. (2001). Mutual knowledge, background knowledge and shared beliefs: Their role in establishing the common ground. *Journal of Pragmatics, 33*(1), 21–44. https://doi.org/10.1016/S0378-2166(99)00128-9

Levelt, W.J.M. (1993). *Speaking from intention to articulation*. MIT Press.

Loock, R. (2013). Extending further and refining Prince's taxonomy of given/new information: A case study of non-restrictive, relevance-oriented structures. *Pragmatics, 23*(1), 69–91. https://doi.org/10.1075/prag.23.1.04loo

López, L. (2016). Dislocations and information structure. In C. Féry & S. Ishihara (Eds), *The Oxford handbook of information structure* (pp. 402–21). Oxford University Press.

Martin, A., Igarashi, Y., Jincho, N., & Mazuka, R. (2016). Utterances in infant-directed speech are shorter, not slower. *Cognition, 156*, 52–9. https://doi.org/10.1016/j.cognition.2016.07.015

Martin, J.R. (1992). *English text: System and structure*: John Benjamins.

–. (2000). Factoring out exchange: Types of structure. In M. Coulthard, J. Cotterhill & F. Rock (Eds), *Dialogue analysis VII: Working with dialogue* (pp. 19–40). Max Niezemar-Verlag.

Martin, J.R., & Rose, D. (2007). *Working with discourse*. Continuum.

Martin, J.R., & White, P.R.R. (2005). *The Language of evaluation: Appraisal in English*. Palgrave.

Martin, J.R., Matthiessen, C.M.I.M., & Painter, C. (1997). *Working with functional grammar*. Arnold.

Martinec, R. (2000). Rhythm in multimodal texts. *Leonardo, 33*(4), 289–97. https://www.jstor.org/stable/1576903

Martínez Lirola, M. (2006). An approximation to the communicative values of reversed-pseudo cleft sentences in Alan Paton's novels. *Revel, Revista Virtual de Estudos da Linguagem*, 4(6), 1–20. http://www.revelhp.cjb.net/

–. (2007). *A systemic functional approximation to the use of cleft sentences and reversed pseudo-cleft sentences in English in a narrative sample written by the South African writer Alan Paton* [Working Paper]. Departamento de Filología Inglesa. Editorial Club Universitario.

–. (2008). Exploring predicated themes from a systemic functional point of view in Alan Paton's novels. *Journal of Literary Studies, 24*(1), 100–27. https://doi.org/10.1080/02564710701789073

Marty, A. (1918). *Gesammelte Schriften, 2 Band, 1 Abteilung: Schriften zur deskriptiven Psychologie und Sprachphilosoplie*. Niemeyer.

Matthiessen, C.M.I.M. (1995). *Lexicogrammatical cartography: English systems*. International Language Sciences Publishers.

McCarthy, M. (1991). *Discourse analysis for language teachers*. Cambridge University Press.

McGregor, W. (1997). *Semiotic grammar.* The Clarendon Press

Miller, E.K., & Buschman, T.J. (2015). Working memory capacity: Limits on the bandwidth of cognition. *Daedalus, 144*(1), 112–22. https://doi.org/10.1162/DAED_a_00320

Miller, G.A. (1956). The magical number seven, plus or minus two: Some limits on our capacity for processing information. *Psychological Review, 63*(2), 343–54. https://psycnet.apa.org/doi/10.1037/0033-295X.101.2.343

Morgan, J.L., Meier, R.P., & Newport, E.L. (1987). Structural packaging in the input to language learning: Contributions of prosodic and morphological marking of phrases to the acquisition of language. *Cognitive Psychology, 19*(4), 498–550. https://doi.org/10.1016/0010-0285(87)90017-X

Muntigl, P. (2009). Knowledge moves in conversational exchanges: Revisiting the concept of primary vs. secondary knowers. *Functions of Language, 16*(2), 225–63. https://doi.org/10.1075/fol.16.2.03mun

Nagel, J. (2014). *Knowledge: A very short introduction.* Oxford University Press.

Needleman, A., & Van de Koot, H. (2016). Word order and information structure. In C. Féry & S. Ishihara (Eds.), *The Oxford handbook of information structure* (pp. 383–401). Oxford University Press.

Newman, S.S. (1946). On the stress system of English. *Word, 2*(3), 171–87. https://doi.org/10.1080/00437956.1946.11659290

Newmeyer, F.J. (2001). The Prague School and North American functionalist approaches to syntax. *Journal of Linguistics, 37*(1), 101–26. https://www.jstor.org/stable/4176644

O'Grady, G. (2010). *A Grammar of spoken English: The intonation of increments.* Continuum.

–. (2014a). An investigation of how intonation helps signal information structure. In W.L. Bowcher & B.A. Smith (Eds.), *Systemic phonology: Recent studies in English* (pp. 27–52). Equinox.

–. (2014b). The use of key in projecting face-threatening acts in televised political debate. *Text and Talk, 34*(6), 685–711. https://doi.org/10.1515/text-2014-0025

–. (2016). Given/new. What do the terms refer to? A first (small) step. *English Text Construction, 9*(1), 9–32. https://doi.org/10.1075/etc.9.1.02ogr

–. (2017a). Theme and prosody: Redundancy or meaning making? *English Text Construction, 10*(2), 274–97. https://doi.org/10.1075/etc.10.2.05ogr

–. (2017b). "I think" in political speech. *International Review of Pragmatics, 9*(2), 269–303. https://doi.org/10.1163/18773109-00901006

–. (2020). Is there a role for prosody within Register studies: And if so what and how? *Language, Context and Text, 2*(1), 59–90. https://doi.org/10.1075/langct.00021.ogr

–. (2021). Intonation and exchange: A dynamic and metafunctional view. *Lingua, 261*, 102794. https://doi.org/10.1016/j.lingua.2020.102794

–. (2022). A Metafunctional analysis of two televised U.K. political interviews. In O. Feldmann (Ed.), *Adversarial political interviews: Worldwide perspectives during polarized times* (pp. 149–70). Springer.

–. (2024). Theme in spoken language: When a tone group is not a clause. *Journal of World Languages, 10*(1), 76–101. https://doi.org/10.1515/jwl-2023-0043

O'Grady, G., & Bartlett, T. (2019). Linearity and tone in the unfolding of information. *Acta Linguistica Hafniensia, 51*(2), 192–221. https://doi.org/10.1080/03740463.2019.1668621

–. (2023). *The language dynamic.* Equinox.

Oxford University Press. (n.d.). "Information." *Oxford English dictionary.* Retrieved March 31, 2022, from https://www.oed.com

Payne, E., Post, B., Astruc, L., Prieto, P., & Vanrell, M. (2019). A cross-linguistic study of prosodic lengthening in child-directed speech. *Proceedings of the International Conference on Speech Prosody.* <https://ora.ox.ac.uk/objects/uuid:5c9cc13f-af92-4574-9ab7-0f551cdbdcc2/download_file?file_format=pdf&safe_filename=A%2Bcross-linguistic%2Bstudy%2Bof%2Bprosodic%2Blengthening%2Bin%2Bchild-directed%2Bspeech.pdf&type_of_work=Conference+item>

Pike, K.L. (1982). *Linguistic concepts: An introduction to tagmemics.* University of Nebraska Press.

–. (2015). Language as particle, wave and field. In *Selected writings* (pp. 129–43). De Gruyter. (Original work published 1959)

Ping, A.L. (2005). Talking themes: The thematic structure of talk. *Discourse Studies, 7*(6), 701–32. https://doi.org/10.1177/1461445605055423

Premack, D., & Woodruff, G. (1978). Does the chimpanzee have a theory of mind? *Behavioral and Brain Sciences, 1*(4), 515–26. https://doi.org/10.1017/S0140525X00076512

Prince, E. (1978). A comparison of wh-clefts and it-clefts in discourse. *Language, 54*(4), 883–906. https://doi.org/10.2307/413238

–. (1981). Toward a taxonomy of given-new information. In P. Cole (Ed.), *Radical pragmatics* (pp. 223–54). Academic Press.

–. (1992). The ZPG letter: Subjects, definiteness, and information-status. In W.C. Mann & S.A. Thompson (Eds.), *Discourse description: Diverse linguistic analyses of a fund-raising text* (pp. 295–326). John Benjamins.

Quirk, R., Greenbaum, S., Leech, G., & Svartik, J. (1985). *A comprehensive grammar of the English language* (2nd ed.). Longman.

Ravelli, L.J. (1995). A dynamic perspective: Implications for metafunctional interaction and an understanding of theme. In R. Hasan & P. Fries (Eds.), *On subject and theme: A discourse functional perspective* (pp. 187–234). John Benjamins.

Raymond, G., & Heritage, J. (2006). The epistemics of social relations: Owning grandchildren. *Language in Society, 35*(5), 677–705. https://doi.org/10.1017/S0047404506060325

River Thames frost fairs. (2024, December 26). In *Wikipedia*. https://en.wikipedia.org/w/index.php?title=River_Thames_frost_fairs&oldid=1265431491

Rochemont, M. (2016). Givenness. In C. Féry & S. Ishihara (Eds.), *The Oxford handbook of information structure* (pp. 41–63). Oxford University Press.

Rooth, M. (2016). Alternative semantics. In C. Féry & S. Ishihara (Eds.), *The Oxford handbook of information structure* (pp. 9–40). Oxford University Press.

Rothermich, K., Harris, H.L., Sewell, K., & Bobb, S.C. (2019). Listener impressions of foreigner-directed speech: A systematic review. *Speech Communication, 112*, 22–9. https://doi.org/10.1016/j.specom.2019.07.002

Sasse, H.J. (1987). The thetic/categorical distinction revisited. *Linguistics, 25*(3), 511–80. https://doi.org/10.1515/ling.1987.25.3.511

Schegloff, E. (1996). Turn organization: One intersection of grammar and interaction. In E. Ochs, E.A. Schegloff & S.A. Thompson (Eds.), *Interaction and grammar* (pp. 52–13). Cambridge University Press.

Schmerling, S.F. (1976). *Aspects of English sentence stress.* University of Texas Press.

Schumacher, P.B., & Baumann, S. (2010). Pitch accent type Affects the N400 during referential processing. *Neuroreport, 21*(9), 618–22. https://doi.org/10.1097/wnr.0b013e328339874a

Searle, J. (1969). *Speech acts: An essay in the philosophy of language.* Cambridge University Press.

Selkirk, E. (1984). On the major class features and syllable theory. In M. Aronoff, R. Oehrle, F. Kelley & B. Wilker Stephens (Eds.), *Language sound structure* (pp. 107–20). MIT Press.

Shannon, C.E. (1948). A mathematical theory of communication. *Bell System Technical Journal, 27*(3), 379–423. https://doi.org/10.1002/j.1538-7305.1948.tb01338.x

Shimojo, M. 2024. *Salience of information in Japanese: Discourse and the Syntax–Pragmatics Interface.* Cambridge University Press.

Sinclair, J.M. (2004). *Trust the text: Language corpus and discourse.* Routledge.

Sinclair, J.M., & Mauranen, A. (2006). *Linear unit grammar: Integrating speech and writing. Studies in corpus linguistics Vol. 25*. John Benjamins.

Sperber, D., & Wilson, D. (1995). *Relevance: Communication and cognition* (2nd ed.). Wiley-Blackwell.

Stalnaker, R. (1974). Pragmatic presuppositions. In M. Munitz & P. Under (Eds.), *Semantics and philosophy* (pp. 197–213). New York University Press.

–. (2002). Common ground. *Linguistics and philosophy, 25*, 701–21. https://doi.org/10.1023/A:1020867916902

Strawson, P. (1964). Identifying reference and truth values. *Theoria, 30*(2), 96–118. https://doi.org/10.1111/j.1755-2567.1964.tb00404.x

Svoboda, A. (1983). Thematic elements. *Brno studies in English, 15*(1), 49–85. http://hdl.handle.net/11222.digilib/104005

Szczepek Reed, B. (2007). *Prosodic orientation in English conversation.* Palgrave.

–. (2010a). *Analysing conversation: An introduction to prosody.* Macmillan.

–. (2010b). Intonation phrases in natural conversation: A participants' category? In D. Barth-Weingarthen, E. Reber & M. Selting (Eds), *Prosody in interaction* (pp. 191–212). John Benjamins.

Taboada, M., & Lavid, J. (2003). Rhetorical and thematic patterns in scheduling dialogues: A generic classification. *Functions of Language, 10*(2), 147–78. https://doi.org/10.1075/fol.10.2.02tab

Taglicht, J. (1984). *Message and emphasis: On focus and scope in English.* Longman.

Taylor, C. (2016). *The language animal.* Belknap Press.

Tench, P. (1990). *The roles of intonation in English discourse.* Peter Laing.

–. (1996). *The intonation systems of English.* Cassell.

–. (1997). The fall and rise of the level tone. *Functions of Language, 4*(1), 1–22. https://doi.org/10.1075/fol.4.1.02ten

–. (2003). Process of semogenesis in English intonation. *Functions of Language, 10*(2), 209–34.

–. (2014). Towards a systemic presentation of the word phonology of English. In W.L. Bowcher & B.A. Smith (Eds.), *Systemic phonology: Recent studies in English* (267–94). Equinox.

–. (2017). The phoneme and word phonology in systemic functional linguistics. In T. Bartlett & G. O'Grady (Eds). *The Routledge handbook of Systemic Functional Linguistics* (pp. 257–74). Routledge.

Teruya, K. (2004). Metafunctional profile of the grammar of Japanese. In A. Cafferel, J.R. Martin & C.M.I.M. Matthiessen (Eds), *Linguistic typology: A functional perspective* (pp. 185–251). John Benjamins.

Thibault, P.J. (2004a). *Brain, mind and signifying body: An ecosocial semiotic theory.* Equinox.

–. (2004b). *Agency & consciousness in discourse: Self-other dynamics as a complex system.* Equinox.

–. (2011). First-order languaging dynamics and second-order language: The distributed language view. *Ecological Psychology, 23*(3), 210–45. https://doi.org/10.1080/10407413.2011.591274

–. (2017). The reflexivity of human languaging and Nigel Love's two orders of language 1. *Language Sciences, 61,* 74–85. http://dx.doi.org/10.1016/j.langsci.2016.09.014

–. (2020a). *Distributed languaging, affective dynamics, and the human ecology volume 1: The sense-making body.* Routledge.

–. (2020b). *Distributed languaging, affective dynamics, and the human ecology volume 2: Co-articulating self and world*. Routledge.

–. (2021). Selves, interactive representations and context: A systemic functional linguistic account of process in language and world. *Language, Context and Text, 3*(1), 33–92. https://doi.org/10.1075/langct.00032.thi

Thompson, G. (2013). *Introducing functional grammar* (3rd ed.). Routledge.

Thompson G., & Thompson, S. (2008). Theme, subject and the unfolding of text. In G. Forey & G. Thompson (Eds.), *Text type and texture* (pp. 45–69). Equinox.

Vallduví, E. (1992). *The informational component*. Garland.

Vallduví, E., & Engdahl, E. (1996). The linguistic realisation of Information packaging. *Linguistics, 34*(3), 459–519. https://doi.org/10.1515/ling.1996.34.3.459

Van Leeuwen, T. (2011). Rhythm and multimodal semiosis. In S. Dreyfus, S. Hood & M. Stenglin (Eds.), *Semiotic margins: Meanings in multimodalities* (pp. 168–76). Bloomsbury.

Van Valin, R.D., & LaPolla, R.J. (1997). *Syntax: Structure, meaning, and function*. Cambridge University Press.

Voloshinov, V.N. (1973). Language, speech, and utterance. In V.N. Voloshinov (Ed.), *Marxism and the philosophy of language* (pp. 65–82). Harvard University Press.

Wagner, M. (2016). Information structure and production planning. In C. Féry & S. Ishihara (Eds.), *The Oxford handbook of information structure* (pp. 541–61). Oxford University Press.

Ward, G.L., & Prince, E.F. (1991). On the topicalization of indefinite NPs. *Journal of Pragmatics, 16*(2), 167–77. https://doi.org/10.1016/0378-2166(91)90079-D

Watson, D., & Gibson, E. (2004). The relationship between intonational phrasing and syntactic structure in language production. *Language and Cognitive Processes, 19*(6), 713–55.

Weil, H. (2009). *The order of words in the ancient languages compared with that of modern languages*. C.W. Super (Trans). BiblioLife. (Original work published 1887).

Wichmann, A. (2000). *Intonation in text and discourse: Beginnings middles and ends*. Longman.

Index